About the editors

Kees Koonings is associate professor of development studies in the Faculty of Social Sciences at Utrecht University. He is also professor of Brazilian studies in the Faculty of Social Sciences at the University of Amsterdam and attached to CEDLA (the Centre for Latin American Research and Documentation). He has published on development issues, ethnicity, the military, democracy and violence in Latin America. He is currently working on the armed conflict and peace process in Colombia and on urban violence and pacification in Brazil.

Dirk Kruijt is professor emeritus of development studies in the Faculty of Social Sciences at Utrecht University. He has published on poverty and informality, military governments, guerrilla movements in Central America, and war and peace in Latin America. He is currently working on the history of Cuba's relationship with the armed left in Latin America.

Other Zed books edited by Kees Koonings and Dirk Kruijt

Societies of Fear: The legacy of civil war, violence and terror in Latin America

Political Armies: The military and nation building in the age of democracy

Fractured Cities: Social exclusion, urban violence and contested spaces in Latin America

Armed Actors: Organised violence and state failure in Latin America

Megacities: The politics of urban exclusion and violence in the global South

VIOLENCE AND RESILIENCE IN LATIN AMERICAN CITIES

Edited by Kees Koonings and Dirk Kruijt

Z

Zed Books
London

Violence and Resilience in Latin American Cities
was first published in 2015
by Zed Books Ltd, The Foundry, 17 Oval Way,
London SE11 5RR, UK

www.zedbooks.co.uk

Typeset in Plantin and Kievit by Swales & Willis Ltd, Exeter, Devon
Index: Michael Solomons
Cover design: www.stevenmarsden.com
Cover photo © Stephan Vanfleteren/Panos

A catalogue record for this book is available from the British Library.

ISBN 978–1–78032–457–9 hb
ISBN 978–1–78032–456–2 pb
ISBN 978–1–78032–458–6 pdf
ISBN 978–1–78032–459–3 epub
ISBN 978–1–78032–460–9 mobi

We dedicate this book to the memory of Menno Vellinga (1939–2015),
scholar, pioneer of Latin American studies in The Netherlands,
dear friend and colleague.

CONTENTS

FIGURES, TABLES AND BOX

Figures

Tables

Box

ABOUT THE CONTRIBUTORS

Lilian Bobea is adjunct professor of sociology at Bentley College Boston, and a senior research fellow at Facultad Latinoamericana de Ciencias Sociales (FLACSO) – Sede República Dominicana.

Roberto Briceño-León is professor of urban sociology at Universidad Central de Venezuela, and director of the Laboratorio de Ciencias Sociales (LACSO), Caracas.

Alan Gilbert is emeritus professor of geography at University College London.

Rivke Jaffe is associate professor at the Centre for Urban Studies, University of Amsterdam.

Abelardo Morales Gamboa is professor of sociology at the Universidad Nacional de Costa Rica, and a senior research fellow at Facultad Latinoamericana de Ciencias Sociales (FLACSO) – Sede Costa Rica.

Wim Savenije is a senior research fellow at Facultad Latinoamericana de Ciencias Sociales (FLACSO) – Sede Argentina.

Chris van der Borgh is associate professor at the Centre for Conflict Studies, Utrecht University.

ABBREVIATIONS

18st	18th Street Gang (San Salvador)
ACR	Agencia Colombiana para la Reintegración (Colombia)
AMC	Área Metropolitana de Caracas (Venezuela)
AMSS	El Área Metropolitana de San Salvador (San Salvador)
AUC	Autodefensas Unidas de Colombia (Colombia)
BACRIM	*bandas criminales emergentes* (Colombia)
CAI	Centro de Atención Inmediata (Colombia)
CEDLA	Centro de Estudios y Documentación Latinoamericanos (University of Amsterdam)
CICPC	Cuerpo de Investigación Científicas, Penales y Criminalísticas (Venezuela)
CMU	Crime Management Unit (Jamaica)
CNFL	Compañía Nacional de Fuerza y Luz (Costa Rica)
CONAVI	Consejo de Seguridad Vial (Costa Rica)
COPP	Código Orgánico Proceso Penal (Venezuela)
CORREPI	Coordinadora Contra la Represión Policial e Institucional (Argentina)
CPI	Commissão Parlamentar de Inquerito (Brazil)
DFID	Department for International Development (UK)
DIBISE	Dispositivo Bicentenario de Seguridad (Venezuela)
DSP	Democratic Security Plan (Santo Domingo)
EAP	economically active population
ECLAC	Economic Commission for Latin America and the Caribbean
ELN	Ejército de Liberación Nacional (Colombia)
ERPAC	Ejército Revolucionario Popular Anticomunista (Colombia)
EU	European Union
FANB	Fuerzas Armadas Nacionales Bolivarianas (Venezuela)
FARC	Fuerzas Armadas Revolucionarias de Colombia (Colombia)
FLACSO	Facultad Latinoamericana de Ciencias Sociales
GAM	Gran Área Metropolitana (Costa Rica)

GDP	gross domestic product
GIS	geographic information system
IBGE	Instituto Brasileiro de Geografia e Estatística (Brazil)
IDRC	International Development Research Centre (Canada)
IMF	International Monetary Fund
INDEC	Instituto Nacional de Estadística y Censos (Argentina)
INDECOM	Independent Commission of Investigations (Jamaica)
INE	Instituto Nacional de Estadística (Venezuela)
INEGI	Instituto Nacional de Estadística y Geografía (Mexico)
INEI	Instituto Nacional de Estadística e Informática (Peru)
JCF	Jamaica Constabulary Force (Jamaica)
JDF	Jamaica Defence Force (Jamaica)
JLP	Jamaica Labour Party (Jamaica)
JSIF	Jamaica Social Investment Fund (Jamaica)
KMA	Kingston Metropolitan Area (Jamaica)
LACSO	Laboratorio de Ciencias Sociales (Venezuela)
MAS	Movimiento al Socialismo (Bolivia)
MLV	Municipios Libres de Violencia (San Salvador)
MP	member of parliament
MS	Mara Salvatrucha (San Salvador)
MTPE	Ministerio de Trabajo y Promoción del Empleo (Peru)
NGO	non-governmental organisation
OIJ	Organismo de Investigación Judicial (Costa Rica)
PAC	Partido Acción Ciudadana (Costa Rica)
PCC	Primeiro Comando da Capital (Brazil)
PLN	Partido de la Liberación Nacional (Costa Rica)
PNB	Policía Nacional Bolivariana (Venezuela)
PNC	Policía Nacional Civil (San Salvador)
PNP	People's National Party (Jamaica)
PNUD	Programa Naciones Unidas del Desarrollo (Colombia)
SEDESOL	Secretaría de Desarrollo Social (Mexico)
SUIVD	Sistema Unificado de Información de Violencia y Delincuencia (Colombia)
UN	United Nations
UNDP	United Nations Development Programme
UN-Habitat	UN Human Settlements Programme
UNODC	United Nations Office on Drugs and Crime
UPP	Unidades de Policia Pacificadora (Brazil)

1 | URBAN FRAGILITY AND RESILIENCE IN LATIN AMERICA: CONCEPTUAL APPROACHES AND CONTEMPORARY PATTERNS

Kees Koonings and Dirk Kruijt

Over the past decades Latin America[1] has not only become the most urbanised region of the global South. It has also produced the highest rates of the urbanisation of poverty, exclusion and violence. New, predominantly urban actors in that violence emerged after the disappearance of the military dictatorships and the implementation of negotiated peace agreements in Central America. Gangs, urban vigilantes, organised crime, lynching parties, private security companies and violent law enforcement agencies are the actors that deploy violence and reproduce insecurity, fear and distrust in many Latin American cities (Caldeira 2000; Rotker 2002). The broader social, political and spatial impact of urban violence includes a widespread distrust in the law enforcement capabilities of the state, paradoxically combined with broad support for zero tolerance policing by the very same state (Bailey and Dammert 2006). It has also brought forth the establishment of extra-legal power and control in many urban areas by gangs, drugs factions or vigilantes (Arias 2006; Jones and Rodgers 2009). This in turn further deepens established and new patterns of socio-spatial urban fragmentation which mean that the actual 'encounters with violence' (Moser and McIlwaine 2004) are unevenly spread across the cityscape but the fear of insecurity has become a generalised feature of urban society (Glebbeek and Koonings 2016).

This state of affairs can be called 'urban fragility'. We follow Beall, Goodfellow and Rodgers (2011; see also Beall 2007; 2009) in their argument that there is a dual relationship between cities and fragile settings (the latter mostly related to states or regions). On the one hand, violence has become increasingly urban, and cities are often the theatre of what they call 'civic conflict' (Beall et al. 2011: 10–11), with disruptive consequences for those cities, their inhabitants and their governance structures. On the other hand, cities are also sites of 'generative civic engagement' (ibid.: 4) and innovative formats for social mobilisation, political participation and creative governance (Beall 2009).

This is the other side of the coin. Latin American cities are not only about fragility. They are, of course, spaces where non-violent forms of engagement, mobilisation and participation have been developed and often successfully implemented. Rodgers, Beall and Kanbur (2012) resist what they call one-sided 'dystopian' (or 'utopian') perspectives on Latin American urban development. They make a plea for a recovery of a 'holistic' interpretation of Latin American cities:

> Certainly, the current vision of 'fractured cities' obscures the
> fact that cities are social, economic, political and cultural systems
> that bring different (and often contradictory) processes together,
> and unless we focus our attention more on the interrelatedness
> of these different processes within cities, our analysis
> – and concomitant policy initiatives – will unavoidably remain
> inadequate. (ibid.: 18)

We propose here to pursue a specific kind of interrelatedness, namely the specific responses and alternatives to urban fragility. We call this 'urban resilience'. Put simply, resilience means that communities, networks, grassroots organisations, and public and non-governmental support structures mobilise to create alternative, non-violent spaces and practices in cities. We will elaborate on this concept later in this chapter, by proposing a typology of urban resilience. At this point, it is important to understand that fragility and resilience are, in most cases, mutually constitutive processes that combine to shape the dynamics and variations of urban processes and their outcomes in any given place at any given moment in time. The city cases presented in this book were selected to offer different examples of this interplay. Although one consideration for selection has been differences in relative qualities of fragility and resilience, we also suggest that it is not always meaningful to make a distinction between more or less violent or safe cities. Violence and security differ in degree as well as in kind. 'Unsafe' cities in terms of average homicide rates, such as Medellín, may simultaneously be presented as showcases of urban regeneration (Martin 2012). A 'safe' city such as San José may at the same time be perceived as being under threat from social fragmentation and the activities of gangs and criminal groups (see Abelardo Morales Gamboa in Chapter 6 of this volume). Other cities, including city cases analysed in this book, show different panoramas of the dynamic interplay between danger and safety, or fragility and resilience.

In this chapter, we elaborate the notions of fragility and resilience and connect these to the main findings offered by the city cases assembled in this book, although we will refer not only to the cities to which separate chapters are dedicated. These cases have been selected not only because they exemplify different scenarios, but also, and more prosaically, because some of these cities have not often been included in volumes of this nature. We also take into account the overview we provide in Chapter 2 of five megacities in the region – Buenos Aires, Lima, Mexico City, Rio de Janeiro and São Paulo – although our overview is, admittedly, quite general.

Starting point: the basic contours of urban violence in Latin America and the Caribbean

During the decades of civil war and dictatorship, from the 1960s to the 1980s, violence was mostly political (Koonings and Kruijt 1999; 2002; 2004), instigated on behalf of the state by military forces, paramilitary units, and police forces and policing extensions (Van Reenen 2004). The era of political violence also generated pseudo-official and illegal security and repression outfits such as death squads operating in the interstices of political repression. These political violence actors confronted the real and imagined enemies of the insurgent left: guerrillas and militias. These were often part of structured revolutionary political-military organisations (Kruijt 2008), but they also operated as offshoots of oppositional social movements and political parties (Wickham-Crowley 1992).

These times now seem long gone. Only Colombia continues to be the stage of this classic repertoire of political violence. But Colombia is also a country in which the old political violence has seamlessly morphed into the new violence of urban crime, homicides, gang control of neighbourhoods, and repressive, often lethal policing. Colombia shares with the rest of Latin America the fundamental paradox of combining high levels of violence with the consolidation of the notions, institutions and rules (if not always the practice) of democratic governance and citizenship. The initial observation to be made regarding this paradox is that, since 1990, Latin America has become more violent. To give some examples: in 2009 alone, there were over five times more deaths caused by routine police violence in Rio de Janeiro than the number of politically killed or disappeared in 21 years of military rule in Brazil (Koonings 2014: 159). Gang and police violence in El Salvador since 1992 has killed more people than the civil war between 1979 and 1992. This urban violence has at least two characteristics: the high proportion of deaths by small firearms; and the overrepresentation of the young population segment between age 12 and 29, mostly male – both as victims and as perpetrators.

This has all been well established in the scholarly literature and in reports of international agencies such as the World Bank, the United Nations Development Programme (UNDP), the United Nations Office on Drugs and Crime (UNODC) and other UN agencies. The UNDP *Regional Human Development Report 2013–2014* again ascertained that Latin America was the only region with rising homicide rates between 2000 and 2010. There are some countries and megacities where violence decreased, such as Colombia, which had declining violence indicators in Bogotá and (between 2003 and 2007) Medellín, or where it stabilised, as in Brazil, which saw declining murder rates in Rio de Janeiro and São Paulo. Such trends are offset by rising violence in Mexico, Central America's 'northern triangle' (Guatemala, Honduras, El Salvador) and Venezuela. So, for the region as a whole, the average trend of lethal violence is rising. The opening paragraph of the most recent *Regional Human Development Report* states:

> Between 2000 and 2010, the murder rate in the region grew by 11 percent, whereas it fell or stabilized in most other regions in the world. In the last decade, more than one million people have died in Latin America and the Caribbean as a result of criminal violence. [...] robberies have almost tripled over the last 25 years. On a typical day in Latin America, 460 people suffer the consequences of sexual abuse, most of them women. Violence and crime directly harm the rights that are at the core of human development: life itself and the physical and material integrity of people. (UNDP 2013: v)

A central dimension of the recent and current patterns of violence in Latin America (and in parts of the Caribbean) is its urban setting. Many Latin American cities have developed into theatres of low intensity warfare. Latin America is the most urbanised developing region in the world, with 80 per cent of its population living in cities (UN-Habitat 2012). Moreover, despite the recent drop in poverty and income inequality, to be addressed in more detail later, Latin America is still one of the most unequal regions in the world and 80 million people are still living in extreme poverty (World Bank 2013: 7).

Of the world's ten deadliest cities indicated by the UNODC *Global Study on Homicide* (2013b), only two are found outside Latin America and the Caribbean. The unequal and fragmented pattern of urbanisation predominant in Latin America since the 1950s turned the cities into the domain of 'informal citizenship' or second-class citizenship (Kruijt et al. 2002; Koonings and Kruijt 2007; Holston 2008). While poverty and second-class citizenship do not directly generate systematic or organised violence, as will be documented extensively in this volume, persistent social exclusion and possibilities for alternative extra-legal sources of income and power, combined with an absent, corrupt or failing state in particular urban territorial or social settings, are conducive to violence and insecurity. As a result, cities have become the prime domain of the 'new violence' in Latin America (Pereira and Davis 2000; Briceño-León and Zubillaga 2002; Koonings 2012).

The backdrop for this is provided by interrelated processes of social exclusion in various urban domains: first, unequal access to livelihood opportunities; second, unequal social capital and civil society organisations; and third, skewed public decision making and urban management. In many cases this has been embedded within a culture of stigmatisation and discrimination, based on ethnic and geographical characteristics – particularly popular neighbourhoods where substantial numbers of poor, indigenous and black people live. At the turn of the century, this was conceptualised as 'new violence' (Koonings and Kruijt 1999; Kruijt and Koonings 1999; Pereira and Davis 2000; Rotker 2002; Rotker et al. 2002; Moser and McIlwaine 2004) But at present, this 'newness' is no longer a relevant distinction. What was new prior to 1995 or 2000 is now normal – and sufficiently normal to be mentioned in the Latinobarómetro report of 2013 as the most important national problem in Argentina, Bolivia, Chile, Ecuador, El Salvador, Guatemala, Honduras, Mexico, Peru, Uruguay and Venezuela.

As far as the new violence actors are concerned, the repressive military and insurgents of the past have been replaced by new sets of actors: criminal and social armed actors as well as official security forces engaged in public order and law enforcement (Koonings 2001; Koonings and Kruijt 2004; 2007a). A wide variety of armed actors are responsible for urban violence, most of them non-state groups but not all. In Latin American cities, a clear-cut categorisation of armed actors quickly becomes impossible. In particular, the conventional distinction between legal and criminal, state and non-state, disappears under the weight of 'hybrid states' (Jaffe 2013) and 'violent democracies' (Arias and Goldstein 2010a). Non-state armed actors, such as organised crime groups and vigilantes, often work in close symbiosis with state actors such as the military and the police (Glebbeek and Koonings 2016).

The violence that is closest to the everyday life of citizens in Latin American cities, and especially those in shanty towns and *barrios populares*, is linked to small-scale and larger criminal organisations. In these urban zones, drug bosses and their gangs often have de facto power. At the other end of the continuum of urban violence, in the classical Weberian sense, is the legitimised application of violence or coercion by formal state armed actors within the public domain. In Latin American cities this function is supposed to be performed by the police, but often urban public security and law enforcement depends on collaboration with the military. Latin American police forces in particular have a negative reputation (Kruijt 2011; Koonings 2012: 262–3): they are often neglectful, incompetent or ineffective, and operate in arbitrary and violent ways. There are very few political incentives for good police performance and conduct. Efforts to improve or reform police forces over the past two decades have largely been unsuccessful (Glebbeek 2003; Bailey and Dammert 2006; Uildriks 2009).

Indeed, in their response to violence, governments, politicians and law enforcement agencies have been facing increasing pressure to address crime, violence and insecurity through repressive strategies, based on *mano dura* or zero tolerance. Here, the emphasis is on punishment and force, police intervention and an expanding penal system. These strategies are based on the idea of criminal violence and insecurity as social and political threats that can be contained only by force. In some countries, militarised police forces or even the armed forces are intervening, as in Brazilian cities; in Mexico this is the case with respect to the drug corridors and the northern frontier cities.

In countries such as El Salvador and Guatemala, combined army and police patrols are the norm. Additionally, since law enforcement operates in a socially differentiated and ineffective way, urban citizens often resort to organising private security and private justice.

These basic contours of Latin American urban violence persist despite recent trends in the region that indicate positive changes, not only in terms of economic growth and the reduction of poverty and even income inequality, but also in terms of social mobilisation, civic engagement and political participation. In order to contextualise at least something of the delicate balance between insecurity, violence, vulnerability and resilience, in the next section we present several tendencies and characteristics that can be observed over the last 15 years. The purpose of this is to dismiss simple notions about the direct causal connection between average (macro) economic and social indicators and the specific mechanisms of fragility and resilience in urban settings. We do think, however, that positive macro-developments may contribute to the creation of more favourable opportunities for urban resilience (UN-Habitat 2012; World Bank 2013).

General contemporary trends in Latin America

We will discuss specifically three positive overall trends in the region that potentially add to the equation of generative civic engagement in cities: first, poverty reduction and class transformation; second, the upgrading of shanty towns, slums and the urban periphery in general, including the improvement of urban infrastructure and services; and third, the emergence of 'democracy of the street' and new social movements.

Poverty reduction across the region   According to the most recent data from the Economic Commission for Latin America and the Caribbean (ECLAC), there has been a consistent decrease in poverty during the last two decades. In comparison with the year 1990, when 48 per cent of the population was poor in terms of income, by 2012 this percentage had decreased to 29 per cent (ECLAC 2013a: 18). The most spectacular leaps occurred in the countries shown in Figure 1.1.

The overall increase in income also had another effect, clearly visible in the two largest economies and societies of the region. In Brazil, where the poverty rate decreased from 38 per cent in 2002 to 25 per cent in 2011, the Fundação Getúlio Vargas published in 2012

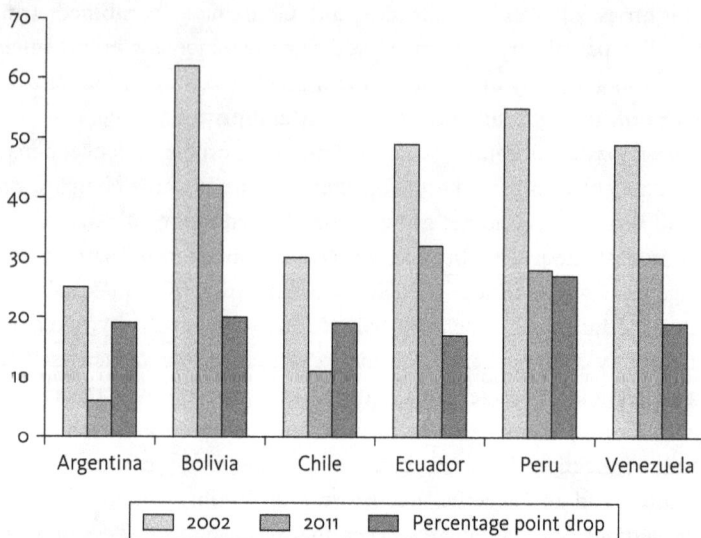

1.1 Reduction in poverty rates between 2002 and 2011 in selected countries (*source:* ECLAC (2013a: 18)).

a study indicating that more than 50 per cent of the population could be classified as 'middle class' (Neri 2012). According to the Instituto Nacional de Estadística y Geografía (INEGI) in Mexico, where the reduction was less marked (the poverty rate was still 30 per cent or more in 2012), the middle-class proportion of the population swelled from 38 per cent in 2000 to 42 per cent in 2010.[2]

Although Latin America and the Caribbean as a region is among the world's most unequal in terms of income distribution (the wealthiest 20 per cent of households receive 47 per cent of total income, according to 2012 data), Latin American countries experienced some of the largest reductions in poverty levels. Since 2002, poverty in Latin America has dropped 16 percentage points and indigence by 8 percentage points (ECLAC 2013b). The most significant contribution to this pattern of poverty reduction has been labour income. In a more detailed study of the situation in Argentina, Brazil, Ecuador, Paraguay, Peru and Uruguay, labour income accounted for at least three-quarters of the variation in total per capita income. Transfers including pensions and retirement provisions and other income-enhancing measures also relieved the general poverty level (ECLAC 2013a: 17).

Upgrading of slum cities and the urban periphery and improvement of provisions The growth of Latin American urban agglomerations from the 1950s and 1960s onwards can largely be explained by the rapid and substantial expansion of slum cities and the urbanisation of the cities' peripheries in the form of shanty towns or slum sister cities. The first migration waves to the major cities and the massive influx of first- and second-generation urban migrants contributed to the nearly exponential urban explosion in the region from the 1970s and 1980s. However, the generalised urban poverty and indigence were alleviated, at least to some extent; this resulted from the gradual improvement in livelihoods, increased levels of income and consumption and the benefits of expanding public services (education, public health, basic transport facilities), the impact of both conditional cash transfers and *bonos* (social welfare reforms such as the *Bolsa Família* programme in Brazil and parallel programmes administrated by most national governments starting in the late 1990s or early 2000s), and the effect of remittances earned by family members who had migrated abroad (Fiszbein et al. 2009; Fajnzylber and López 2007).

During the last five decades, a process of urban transformation has taken place in the oldest – and then the newer – shanty towns: highways from the city centre to the 'new urbanisations', improved transportation, electricity, neighbourhood hospitals, primary and secondary schools and even university facilities, improved avenues, shopping malls, bank offices, popular supermarkets, discotheques and police stations (Muggah 2012: 61–4). In Rio de Janeiro and other Brazilian cities (São Paulo and Belo Horizonte, for example), regional and municipal authorities have provided considerable funding for new real estate and infrastructure projects, and have also created social capital in the local communities via participatory planning and decision making (Koenders and Koonings 2012: 25). In a repeat study of Rio's (former) shanty town inhabitants, Perlman (2005; 2010) found that only 34 per cent of her former interviewees still lived in their original neighbourhood, whereas 25 per cent had found a residence in one of the municipal upgrading projects in the urban periphery.

A local middle class has developed in the former slum areas and a 'local' elite has evolved, whose residential environment and other construction projects reflect the emerging class structure in the former squalid conurbations or the sister cities of the poor. This has occurred in Bolivia (Tassi et al. 2011; Spedding Pallet et al. 2012), in Peru (Matos

Mar 2004; Kruijt and Degregori 2007; Ypeij 2013) and in Ecuador (Klaufus 2009; 2012). The same observations can be made in the case of the metropolitan areas of the Central American countries (Savenije 2009; Gutiérrez Rivera 2012; Levenson 2013a). In the metropolises of Argentina, Colombia, Mexico and Brazil, similar processes took place. Other improvements took place in the cities considered to be the violence capitals of Latin America: Medellín and Rio de Janeiro.

In Medellín, during two consecutive municipal administrations, mayors Fajardo and Salazar conceived a way out for members of the rival armed groups that were engaged in territorial disputes and mutual warfare: paramilitary *bloques*, guerrilla *frentes* and *sicario* bands. Their programme for disarmament and the reintegration into local society of all these demobilised individuals was explicitly combined with neighbourhood integration and security programmes: district and infrastructure improvement, street upgrading by asphalting the roads, the construction of public transport systems (metro, cable cars, and even public escalators), increased police presence, social and political participation, and educational and cultural projects for community enhancement. Some key elements – including connecting the urban rail transport system with a 3.5 kilometre cableway to the Complexo Alemão and other *favelas*, involving former drug traffickers in local non-governmental organisations (NGOs), and creating a new police force (the Unidades de Policia Pacificadora or UPP) – were incorporated after the 2010 'pacification operations' in Rio de Janeiro. In both cities, private investment in house improvements and municipal investment in recreation and culture contributed to a rise in welfare and employment, increased local business and the feeling of 'belonging to the city'.[3] Conditions for owning real estate, in particular housing, improved and its value in the former slum environments increased noticeably in both cities.

Emergence of 'democracy of the street' and new social movements   There is an interesting phenomenon that materialised in different forms after 2000: the emergence of powerful, however short-lived, social movements and popular protest demonstrations against failing government policies or presidents who paid insufficient attention to in-depth investment in employment, education and public health. These movements were not an offshoot of more institutionalised social organisations (such as the Movimento sem Terra in Brazil) but were expressions of civilian protest in the form of marches or occupations of public spaces. Most non-electoral changes of the presidency in the past 15 years have resulted from this kind of ad hoc movement in which traditional political parties or institutionalised social bodies scarcely participated (Alba Vega and Kruijt 2007). They represent the newly discovered capacity of civilians to participate in forms of protest: street marches and roadblocks, for instance.

In Ecuador, for example, popular marches cut short the government of Jamil Mahuad. In 2003, the new Ecuadorian president, Gustavo Noboa, had to request political asylum in the Dominican Republic after demonstrations. His successor, Lucio Gutiérrez, had to step down in 2005 after popular protest marches. In Peru, President Alberto Fujimori (1990–2000) had to escape the country after months of protest marches and sit-in strikes in the country's avenues and central squares. The leader of these marches, Alejandro Toledo, who was subsequently elected president, also had to confront a series of regional marches and protest demonstrations in 2002 and 2003, and until the end of his term. In Venezuela, an attempted military coup failed when, two days later, popular movements brought the already imprisoned President Chavez back to the presidential palace in 2002. In Argentina in 2001, popular discontent that exploded in disturbances and marches led to the fall of four presidents in a period of two weeks.

In Bolivia, consecutive urban and rural popular protests occurred between 2000 and 2005: an urban 'water war' in Cochabamba was followed by marches in the highland departments, the blocking of the principal national highways and a national strike by the teachers' union; a second conflict, caused by a drug eradication programme in the Chapare region, ended in a bitter confrontation between the coca cultivators and the government; land conflicts in the eastern department of Santa Cruz initiated the third wave of clashes and land occupations, and so on. Again, the consequences were felt nationwide, in terms of instability and uproar, and resulted in the turbulent ousting of two consecutive presidents in 2003 and 2005. After elections, the Movimiento al Socialismo (MAS), an umbrella association of several indigenous and popular movements headed by Evo Morales, took over power. After the re-election of the president, the MAS government was also confronted by new popular protest, regional marches and roadblocks (Crabtree 2005; Crabtree and Chaplin 2013).

In 2013, Brazil became the setting for enormous marches that started apparently as a protest against a bus fare increase in São Paulo but swiftly transmuted to encompass a much larger body of social issues: improvements in social provisions, public services, better education and public health. The marchers also demanded good government, protested against huge government spending in construction works and infrastructure on behalf of the FIFA World Cup, and demanded the prosecution of corrupt practices in politics. This time students, the young and the well educated were mobilised, operating in near-leaderless movements, communicating by social media and smart phones, and preventing the co-optation of their protest by older and more political social organisations. Subsequently, unions and the social movements of the organised left arranged demonstrations as well, channelling the previous demands into more policy-adaptive measures on transport, public health, education and transport; President Dilma Rousseff, 'listening to the voice of the street', announced a programme of political reforms and improved public health and educational policies.

Persistent sources of urban fragility

The three constructive tendencies mentioned above are, however, accompanied by two characteristics that have also continued to raise increasing concern in the region during the last decades. These characteristics mostly, albeit not exclusively, affect the urban domain in Latin America, where they provide a continuous foundation for forces and agents of fragility.

Sustained or rising levels of crime and violence   Crime, and in particular lethal violence, is persistent in Latin America and the Caribbean and is the subject of the recent UNDP *Regional Human Development Report 2013–2014*. In light of the widespread concern about violent crime and insecurity, the report opens with a poignant observation:

Latin America is the only region in the world where lethal violence increased between 2000 and 2010. While homicide rates in most regions of the world have fallen by as much as 50 percent, in Latin America they increased by 12 percent. In a decade, more than one million people have died in Latin America and the Caribbean as a result of criminal violence. (UNDP 2013: 1)

A recent UNODC study (2013b) also mentions a continuing high level of crime and violence in Latin America and the Caribbean. In comparison with non-regional countries with a high murder incidence, the Latin American and Caribbean situation is much more sombre. Whereas the peak homicide rate per 100,000 inhabitants in African countries is between 31 per 100,000 in Congo (2008), 31 in South Africa (2011) or 35 in Namibia (2011) and 57 per 100,000 in Côte d'Ivoire (2008), in the Caribbean Jamaica had a figure of 62 per 100,000 in 2008. (Asian countries have a much lower rate.) The highest country rates per 100,000 inhabitants are those of El Salvador (95 in 1998 and 70 in 2011) and Honduras (42 in 1999 and 92 in 2011). In Venezuela, the increase was also dramatic: from 19 in 1998 to 45 in 2011. In Guatemala, which was considered to be the most dangerous country in Central America for many years, the proportion declined from 46 in 2008 to 39 in 2011. A much larger reduction occurred in Colombia: 60 in 1998 and 32 in 2011. The two largest countries have relatively low figures: Brazil (22 in 2011) and Mexico (10 in 1998 and 24 in 2011). A jump in the Mexican homicide rate occurred in 2008 when the effects of the 'war on drugs' became visible in the upscaling of mafia-related murders (Polanska 2010).

At the level of the largest cities in the region, the pattern is quite different: there is a staggering ratio of 122 per 100,000 in Caracas (in 2009), 116 in Guatemala City (2010), 106 in Belize City (2010), 94 in San Salvador (2009) and 73 in Tegucigalpa (2009) – even Basseterre in St Kitts and Nevis had 47 murders per 100,000 population in 2010 – compared with the numbers in Bogotá (23 in 2005 and 17 in 2010) and São Paulo (21 in 2004 and 11 in 2009). Other large metropolitan areas had lower homicide ratios: Mexico City (eight in total during the years 2004–09), Montevideo (seven in 2007) and San José de Costa Rica (also seven in 2006). Buenos Aires (four on average for the years 2005–08) and Lima (four in 2004; no more recent data provided) share a very low proportion.

Drugs and organised crime   In several countries in the region (Colombia, Mexico and the northern triangle of Central America), violence is directly related to the production of and trade in drugs. In terms of production, the situation in the three cocaine-producing Andean countries (Bolivia, Colombia and Peru) has hardly changed in the last few years (UNODC 2013a). Recently, Peru overtook Colombia, although by only a small margin, as the largest producer and exporter. Only in terms of consumption does the panorama vary. Traditionally, the principal markets were in the United States and the European Union (EU). However, in the period 2004–05, the United States accounted for 49 per cent of the worldwide consumption of cocaine and the EU 25 per cent. Latin America, with its lower street prices and shorter trade chains, accounted for 15 per cent of world consumption and Africa for 7 per cent. However, in a couple of years consumption underwent a process of globalisation. In 2011, Latin America (25 per cent) and Africa (15 per cent) together consumed 40 per cent, and the market share of the United States (27 per cent) of the world cocaine production dropped considerably (ibid.: 38). At present, the level of consumption in Latin America's metropolises is the same as that of the larger cities in Europe and the United States.

Extreme drug-related violence is directly linked to the two Latin American countries that declared a 'war on drugs': Colombia and Mexico. It is also linked, but to a different degree, to coca- or cocaine-producing countries. However, when compared with Colombia, it is remarkable that the two other cocaine-producing countries (Bolivia and Peru), where coca producers are not immediately considered as state enemies, are much less homicidal. Brute force is also common in the countries that form the corridor between the Colombian and Mexican cartels and gangs: El Salvador, Guatemala and Honduras. In these five countries, organised drug crime is the major cause of murder, fear and political corruption (Kruijt 2011).[4]

When the Mexican government declared its war on drugs in 2007, cartels of all sizes triggered a murder explosion. 'Mini-wars' materialised at the local and regional level between the cartels themselves, as well as between the Mexican law and security institutions and organised crime (Benítez Manaut et al. 2009; Benítez Manaut 2010). In many countries, the groups behind organised crime are known as 'mafias': Brazilian mafias, Colombian mafias, Venezuelan mafias. Strong and recognisable cartels have been established only in Mexico, with 'local' branches in Guatemala and Honduras. In other countries, there has been a gradual transformation of militarised mini-armies into youth gangs, criminal bands and local territorial militias.

In Colombia, a variety of armed actors – especially paramilitary groups and criminal gangs and, to a lesser degree, guerrilla forces – took power in disputed regions where intensive coca cultivation takes place.

Although the precise magnitude of the phenomenon is unknown, it is common knowledge that drugs-derived corruption money pervades the institutional fabric of Colombia at most levels. The use of violence and intimidation induces or paralyses action by civil servants and law enforcement officers in ways that suit the interests of the 'old' and 'new' violence groups. Corruption and coercion are major causes of institutional erosion, especially at the local level (López Hernández 2010).

The northern triangle of Central America – El Salvador, Guatemala and Honduras – is probably the most affected region in terms of violence, weakened public institutions and infiltration of the economy, society and political system by organised crime. Of these, Guatemala is probably the most affected country. As in Mexico, the Guatemalan criminal groups as well as youth gangs use brute force and violence as an operational culture. The number of murders related to these gangs increased between 2000 and 2010 from around 2,000 to 6,000. Also as in Mexico, the cartels use carrot-and-stick tactics to dominate or to infiltrate. When confronted with resistance, extreme violence is used. Of course, they use enforcers against enemies and adversaries. Of course, they murder local police officers. But in general they attempt, systematically, to bribe the local police and the local public sector officers; to accommodate the power structures of local powerbrokers and mayors; and to infiltrate, as benefactors, local and regional social movements.

The most recent Latinobarómetro report (2013: 61–6) mentions 'delinquency', 'unemployment' and 'corruption' as the most important national problems. In most countries, the problem of delinquency is common: in Argentina, 35 per cent of Latinobarómetro's respondents mentioned this, in an open question, among the 'most important problems'. For other countries, similarly high responses were reported: Bolivia (34 per cent), Chile (23 per cent), Ecuador (31 per cent), El Salvador (21 per cent), Guatemala (30 per cent), Honduras (28 per cent), Mexico (28 per cent), Peru (35 per cent), Uruguay (36 per cent) and Venezuela (47 per cent).

Urban resilience

Urban violence has perverse political consequences at the local, national and even transnational level. It reframes the conventional urban paradigm of progressive modernity and inclusive non-violent politics. It leads to fractured citizenship and the systematic distortion of democratic governance and the rule of law. At the local level, it fractures public space and the privatisation of security. It has produced cultural geographies of segregation, stigmatisation and fear in Latin American cities, in which the existence of 'dangerous others' confounds class, race and cultural constructs of deviance. At the national level, it provokes zero tolerance policies of public security that do little or nothing to tackle the real causes of urban violence, and that harm the security interests of the cities' most vulnerable inhabitants (Glebbeek and Koonings 2016). Transnationally, urban violence is increasingly seen as contributing to state failure, terrorism and global instability.

So, what are the chances for resilience in this gloomy environment? Resilience – the capacity to cope, mitigate, bounce back, recover or restore in face of severe violence – has to be sought in good urban governance and the mobilisation of resources available to communities, local agencies and administrations (Moser and McIlwaine 2004; Muggah and Jutersönke 2012; Denyer-Willis and Tierney 2012). It supposes that there are inclusive policies to counter and dismantle the structural ingredients of 'criminogenic environments' – as Lilian Bobea calls them (Chapter 8 in this volume) – and to neutralise the effects of what Perlman (2010) calls the 'violence stew'. This 'stew' includes: first, the spatial organisation of lucrative illicit businesses, such as the trade in drugs and arms; second, the ability of gangs to translate their access to money, arms and firepower into open control over peripheral urban areas; third, the presence of a common or militarised police force that combines violent operations against gangs with simultaneous involvement in illicit activities through corruption or extortion; and fourth, the absence of a trusted police force and of local intelligence about crime and its perpetrators. Countering policies are also in need of complementary national and municipal public policies, such as the creation of substantial sources of youth employment, wide-scale conditional cash transfer programmes, housing and neighbourhood renewal, breakfasts in public schools and micro-credit to local entrepreneurs.

For this reason, recent attention has increasingly been focused on the mechanisms that allow cities (as integrated social systems) as well as specific populations, spaces and institutional domains to resist or recover from violence and insecurity. This has been captured by the notion of 'urban resilience'. The work of Caroline Moser and Cathy McIlwaine (Moser and McIlwaine 2004; McIlwaine and Moser 2007) has uncovered strategies used by (vulnerable) urban populations to cope with violence and insecurity. In a similar vein, research on urban social movements and local politics has stressed the importance of social and cultural capital as well as participatory arrangements within urban democracy as being important factors in mitigating exclusion, violence and insecurity (Avritzer 2002; Koonings 2004; Wampler 2009). Urban governance is clearly an important hub for understanding degrees of vulnerability or resilience to violence.

Building on these considerations, we propose a typology of resilience based on, on the one hand, modalities in terms of scope, reach and transformational potential, and, on the other, different levels of aggregation within cities, which imply different sets of actors (see Table 1.1). 'Coping' means that prevailing levels of violence, coercion, insecurity and fear are not in themselves altered but accepted, circumvented or protested. 'Mitigation' goes a step further by (partially) dampening violence and insecurity, mainly through reactive protective action. Recovery, prevention and transformation imply more durable and systemic processes that remove violence and insecurity by trying to restore or preserve conditions of non-violence, or by more ambitious changes that address simultaneously various factors of fragility. The distinction between levels of aggregation does not mean that there are no interfaces between them; of course, these do exist. It may even be argued that synergetic interfaces are a crucial condition for sustainable and city-wide resilience. In Table 1.1, we have filled the typology cells with generic examples, but these do not claim to be exhaustive. We also acknowledge that some of the examples might fit other types (or more than one type); therefore, the typology is tentative and the examples heuristic rather than derived from rigorous analysis.

The concept of resilience is not without its controversies. In a more radical vein, resilience is rejected as a stop-gap notion to fill the holes created by neoliberal urbanism (understood roughly along the lines of our concept of fragility). Seen in this way, resilience points either towards strategies to make cities more liveable within the parameters of neoliberal urbanism, or to coping responses available to the urban excluded without enabling these urban categories to challenge the root causes of fragility. Slater (2014) therefore rejects urban resilience as a guise for gentrification, stating that:

The insidious work of urban resilience lies in the obvious and, to its proponents entirely logical policy suggestion the word carries: 'urban dwellers of the world, brace yourselves for austerity [or environmental catastrophe] and everything will be fine in the end!'

We feel, however, that such a take on the concept is one-sided or reductionist because it denies any possibility of active engagement or mobilisation by non-elites (the famous 'subaltern') being valuable in itself. It portrays those affected by fragility as passive subjects that only 'survive'. However, as suggested by Simone (2013), modes of survival, or 'endurance', are important resources for the underprivileged in global cities, not only in the sphere of socio-economic survival but also with respect to collective action. MacKinnon and Driscoll Derickson (2013) favour the term 'resourcefulness' over resilience to conceptualise such capabilities, but we do not accept their rejection of the idea that places (in our discussion cities or urban neighbourhoods) can be meaningfully seen as resilient. Obviously, the spatial (and physical) aspects of urbanism are the outcome of political processes, governance decisions and social mobilisation; yet, the spatial layout of cities and the integrating or exclusionary effects of the use of space, the built environment, infrastructure and other systemic aspects of cities in turn delineate patterns of urban sociability, participation or conflict.

Our reading of this debate is that resilience comes in gradations: the capacity to deal with fragility may range from resourcefully responding to, without challenging, the dominant mechanisms of fragility – or even sustaining them – to actively engaging for transformation. It is obvious that resilience means different things to different populations in different urban settings. In addition, the repertoires of resilience cannot be seen in isolation from the broader economic, social and political context. The typology in Table 1.1 tries to capture this gradated and multidimensional quality of the notion.

Dimensions of resilience are shaped by different processes. At this point, we want to briefly indicate some of these in order to support the building blocks of the typology. The city cases in this volume represent these processes in different ways. The authors of the city chapters have been invited to apply them according to their own criteria and based on an expert assessment of their relevance in each case. We therefore do not claim that this book offers a fully rigorous 'structured' or 'focused'

TABLE 1.1 Urban resilience to violence and insecurity

Modalities of resilience	Levels of resilience		
	Households, neighbourhoods, communities	Institutions, governance, civil and political elites	The urban system: the built environment, urban space, urban culture
Coping (including 'negative coping': the ordering power of extra-legal agents of violence)	Accommodation Compliance Avoidance Resistance	Zero-tolerance repressive policing Vigilantism Private security Criminal governance	Internet-based danger mapping
Mitigation	Protective physical and social practices (locks and bars, neighbourhood watch)	Ad hoc surveillance of urban spaces Humanitarian relief for affected urban populations	Gated communities Urban relocation
Recovery	Non-violent spaces Churches Women's empowerment	Pacification Peace communities	Urban upgrading Infrastructure
Prevention	Gang truces	Community policing	Accessible and well-maintained public spaces
Transformation	Positive livelihood opportunities Building social capital	Citizen security policies Participatory governance	Integration of citizen participation, inclusive public spaces and governance

comparison of the six city cases (and the five megacities analysed in Chapter 2).

Livelihood, collective consumption, public services   These factors form the backdrop of social exclusion. Livelihood in Latin American cities is increasingly precarious and dominated by informal work (Roberts 2005). The erosion of so-called corporatist arrangements has greatly reduced service provision to the urban poor by national and local states. Young males in peripheral neighbourhoods in particular face the disappearance of opportunities for social mobility and status improvement (Cruz 2007). The public sector is losing presence and credibility as a provider of collective goods.

Criminal capital: commodities, organisations and networks   The drugs and arms trades have developed into key economic sectors for employment and income in excluded urban environments. At the same time, these activities link cities to wider transnational networks of production and exchange dominated by organised crime (Kruijt 2011; López Hernández 2010; Briscoe and Rodríguez Pellecer 2010; UNODC 2013a). At the micro-level of city neighbourhoods, and even at the macro-level of entire regions and even states, criminal networks, paramilitary forces, informal armed actors and youth gangs are key conduits for the generation and distribution of wealth, (male) status and power (Arias 2006; Bobea 2011; Dreyfus 2009; Flores Pérez 2009; Gutiérrez Rivera 2012; Jones and Rodgers 2009).

Law enforcement and public security strategies   The state's law enforcement strategies face a number of dilemmas. Electoral motives often drive repressive crime-fighting strategies as security priorities locally, and increasingly also nationally. Most of the time, security forces follow militarised models in terms of organisation, doctrine and tactics. Preventive and community-oriented law enforcement based on citizen security is an exception. This is the most important 'governance void' that helps explain the causal link between exclusion and violence (Kruijt and Koonings 1999). In response, citizens take the law into their own hands (Snodgrass Godoy 2006) and criminal groups or informal armed actors (such as the Colombian paramilitary, the Mexican cartels, the militias in Rio de Janeiro, or the Primeiro Comando da Capital or PCC in São Paulo) take over de facto organisation of 'order and security' (Arias and Davis Rodriguez 2006; Denyer-Willis 2009). At best, this is viewed with ambiguity by affected urban residents. The wealthier classes resort to private security firms and gated communities (Caldeira 2000).

Stigmatisation, identities and reputations The double-edged sword of stigmatisation means that, on the one hand, poor and often violent neighbourhoods are seen as 'dangerous' and 'no-go' areas populated by criminal 'elements' amidst a human debris of outcasts (M. Davis 2006). Criminals and the urban poor are broadly categorised as social 'enemies'. On the other hand, denizens of popular neighbourhoods (who prefer to call these 'communities' rather than slums; see Goldstein 2003; Perlman 2010) nurture a deep-seated distrust against the representatives and institutions of law and order. The police in particular are often seen as the most threatening enemy of the poor. It is no surprise that local informal and criminal armed actors manage to project their image as protectors of the population, despite the ruthlessness of their tactics; at the same time, these armed actors facilitate alternative identities, especially for male juveniles (Zaluar 2004a; Zaluar and Alvito 2006).

Social capital, networks and movements While non-violent social capital is often under pressure from the 'negative' or 'perverse' social capital mentioned above (Zaluar 2000), local networks, neighbourhood groups and grassroots movements are important factors in resisting the containment of crime and violence. These groups seek local development, often through the provision of collective goods and the organisation of local security (Holston 2008). It has become increasingly clear that the institutionalisation of social capital in alliance with the state is one of the most important factors in mitigating insecurity and violence and hence in urban resilience. Countries such as Cuba, Nicaragua and Peru show that neighbourhood committees that are supported by (or cooperate with) the state can be important tools to counter urban violence (Kruijt and Degregori 2007). In many cases, churches (especially evangelical protestant congregations) play a major role in creating nonviolent spaces and options (for instance, for former gang members).

Gender Violence in Latin American cities is overwhelmingly pursued by (young) men. If we look, for instance, at gang violence, it is clear that active participation and ensuing fatality rates among (young) men are far higher than among women. In general, indicators such as the homicide rate for men are much higher than for women, even if we look at vulnerable categories and areas. In addition, gendered cultural mechanisms contribute to gang violence, such as masculinity norms guiding violent behaviour of male gang members (Zaluar 2004a). Female gang members do exist and young women operate in the orbit of gangs in a variety of supportive roles (Gay 2005; Levenson 2013b: 96–7). Recent research, however, tends to show the domination of men and masculinity in street gangs and organised crime, or as perpetrators of urban violence more generally. In this respect, the issue of feminicide has drawn much attention, notably in the cause célèbre of Ciudad Juárez but also in Guatemala (Sanford 2008; Carey and Torres 2010). In the literature on urban violence in Latin America, relatively little attention is paid to the issue of domestic violence. It is safe to say that domestic and sexual violence remains an under-researched and therefore largely hidden phenomenon and a number of social and cultural factors constrain women in challenging violence perpetrated by men in the private domain (Alcalde 2006). With respect to resilience, a gendered approach suggests that women are powerful agents for non-violence. For instance, ACR (Agencia Colombiana para la Reintegración, the Colombian state agency for the reintegration of demobilised combatants) has found that reconciliation with mothers and female relatives is essential for motivating demobilised men to reintegrate into non-violent civil life (Koonings et al. 2013). Moser and McIlwaine (2004) have analysed the prominent role of women in building social capital amidst the violence and insecurity that affect Colombian and Guatemalan cities. The same applies to social movements: as a prominent example we mention the so-called Mujeres de Negro (Women in Black) movement in Northern Mexico that challenges the inaction and lack of accountability of state institutions and political elites in the face of the proliferation of violence against women (Wright 2005).

Politics and participation While it is often asserted that city politics are dominated by local economic and political elites that do not give high priority to urban social integration, an increasing number of examples of participatory politics in Latin American cities suggests that giving voice to the urban poor makes specific public policies (such as investments and service provision) more attuned to the priorities of poor communities. More importantly, these arrangements may alter the nature of politics and the relationship between poor neighbourhoods, their inhabitants and the state (Koonings 2004; Moser and McIlwaine 2004; Mathieu and Rodríguez Arredondo 2009; Mathieu and Niño Guarnizo 2010). It is suggested that this will also change the dynamics of urban insecurity and violence, although systematic empirical evidence on this causal connection is not available.

Urban management and public space   The case of Bogotá is often used to underline the importance of sustained urban management based on conceptions of civic culture and inclusion in containing the violence that marked this city until the early 1990s. Investment in public spaces, security and participation have resulted in a widely acclaimed urban transformation (Gilbert 2006; see also his chapter in this book). Comparable processes took place in Medellín after 2003 under the consecutive administrations of Fajardo and Salazar, who tried to combine the de-activation of armed groups with broader investments in infrastructure, social capital, political participation, public space and culture. These two cities are remarkable because the reorientation of urban management has been tried against a backdrop of ongoing armed conflict. However, a number of Latin American cities have been the scene of similar transformations within the framework of democratic transitions and decentralised politics (Avritzer 2002; Silva and Cleuren 2009).

The city cases: rationale and overall findings

In this volume, we seek to study the complex interplay between fragility and resilience in Latin American cities. We look at the factors that shape vulnerability and resilience to violence and insecurity. We choose to include, as a starting point, three pairs of cities that for different reasons (size, location, social structure) may be considered to be similar, but we highlight important differences and, indeed, contrasts. We invited the authors to look at a number of city cases that have been addressed less often in recent literature. In addition, we provide in the next chapter an overview of the textbook cases of exclusion, insecurity and violence in the more frequently studied Latin American megacities: Buenos Aires, Lima, Mexico City, Rio de Janeiro and São Paulo. The remaining six chapters provide paired comparisons of Latin American and Caribbean capital cities. They are grouped together in Table 1.2 with our reasons for their selection and comparison.

TABLE 1.2 Motivation for the comparison of six paired cities

Two large South American national capital cities and their metropolitan areas. These two cases, in the neighbouring countries of Venezuela and Colombia, represent a relative historical 'inversion' of the pattern of violence and insecurity. They are also roughly similar in size, average welfare and social structure but show important political and institutional differences and contexts.	Caracas (Chapter 3) Bogotá (Chapter 4)
Two medium-sized capital cities of small nations in Central America with urban primacy and centre-left national governments, but important differences in average welfare and politico-institutional dynamics. Furthermore, El Salvador is part of the high-violence 'northern triangle' of Central America while Costa Rica nurtures a legacy of relative non-violence and social inclusion.	San Salvador (Chapter 5) San José (Chapter 6)
Two capitals of island nations in the Caribbean with similar degrees of urban primacy and certain shared characteristics of socio-economic development but different politico-institutional arrangements and different dynamics of interaction between violence agents, politics and the governance of security.	Kingston (Chapter 7) Santo Domingo (Chapter 8)

In addition to these cases, in Chapter 2 we will present an overview of the changing connections between poverty, exclusion, stigmatisation, violence and resilience in five megacities. Here, it is not so obvious whether some of these megacities are cases of 'low violence' and others of 'high violence'. Initially, we saw Lima as the counterpoint megacity in which substantial contextual factors related to poverty and inequality did not coincide with high and sustained levels of insecurity (Kruijt and Degregori 2007). However, São Paulo and Rio de Janeiro, textbook cases of high levels of violence and insecurity in the 1990s, have gone through apparently important changes over the past decade. Buenos Aires returned to low levels of violence after an upsurge during and after the crisis years of 2001–02, while Mexico City seems to be an enclave within a country that, in a certain sense, is torn apart by drug-related armed confrontations. Therefore, the five megacities offer important testing grounds for assessing factors of fragility and resilience.

Rather than presenting the conventional sequence of chapter abstracts, we will conclude this opening chapter with a discussion of the main findings of the book. First, we will group these findings under the headings of fragility and resilience, and second, we will finish with some concluding reflections on their interplay.

Urban fragility　A first aspect of fragility that emerges out of the case studies is the contextual factor of growing social inequality, sometimes reinforced by decades of neoliberal macro-policies. This is specifically mentioned in relation to the Central American and Caribbean capitals, but is also relevant to Buenos Aires and Caracas during the 1990s as a contextual factor that has contributed to urban fragmentation and violent protests accompanied by politically motivated looting in the case of Buenos Aires (Auyero 2006) and social and political upheaval, including looting, in the case of Caracas (Briceño-León, Chapter 3). Of course, Bogotá (Gilbert, Chapter 4) and Lima (Chapter 2) have also faced national neoliberal economic policies over the past 20 years, but, at the city level, specific social, political and institutional conditions offered a counterweight to this fragility-enhancing context, as we will see below. In the other cases, the lack of national and local employment policies and the weakening of public service provision at the city level, such as educational facilities and public healthcare, appear to be fragility-inducing contextual variables.

Second, the case studies bring up the question of spatial segregation of cities, not only with respect to the lower-income or popular neighbourhoods but also through the growth of gated communities as 'fortified security enclaves' in upper-middle-class and elite areas. This is reinforced by the fact that most formal, more or less 'decent' policing is carried out in the elite and urban middle-classes neighbourhoods and also by the fact that poor people cannot afford the services of private police in their *barrios*.

Third, deficient urban planning and administration, which could have countered urban segregation and fragmentation, is noted in most chapters, but especially in the case of San José (Morales Gamboa in Chapter 6). In the case of Costa Rica, the metropolitan expansion of the country's capital resulted in the absorption of three other provincial capitals, each one with different traditions of spatial planning and urbanisation. The spurious nature of urban communal identities, accompanied by urban property speculation, unplanned urbanisation and even ungoverned spaces, resulted in a complicated and complex administrative system, conducive to illegality and indifference. Still, in comparison with other capital cities in the region, San José is a low-crime and low-violence city.

This, fourth, contributes to the emergence of 'criminogenic' micro-systems (Bobea in Chapter 8) in poor and popular neighbourhoods, enhanced by the abundance of young unemployed males and the widespread availability of small arms and alcohol, a variable mentioned explicitly in the cases of Bogotá, Caracas, San Salvador, Kingston and Santo Domingo. These local criminogenic factors intersect with the impact of the increased presence of local, national and transnational drug trafficking and drugs routes to Mexico and the US; this is discussed in all chapters, but especially in the chapters on the Central American and Caribbean capitals, which are drug corridors to Mexico and the USA. This is a propitious environment for the establishment of (often heavily armed) youth and street gangs, known as *maras*, *pandillas* and *naciones*. Their presence is highlighted in most of the cases and results in explicit violence between gangs, between gangs and the forces of public order, with organised vigilantes (such as Rio de Janeiro's *milícias*) and against residents. Even in cases where urban criminal organisations uphold a certain degree of order, with the tacit complacency of the state, this is backed up by the direct and ruthless application of violence and can therefore be interpreted as a continuous threat of possible victimisation. Also, these forms of criminal governance constitute a source of the public's generalised sense of insecurity, although in some cases – such as Kingston's dons (Jaffe in Chapter 7) – they are founded on a certain degree of legitimacy and loyalty to the criminal leadership.

A fifth and major factor, noted in all the cities covered, is deficient policing. This comprises a panoply of issues, such as public policies of *mano dura* (zero tolerance) implemented by militarised and repressive police forces, the proliferation of rogue police units, and abusive profile- or stigma-based policing of actual or perceived crime-inclined youth. A particularly poignant case is that of Caracas; three decades ago it was one of the safest capital cities in Latin America, but is currently an agglomeration infested by crime and violence (Briceño-León in Chapter 3). An initial event was the *Caracazo* in 1989, a sudden situation of rioting and looting with incongruent police acting during a politically turbulent situation. The coup attempt led by Lieutenant Colonel Hugo Chávez in 1992 was another watershed: an intra-military conflict accompanied by popular upheaval that left the country and its capital divided. The situation was aggravated by the Venezuelan national policy of implementing a new penal code that resulted in the massive release of arrested suspects prior to their trials, a kind of anti-normative government style, and a nearly obligatory system of public underreporting of crimes and violence.

Finally, we note a sixth element: the stigmatisation of entire cities, as exemplified by Kingston as a 'murder capital'. Similar lasting reputational stains have been applied to Bogotá, Cali, Caracas, Ciudad Juárez, Guatemala City, Medellín, Rio de Janeiro, San Pedro Sula, San Salvador, São Paulo and Tegucigalpa. In some cases (including Bogotá; see Gilbert in Chapter 4) this reputation is untrue, but the 'feeling' of public insecurity remains. As we will mention in Chapter 2, a city such as Lima also suffers from an unjustified reputation of violence: its residents still report crime and insecurity as their basic problem. The same stigmatisation process can be perceived in a more general sense with respect to the *favelas*, *barriadas* and urban peripheries; in short, the neighbourhoods where poor, indigenous and black people or migrants are a considerable proportion of the local population. In the case of Kingston, the stigmatisation as 'criminal' is even attached to all 'dark-skinned low-income men living in inner-city neighbourhoods' (Jaffe in Chapter 7).

Urban resilience With respect to urban resilience, the following factors and processes appear to be essential. This inventory starts with 'good governance' and 'good public administration' of the national and municipal authorities. What warrants the possibly overly normative adjective of 'good' here is that such governance and policies concern citizens' rights and citizen security, focus on public safety and include the provision of employment opportunities, local educational and public healthcare facilities, and efficient public transport that is accessible to the urban popular classes in particular. In sum, inclusive social policies are considered to be the *sine qua non* in all the city cases reviewed in this book.

Directly following from this is the importance of 'good policing', meaning policing that is effective at and integral to the level of neighbourhoods. The case of Lima (Chapter 2) demonstrates that such policing, in combination with the presence of local authorities that explicitly support the needs of residents' committees and local civic security groups (sometimes supported by local Catholic and evangelical churches), is indispensable for local trust and confidence building. Community policing and direct contact with police stations and police patrols are key elements as well. A trusted police presence and the accessibility of police institutions, including low-threshold access to special units for violence against women and within households, are deemed to be necessary for people to feel safe and protected. The example of *favela* pacification in Rio de Janeiro inspires mixed responses: it is seen as effectively re-establishing legal state control through 'proximity policing' by some, but as not ending insecurity and distrust due to the specific top-down style of policing and the failure to keep drug gangs at bay by others (Koonings 2014).

In some cities, the publication of actual crime statistics and residents' safety reports are mentioned as being important, especially in the case of Bogotá (where good statistics and public reporting have played a positive role in the improvement of urban resilience) and Caracas (where the absence of reliable statistics on crime and violence is part of the deficient governability of that violence).

The possibility of establishing truces and negotiations with the leadership of youth gangs are mentioned as contributing to resilience. This has been the case in Bogotá (see Gilbert in Chapter 4) and Medellín, and also in San Salvador and the two Caribbean capitals; in the latter, local gangs are not only abundantly present but also constitute key agents in the sociability of neighbourhoods. Bringing local organised crime into arrangements for resilience is politically and legally controversial, but can be seen as one of the conditions required to change the forces of criminogenesis.

Finally, it is remarkable but not surprising that many chapters mention the phenomenon of passive, reactive resilience, or even adaptation to or compliance with the given situation. These forms of coping and mitigation are especially visible in cities where drug-related crime and violent crime (Caracas and Kingston, and also Rio de Janeiro and São Paulo) or youth gangs (San Salvador and Santo Domingo) are firmly established. In these situations, common patterns of conduct include informal support networks, small self-help organisations run by residents in popular neighbourhoods, and even the passive resilience of residents in these neighbourhoods. People are 'mapping dangerous and unsafe routes and zones' as routine coping strategies in Santo Domingo (Bobea in Chapter 8), rely on self-help justice delivered by criminal dons in low-income neighbourhoods in Kingston (Jaffe in Chapter 7), adapt to the street codes of *mareros*, and meet their 'obligations' by letting themselves be the victims of extortion or even by adapting to living with restricted mobility, enjoying only weekly 'freedom of movement' in the metropolitan shopping malls of San Salvador (Savenije and van der Borgh in Chapter 5). An alternative is moving out of their neighbourhoods; the ultimate solution is migration to the United States as a way of coping, a common strategy for residents of the Central American and Caribbean cities.

Conclusion

In conclusion, with respect to fragility we observe the interplay of the structural contextual factors of poverty, inequality and exclusion and the pattern of vulnerability of specific urban populations who are 'at risk' (such as unemployed youth), the dynamics of criminal capital, the mechanisms of perverse social integration, the weakness of 'public security', and arrangements for the extra-legal enforcement of 'order'. In relation to resilience, we see factors such as the reform of security sectors and policing, urban management and public space, local democracy and participatory politics, and social capital, networks and social movements. We will emphasise, again, that direct relationships between fragility and resilience and poverty and socio-economic inequality are spurious. Furthermore, global crime statistics are insufficient instruments for a clear analysis of urban conditions. The focus of analysis should be the micro-level of (popular) neighbourhoods, neighbourhood clusters or even partial segments of neighbourhoods. At this level, the key elements are connections and interactions, alliances and conflicts, and peaceful and hostile coexistence between local urban actors, such as the local representatives of law and order (especially the police), the residents' neighbourhood organisations (another very important actor) and the general public. At the city level, but also within and between countries, conducive conditions and strategies that are important relate to livelihood opportunities, public services, social participation and spatial integration, all backed up by effective, pro-citizen governance.

2 | EXCLUSION, VIOLENCE AND RESILIENCE IN FIVE LATIN AMERICAN MEGACITIES: A COMPARISON OF BUENOS AIRES, LIMA, MEXICO CITY, RIO DE JANEIRO AND SÃO PAULO

Dirk Kruijt and Kees Koonings

Introduction

In earlier work on urban exclusion and violence, in particular in Latin American and Southern megacities (Koonings and Kruijt 2004; 2007; 2009), we portrayed these metropolitan agglomerations in terms of the consequences of lengthy processes of exclusion, insecurity and violence. The analysis of the situation in large Latin American cities that we brought together – such as Buenos Aires, Caracas, Guayaquil, Lima Metropolitana, Medellín, Mexico City and Rio de Janeiro – covered developments in the 1990s and early 2000s. We sought to assess their shared characteristics of urban misery, poverty and social inequality, but we particularly tried to understand the specific mechanisms and agents involved in what we then thought of as 'new violence' (see also Pereira and Davis 2000). In post-1990 Latin America, at least, violence seemed to have changed from 'political' to 'social and criminal', affecting especially the large urban agglomerations. Urban violence came to characterise the specific profile of unequal, divided and fragmented urbanisation of which Latin America was the front runner in the so-called global South (Briceño-León and Zubillaga 2002).

After 2000, this phenomenon contributed to the paradoxical situation that Latin America had become the only region in the world where (lethal) violence (measured in homicide rates) was still growing (UNDP 2013). The paradox was greatly enhanced by the simultaneous positive turn the region took on a number of economic and social indicators. In part, this reflected the favourable global economic environment; however, it was also the result of domestic and intra-regional socio-political conditions that introduced social concerns in economic governance and public policy. As a result, the gloomy view circulating not so long before, that entire Latin American and Caribbean countries should be considered 'failed states', precisely because of their high levels of desolation and structural violence, has lost traction. In an overview of the Latin American security situation, Tulchin (2010: 7) mentions only the cases of Haiti and Surinam when emphasising the existence of 'territories without government'.

But still the question remains: is the notion of failure (or 'fragility'; see Beall et al. 2011) still applicable to the (large) Latin American cities? Are these not cities where armed actors or organised crime are violently competing with government security institutions for money, power and territorial control? Are Latin American and Caribbean cities not leading global statistics on violence and insecurity (Koonings 2012)? Are they not synonymous with perceptions of insecurity and fear that rule the everyday lives of urban residents (Caldeira 2000)? Are these characteristics not grounded in long-term patterns of inequality and segmentation that dissect Latin American cities in both a spatial and a socio-cultural sense?

However, the notion of failed states or fragile cities is too pessimistic, or at least too one-sided, to adequately analyse the complex relationships in the urban and metropolitan domain between poverty, inequality, exclusion and security. The relative absence or presence of the basic state institutions is not a black-or-white condition but is embedded in complex articulations of legal and extra-legal arrangements of power and governance that tie legitimate politicians and civil servants to extra-legal armed actors, making coercion and violence part of the daily bread of urban politics (Arias 2006; Arias and Goldstein 2010b; Jaffe 2013). In addition, as we argued in the previous chapter, cities can also offer propitious conditions for resilience and resistance by local communities, local administrative agencies (public or non-governmental) and citizens' organisations and initiatives. In other words, as has also been suggested by Beall, Goodfellow and Rodgers (2011: 22), cities can also help to reduce violence and offer 'generative' solutions. Latin American cities are neither 'utopias' nor 'dystopias', but complex and integrated social, institutional and cultural spaces (Rodgers et al. 2012).

In this chapter, we will take a closer look at five of the largest urban agglomerations in Latin America: Buenos Aires, Lima, Mexico City, Rio de Janeiro and São Paulo. These five megacities are very suitable for illustrating the complex unity of adverse and constructive forces at work in cities in the region over the past two decades. It is not our intention to offer an exhaustive empirical assessment of exclusion, violence and resilience.[1] We seek, rather, to use these five cities as examples to caution against simplified views ('urban poverty breeds violence'; 'the state is absent in the violent peripheries'; 'Latin American cities are lethal war zones') and also to show that different, often contradictory trends are visible across space and time, challenging an all too monolithic perspective on the problems faced by large Latin American (and Southern) cities.

The chapter also intends to complement – and serve as backdrop for – the case studies in this book in which we sought paired comparisons of both violence and resilience, matching cities with 'low' and 'high' levels of victimisation and insecurity and making comparisons with other cities that have remained largely absent in recent literature. The 'big four' metropolitan areas of Buenos Aires, Mexico City, Rio de Janeiro and São Paulo are the iconic Latin American megacities that, together with Bogotá and Caracas, were traditionally considered to be the most important examples of deprivation and violence from the 1960s onwards. We also include the example of Lima Metropolitana as a counterpoint example of a large city with high levels of poverty and inequality that has generated violence-reducing forces and arrangements rooted in popular participation in security issues and neighbourhood committees set up to facilitate crime prevention and police protection. During the 1990s, the two Brazilian megacities were symbols of urban warfare, especially in the (in)famous *favelas*, but, in recent years, homicide rates and other indicators of insecurity have been improving (spectacularly in the case of São Paulo). Buenos Aires has emerged from a scenario of impending urban disintegration after the 2001 crisis, while Mexico City is the capital of a country that has been branded the prime battlefront in the western hemisphere's 'war on drugs'. As we will show, these five large urban agglomerations present considerable variation with respect to crime, violence, insecurity and urban governance. We will cover three key aspects: first, we provide a general assessment of recent trends in poverty, inequality and violence; second, we discuss the agents and forces that have shaped violence and insecurity (including on the side of the state); and finally, we examine the sources of resilience available to communities and (local) agencies and administrations, such as social and cultural capital and violence-reducing policy options and interventions.

Poverty, inequality and violence: trends in five megacities since 1990[2]

If we examine the development of poverty and inequality in the five cities over the two decades from 1990 to 2010, we note a gradual downward trend in the incidence of poverty; this trend more or less echoes the national trends visible in Argentina, Brazil, Mexico and Peru mentioned in the previous chapter. The most spectacular decline of (income) poverty took place in Lima. In contrast, Buenos Aires presents a partial exception because of the Argentinean economic collapse in 2001–02 that brought many members of the urban middle class dramatically but temporarily below the poverty line. Only towards 2010 did Buenos Aires return to the relatively low incidence of poverty that has historically been a marker of the Argentinean capital. The decline of poverty in Mexico City has been sluggish after 2000, while Rio de Janeiro and São Paulo roughly followed a more notable poverty reduction trend at the national level after 2003 (Figure 2.1).

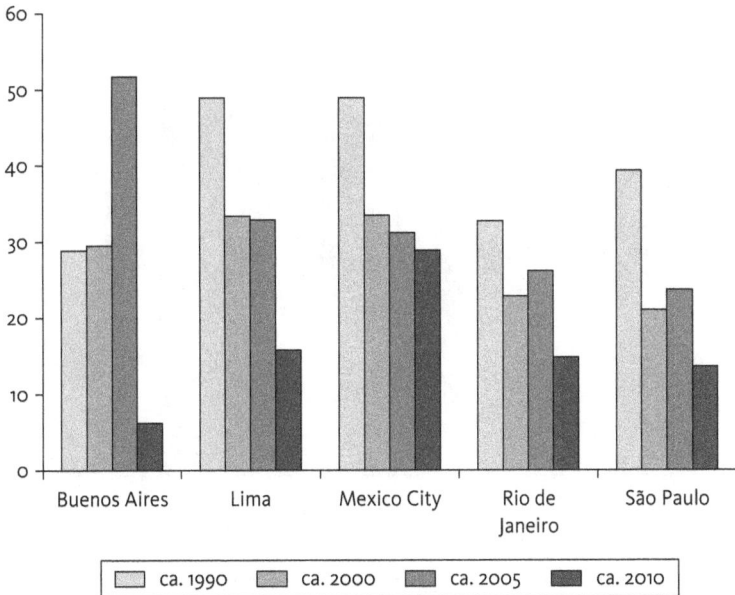

2.1 Trends in poverty for five Latin American megacities (percentage of total population) (*sources*: see note 2).

The picture is more mixed with regard to trends in income inequality. The Gini index rose for all cities except Lima during the 1990s and early 2000s, then dropped for Buenos Aires after 2000 and for Mexico after 2005. Inequality continued to increase in the two Brazilian megacities, a trend that runs counter to the downward trend of the Gini index in Brazil as a whole. Around 2010, Buenos Aires and Lima displayed relatively low levels of income inequality, at least by Latin American standards; Mexico City showed an average level; while Rio de Janeiro and São Paulo continue to face the high levels of inequality that were typical until the early 2000s for Brazil as a whole (Figure 2.2).

This means that, for the five urban agglomerations as a whole, the overall downward trend in poverty levels became visible after 2000 but varied considerably in terms of speed. Similarly, income inequality trends also showed a variation: the two Brazilian megacities continued to display their historical high levels despite the slow decline of inequality in the country.

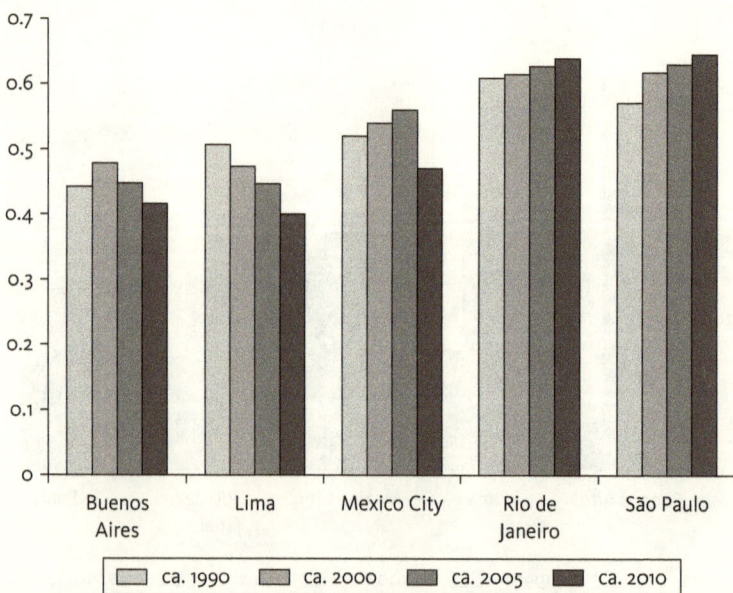

2.2 Trends in income inequality for five Latin American megacities (Gini index) (*sources:* see note 2).

If we match the trends of poverty and inequality with trends in homicide rates during the same two decades (Figure 2.3), it can be readily observed that there is no direct correlation. In fact, each of the five megacities displays a quite unique pattern, but one in which, curiously, decline appears to be the outstanding feature. This suggests two things: first, and not surprisingly, that changes in the homicide rate (taken here as a proxy for violence and insecurity) are dependent on a complex set of specific variables (discussed in Chapter 1) and are not a direct outcome of poverty and inequality (certainly not at the average level for entire cities). Lima is the clearest case in point: the decline of lethal violence in the early 1990s reflects the gradual ending of the armed conflict and the disappearance of Shining Path guerrillas from the urban scene of Lima. From then onwards, levels of violence in Lima remained low, but started to creep up after 2000 despite the faster drop in poverty and inequality. Second, and this may be more surprising, these five megacities do not reflect the average upward trend of lethal violence registered for the Latin American

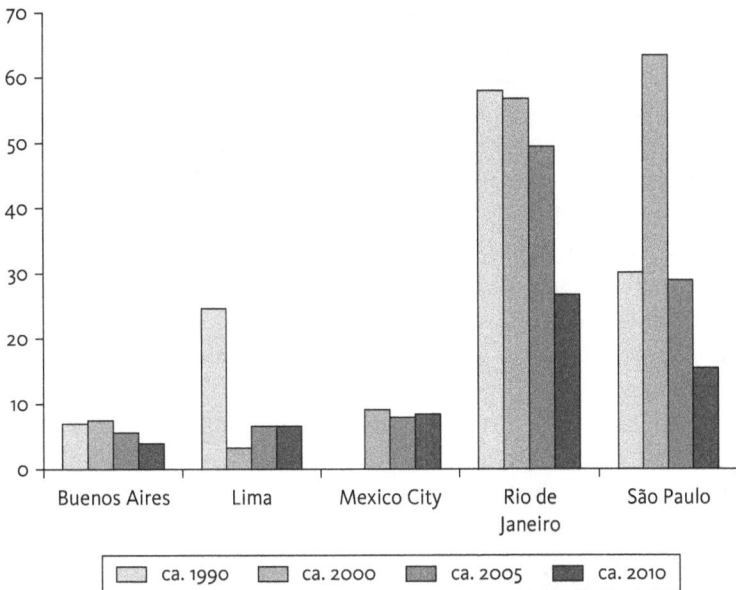

2.3 Trends in annual homicide rates for five Latin American megacities (per 100,000 population) (*sources*: see note 2).

region as a whole after 2000. Both Brazilian cities experienced rising homicide rates in the 1980s and 1990s; the latter decade in particular brought a steep increase for São Paulo. But the fast decline of homicide rates during the past ten years in both cities stands in contrast not only to the previous two decades but also to the Latin American regional trend after 2000. Whereas, during the 1990s, the two cities were still prime examples of the escalation in urban violence in Brazil, after 2000 this trend was reversed, most visibly in the case of São Paulo. Again, as we will see, this must be attributed to a number of city-specific factors and cannot be meaningfully related to the overall behaviour of poverty and inequality trends in both cities.

In a similar vein, the relative low-level stability of the homicide rate in Mexico City indicates that the escalation of violence in the Mexican drug war did not directly translate into increasing violence in the capital city. In sum, the spatial and temporal dynamics of violence in specific city cases respond to a variety of causal factors. In general, and in particular in the case of Brazil and Mexico, urban violence appears to have become more dispersed over the national territory; regional capitals, intermediate cities and smaller towns have been displaying higher homicide rates than the megacities. This also follows a specific logic of territoriality. In the case of Mexico, this is clearly related to the geography of drug trafficking, which uses specific hubs (*plazas*) and corridors to move the merchandise to the US market. In the case of Brazil, Waiselfisz (2011: 57–8) calls this the 'interiorisation' of violence and argues that it can be explained by three factors: the economic and demographic expansion of so-called non-central regions, the increased effectiveness of security policies in São Paulo and Rio de Janeiro, and the improvement of homicide data gathering in smaller towns and rural areas.

It should be made clear, however, that trends in homicide rates have been compiled on the basis of average statistics available for the five cities. The downward trend in the two Brazilian cities in particular – but this applies to all cities – should not hide the fact that specific urban areas display much higher levels of violence, and, furthermore, that these may be sustained even if city averages are dropping. As an example we can use the case of Rio de Janeiro. Cesar and Cavallieri (2002) show how, in 2000, homicide rates within the city varied considerably across five 'planning regions' in the municipality, with the highest density of killings occurring around the centre and the northern periphery. Barcellos and Zaluar (2014) offer an even more detailed example. By looking at the precise location of murders in *favelas* in 2009, they discovered that homicide rates varied widely, between 22 and 129 per 100,000. This could be explained by the high incidence of armed confrontation between gangs and police or among gangs at the perimeter of *favelas*. It is noteworthy that, inside *favelas* firmly controlled by one of the three drug trafficking factions or by militias, homicide rates were low – lower even than the city average.

Such a pattern can be found in many Latin American cities.[3] A second distinctive feature of urban violence in these (and most other Latin American) cities is that it profoundly affects the young male population, among whom homicide rates are substantially higher than for the total population (Waiselfisz 2013). It reflects the fact that urban violence follows a perverse logic of 'reasons, resources and resolve', or, in other words, the motives, means and opportunities for the use of violence (Ohlson 2008). This brings us to the agents that engage in it. Since we focus on social and criminal violence with a minimum degree of organisation, this means looking at (drug) gangs, police and the military, vigilantes, and the various ways in which they interact.

Urban armed actors and the dynamics of violence

Despite the recent decline in homicide rates in Rio de Janeiro and São Paulo, and in view of the much higher intensity of violence in specific urban areas, these two megacities continue to be emblematic of urban violence in Latin America because of the specific combination of agents and factors that drive the violence. This toxic cocktail – or, as Perlman (2005) calls it, 'violence stew' – includes the spatial organisation of lucrative illicit businesses, such as the trade in drugs and arms; the ability of gangs to translate their access to money, and hence to arms and firepower, into open control of, or dispute over, peripheral urban areas; and the presence of a (militarised) police force that combines violent operations against gangs and the neighbourhoods in which they operate with simultaneous involvement in illicit activities through corruption or extortion. This toxic cocktail is embedded in a broader context of political support for zero tolerance and a pervasive urban culture of fear, in most cases permanently nurtured by media reports and 'talk of crime' (Caldeira 2000).

Rio de Janeiro offers the most dramatic stage for urban inequality and exclusion.[4] Especially in the city's southern zone, where upscale neighbourhoods and world famous beaches are postcard material, the ominous presence of *favelas* straddling the nearby *morros* (hill slopes) offers a stark reminder of the social divide that runs through modern urban Brazil. The origins of the *favela* phenomenon date back to the early twentieth century. From the 1920s to the 1960s, the number of *favelas* increased from 26 to around 300, caused by rural–urban migration, natural demographic expansion and industrial development. The geographical area of the *favelas* spread from the central part of the city to the industrialised northern zones and subsequently to the upper-middle-class beach areas. The severe economic crisis of the 1980s gave a further boost to the expansion of *favelas* and other low-income neighbourhoods. In 2000, Rio could count almost 1.1 million *favelados*, 19 per cent of the metropolitan population. The *favelas* form a structural component of the urban geographical and social landscape of Rio de Janeiro.

The basic features of urban poverty and exclusion in Rio de Janeiro are not so much their absolute concentration in separate ghettos, but their insertion into a highly complex pattern of urban fragmentation and integration, conditioned by geography, employment opportunities, active associational life at the neighbourhood level, and vigorous religious transformation with the rise of various neo-protestant congregations (Pandolfi and Grynszan 2003). Violence is another characteristic. Leeds (1996; 2007) has described the origins and consolidation of organised urban violence in Rio de Janeiro. There has been a clear connection between the urban guerrilla phenomenon of the late 1960s and 1970s and the emergence of organised criminal groups that started to take control of parts of the city in the 1980s. Imprisoned urban *guerrilleros* came into contact with detained criminals and drug dealers. They passed on their organisational expertise (vertical command lines and the cell structure) to criminal leaders, who used it first to secure their power within the prisons and then to consolidate drug gangs and syndicates outside.[5] Due to the local expansion in the consumption of drugs among the middle- and upper-class segments of Rio society, in the 1990s almost every *favela* came to be the domain of drug gangs (*quadrilhas*) led by a local *dono* (drug lord). Over time, these gangs consolidated into three major syndicates: the Comando Vermelho (Red Command), the Terceiro Comando (Third Command) and the Amigos dos Amigos (Friends of the Friends). Small arms were bought on a regular basis from corrupt police and firemen (in Brazil, fire departments are part of the state military police force).

Until the mid-2000s, the municipal authorities sought an answer in repressive counter-insurgency operations, the so-called *blitz* operations. During a blitz, heavily armed police officers enter a *favela* to detain certain gangsters, but in practice they mostly fired at random, even killing possible suspects or just (young black) males who happened to be in the wrong place at the wrong time (Pinheiro 1997). Poor people are generally depicted as *marginais* (those supposedly living on the margins of society), a classification not much different from *bandido* (thug or gangster), which makes every *favelado* a potential criminal and thus an enemy of society to whom human rights do not apply. In this sense, there is a continuity between this approach and the politically inspired repression of the 1960s and 1970s (Gay 2005).

In the 2000s, members of the regular police forces and other concerned citizens started to act as voluntary neighbourhood guards. However, their power was firmly grounded in coercion, extortion and extrajudicial killing as well (Gay 2009). The post-2000 militias operate in the tradition of *justiceiros* or *polícia mineira*, and consist of off-duty or retired armed police officers and firemen who claim that they deal with petty crime and local gangs in 'their' communities. After 2000, in a growing number of *favelas*, 'paramilitary' groups appeared as a response to the increasing power of the drug gangs. These groups, the so-called *milícias*, succeeded in taking over communities from gang control. The use of excessive force by *milícias* has been commonplace, since many of them consider themselves to be part of or 'above the law'. This has allowed them to set up their own range of illegal activities. These activities are typically 'rackets' of extortion or monopolies for the sale of goods and services. They include, besides offering protection, the sale of gas bottles, the distribution of (illegally tapped) cable television and internet connections, and the control of local means of transportation such as vans and *mototaxis*. The militias profess to fight the criminal violence of the drug gangs, but they employ the same violence to force their way into communities and to keep control of their 'economic interests'. Those suspected of having links with the drug trade are dealt with in a swift and ruthless way (Cano and Iooty 2008; Machado da Silva 2008). Hence, *milícias* have added a new dimension, that of security provision as criminal racketeering, to the continuum suggested by Huggins (2000: 119–20) from on-duty policing, through corporate private security provision to clients and off-duty moonlighting by policemen, to organised vigilantism and the individual *justiceiro*.

Until 2008, the militias enjoyed a certain amount of institutional and political support. Police units cooperated with militias in certain areas, important local politicians praised their 'patriotic' efforts at restoring security, and a few deputies in Rio de Janeiro's state legislature had ties to militia organisations. However, after the use of violence by militia members in the *favela* Batam against undercover reporters of the local newspaper *O Dia* in May 2008, the state legislature started an official inquiry to unveil the nature and scope of the militia phenomenon. Following the publication of the final report of the Rio de Janeiro State Assembly Inquiry Commission (Commissão Parlamentar de Inquerito or CPI), the authorities denounced the militias while public opinion started to turn against them.[6]

São Paulo offers a different scenario. As in Rio de Janeiro, violence increased sharply during the 1990s. The largest metropolis of South America was characterised by growing crime, gang violence and extrajudicial killing by the police. However, in the late 1990s and early 2000s, the PCC (Primeiro Comando da Capital or First Command of the Capital) emerged as the dominant criminal faction exerting control over much of the vast urban periphery of São Paulo. The PCC originated in the state's prison system after the massacre in Carandirú prison (the Casa de Detenção) in October 1992 when 111 prisoners were killed by guards and police following a prisoners' revolt. The PCC sought to protect prisoners from state abuse and to exert control over the prison population. Subsequently, the PCC moved to the streets, disciplining local gangs, incorporating them into the city- and state-wide network of drug trafficking, and imposing their own discipline on the basis of violence and fear but also through a formal statute that codified the 'law of the *favela*' (Amorim 2007). In sharp contrast with Rio de Janeiro, the PCC achieved a virtual monopoly of coercion in the urban periphery of São Paulo. The PCC enforces its security regime through summary trials and harsh punishment, including execution (Feltran 2010).

It is believed that the PCC and the state (the police and politicians) maintain a silent covenant. When this was broken in May 2006, after the state government announced plans to tighten the security regimes in prisons for incarcerated PCC leaders, violence erupted between the PCC and the police, killing hundreds of people including an unknown number of 'innocent' citizens. From 2007 onwards, things calmed down and settled back into the relative calm of 'criminal security'. Still, as Feltran (ibid.) and Denyer-Willis and Tierney (2012) argue, the reduction in lethal violence is not the same as an increase in security, as distrust of the police and fear of the PCC continue to dominate the daily life of residents in São Paulo's periphery.

In Mexico City, with its relatively low murder rates and even its related absence of drug-related homicides, organised crime and its associated violence are visible in the form of arms dealing, contraband, automobile theft and cannibalisation of car parts, kidnapping and drug trafficking (Pansters and Castillo Berthier 2007: 54). The overall context in Mexico is therefore grim. The most important Mexican security problem is the presence of drug cartels. Benítez Manaut (2010: 187) signals that, over the course of two decades, the Mexican government did not succeed in implementing an effective counter-strategy. Aguayo Quezada and Benítez Manaut (2013: 13) summarise the complicated recent situation as follows: there are wars fought between the actors of organised crime to disrupt each other's business opportunities, transport routes and territorial control. The arrests or killing of mafia leaders results in internal succession battles and some of the initial six powerful cartels have broken down into fragmented regional groups, which means that this war scenario is shifting. Then there is another war caused by the federal government's offensive against organised crime. And there is a third war ongoing: the internal war of state actors against each other over corruption and the penetration of crime within the multiple layers of the three government levels: the federal, the state and the municipal. This third war is where the 'clean' segment of the state confronts the 'contaminated' one. A special cross-border security relationship exists with the USA via the Merida Initiative. During the government of former president Calderón, the armed forces were explicitly engaged in the war on drugs and the police forces were reorganised, with many retired military officers taking posts in the police (Barrachina and Hernández 2012). After assuming office in December 2012, President Peña Nieto announced that he would establish a new 10,000-member National Gendarmerie, expand the federal police by at least 35,000 officers, reorganise Mexico's national security and law enforcement agencies and improve coordination between them (Felbab-Brown 2013: 4).

In comparison with this escalation of the 'war on drugs' in other parts of the country, Mexico City is relatively safe in terms of homicide. Of the 26,037 homicides in 2012, only 1,086 were reported in the capital (INEGI 2013). The metropolitan government implemented a series of anti-poverty programmes from 2000; these included conditional cash transfers such as *Progresa* and *Oportunidades*, which were targeted at families living in extreme poverty, housing and neighbourhood renewal, breakfasts in public schools and micro-credit (Mahon and Macdonald 2010: 214–15). As a consequence of zero-tolerance policing in the central part of the megalopolis, introduced in accordance with the advice of former New York mayor Rudy Giuliani, a process of 'securitisation of urban space' took place in the capital city (Davis 2012; Müller 2013). This programme was initiated by a group of businessmen led by Carlos Slim, Mexico's most successful entrepreneur, and was legalised in the Civic Culture Law. The policing agenda also implied a 'purification' of informal and petty crime activities. A further consequence, which was probably not intended, was a major segregation pattern in housing and an increase in the number of gated communities, a process that started in the 1990s (Monkkonen 2012). However, trust in the metropolitan police did not improve. The public's estimation of police corruption in Mexico is the highest in Latin America (ICESI 2012: 9), and in Mexico City the dissatisfaction rate with police conduct is high: 74 per cent (ibid.: 14). The proportion of inhabitants who are victims of crime in Mexico is highest in Mexico City: 19 per cent in 2008, according to the most recent study (ICESI 2010: 31).

In Buenos Aires, with its quite low overall homicide rates, and in other Argentinean cities and provinces, police violence seems to eclipse that of criminal gangs in terms of its nature, scope and societal repercussions. According to a report by the Coordinating Group against Police and Institutional Repression (Coordinadora Contra la Represión Policial e Institucional or CORREPI), even in 2007 death squads were operating within police forces. This phenomenon was thought to be a thing of past military governments; as it turned out, it still existed during the government of President Néstor Kirchner. According to journalist Pablo Waisberg, the report stated that during the Menem presidency (1989–99), 383 people were killed by state security forces; these numbers rose to 439 under De La Rua's short presidential term (1999–2001) and then to 635 during the first three years of Néstor Kirchner's administration, between 2003 and 2006.[7]

In general, victimisation by police repression was highest in Buenos Aires (48 per cent of the national total; Denissen 2008: 66).[8] Urban insecurity is especially felt in the *villas miserias*, the poor neighbourhoods where the victimisation ratio (mostly property-related) is high. Another parallel phenomenon is the rise and expansion of gated communities and even *barrios cerrados* (closed neighbourhoods) for the upper-middle-class population and the elite (Thuilier 2005: 259–62; Benwell et al. 2013: 156–8).

During the last decade, the Argentinean Gendarmería Nacional has been deployed in urban areas. This is a highly militarised institution and, in general, the local urban police forces were also militarised during the governments of the two presidents Kirchner from 2003 to 2013 (Salles Kobilanski 2012). Previously, the gendarmerie (the border security) and the naval prefecture (policing the territorial waters) had been incorporated within civilian structures (Eaton 2008: 11). An unarmed local police corps in Buenos Aires, the Guardia Urbana, was created in 2004 and was disbanded in 2007 (Lis Ríos 2011). The continuation of police violence in the 2000s was also a rationalisation of the intuitive repressive responses to new forms of organised crime; this was perhaps not reflected in the homicide ratios, but is clearly visible in the number of armed assaults and violent robbery without injury or death – 62 per cent of all reported crimes in May 2015 (LICIP 2015: 6). From the early 2000s, the trade in illegal drugs and the steady rise in the urban consumption of narcotics (which had begun in the 1990s), together with the trade in and illegal sale of arms, posed further challenges that the police could not handle adequately. The theft and dismantling of cars and the trade in illegal car parts were the fastest-growing profitable criminal activities. This business is concentrated in Buenos Aires, where in 2002 more automobiles were stolen than were imported by car dealers (Saín 2004: 134). Ongoing problems include the lack of adequate strategic planning and intelligence, the absence of a coordination institution and the national fragmentation of the Argentinean gendarmerie (Saín 2009: 145–6). 'Control of crime' policies in Buenos Aires are, according to some analysts, mostly rhetorical statements (Beltrane 2012). In 2003, a series of scandals about high-ranking police chiefs involved in crime rings became public (Hinton 2005: 85–6).

Lima Metropolitana still provides an example of relatively unharmed relations between the police and neighbourhood residents.[9] Lima, a well-designed city of 500,000 inhabitants until the end of the 1940s, is now, in 2014, a depressed metropolis of 9 million-plus. Shantytowns (*barriadas*) rather than middle-class neighbourhoods shape the Peruvian capital. A decades-long migration process, reinforced by internal armed conflict (1980–2000), brought about a spectacular urban transformation. The old historical and middle-class neighbourhoods of Lima constitute around 25 per cent of the metropolitan territory. Surrounding this traditional nucleus are three enormous clusters of slum cities that have formed a conurbation known as the north, east and south 'cones' (*conos*), most of the neighbourhoods being former squatter areas that were subsequently consolidated. In 1957, the inhabitants of the city's 56 *barriadas* accounted for less than 10 per cent of the metropolitan population of around 1,375,000. By 1981, Lima had a total population of approximately 6 million and 32 per cent lived in the 408 *barriadas*. The estimated population of Lima in 2004 was 8.5 million, of which 5 million, or 62 per cent, lived in the *cono norte* (around the northern part of the Pan-American Highway), the *cono este* (around the Central Andes Highway) and the *cono sur* (around the southern part of the Pan-American Highway), three areas surrounding the 'old Lima' with its residential middle-class neighbourhoods and its depressing popular districts.[10]

The population of the three new 'cones' mainly comprises the first and second generation of provincial migrants. Scraping a living is the lifestyle of most of its inhabitants. Many of the newcomers are self-employed or start with informal enterprises and artisan production in home *talleres*, cottage industries and commercial activities. Amidst the precariousness and poverty, however, a local 'popular' middle class is emerging and now accounts for an estimated 10 per cent of the population of the northern, central and southern 'cones' (Matos Mar 2004: 134 ff.). New commercial establishments and industrial parks have emerged in the 'cones', financed by local investors. In Villa El Salvador, core of the *cono sur* and originally a self-managed city, the authorities have designed a large industrial area with associated shopping malls, cinemas, restaurants and bank offices.

Still, 25 years ago, violence indicators for Lima were high and the city was in the grip of an overall perception of insecurity. These were the times of Shining Path's efforts to gain a foothold in the city's *barriadas* and to use terror as a weapon against the state and urban civil society. During the armed conflict, Shining Path's guerrilla members tried to conquer popular organisations by using terror: public assaults and executions of the local (female) leadership in the popular neighbourhoods and control and taxation of local petty businesses. The *cono* population established neighbourhood security committees that collaborated with the local police. This internal war reinforced a traditional security institution, the *serenazgos*, armed night watch committees of concerned citizens. These were, in fact, a kind of voluntary neighbourhood police force, under the command of the local police commissariat. Subsequently, it bolstered the creation or continuation of local urban security committees whose members hold a close watch on, for example, the irregular activities of petty criminals and thieves, in close cooperation with the local police. In the more elite and middle-class neighbourhoods, and even in some popular districts, the phenomenon of the local street *guachimanes* (watchmen) is common: for example, a private guardian is paid by homeowners or shopkeepers to ensure their security.

In the mid-2000s, it was a generalised practice that the police leadership tolerated a sort of self-employment that permitted private guardianship within the context of formal police tasks: after one or two working shifts as police officer, an individual could be employed as a private policeman, sometimes even with a uniform and service pistol. Police chiefs sometimes negotiate security or protection contracts with construction firms, restaurants owners, or industrial and commercial entrepreneurs (Rospigliosi 2013).[11] This kind of public–private symbiosis, whatever other effects it may have, at least reduces the necessity of residents in the elite and middle-class neighbourhoods and the tenants in the popular districts seeking security and protection by other means. Extreme violence and high homicide rates in Lima are absent, as is heavily organised crime. However, a recent report about citizens' security (IDL 2012: 21, 25–6) indicates that there is a high perception of insecurity in Lima (70 per cent in 2012) but a low incidence of homicide and extreme violence.

Huge fraud or large-scale corruption is not associated with the police force. Police officers are chiefly recruited from the popular neighbourhoods and generally they spend many of their years on the force in their own locality. They are considered – and consider themselves – to be members of the civilian population, interested in problem solving and not in abusive practices. In the early 2000s, reform was initiated to de-militarise police forces, to promote popular participation in local security committees, and to facilitate the integration of police officers, representatives of relevant government bodies and local popular representatives (Costa and Basombrío 2005).

This does not mean, of course, that street gangs and gang violence are absent in Lima. But compared with the other cities discussed here, the phenomenon is much less disruptive. Research data are fragmentary, but seem to indicate that Lima gangs are predominantly composed of groups of adolescents who 'hang out' on the streets of their *barrio* with which they identify, while engaging in relatively low-level violence such as harassment and petty crime. They are seen by residents and the authorities as a nuisance and a social problem rather than a severe security threat (Munar et al. 2004; Villegas Alarcón 2005). Mejía Navarette (2005) discusses environmental factors that contribute to adolescent males joining a *pandilla*, such as problems in the family, at school and in finding work, and the influence of mass media. On paper, public approaches to the *pandilla* phenomenon prioritise prevention, although the prevailing legislation (the *Ley contra el Pandillaje Pernicioso* of 1998) is said to contribute to the criminalisation of the youth gangs and the preventive approach of the police is often undermined by insufficient resources and procedures (Villegas Alarcón 2005: 80). Lima's *conos* are not urban territories where heavily armed gangs or militias have carved out their nested forms of sovereignty, but areas where street gangs are mainly seen as a social problem to be dealt with by the system of public security at the city and neighbourhood levels, although they are regarded with a certain amount of concern.

Urban resilience

Among the five megacities discussed in this chapter, Lima has the most elaborate and apparently most effective system of resilience against urban violence and insecurity. In this section, we will use the concept of resilience presented in the previous chapter to highlight instances in each of the five cities. Of course, constraints of space and data do not allow us to cover them in a holistic or comprehensive way. Rather, we seek to identify key examples to underscore our basic point, which is that resilience is the outcome of the interplay between specific conditions, agents and interventions at different levels of the city.

Urban resilience means the capacity to 'bounce back', to recover, or to restore (Muggah and Jutersönke 2012). This means that communities, networks, grassroots organisations and public and non-governmental support structures mobilise to create alternative, non-violent spaces and practices in cities. In Chapter 1, we presented a typology of urban resilience that connects different levels (households and communities, urban administration and urban systems) to different modalities of resilience defined by what we could call 'reach' and 'impact'. We talk of coping and mitigation when violence and insecurity are dominant, so that residents, communities and authorities seek to facilitate a certain degree of normal functioning within this context. This type includes what we call 'negative' or 'perverse' resilience: the control of violence and insecurity depends directly on the agency of violent actors themselves. Recovery and prevention refer to a situation in which violence is significantly reduced and controlled due to the prevalence of non-violent practices. Transformation is clearly the most ambitious form of resilience; here, not only are the factors and actors that lead directly to violence eliminated, but also the background factors relating to socio-economic conditions, non-violent social capital and institutions, and public governance for citizenship security and rights are firmly established.

Of the five cities analysed in this chapter, Lima comes closest to the transformation type, especially if we consider the wave of political violence unleashed in the city by Shining Path in the late 1980s and early 1990s. By the 1980s, Lima's municipal authorities already actively supported popular committees, such as mothers' committees and *comedores populares* (the community-run canteens for low-cost food in the *barriadas*). Women's participation in leadership functions became common. Around the associations of slum residents, the mothers' committees and the self-managed canteens, other institutional networks evolved, forming an overlapping network of popular support organisations in the *barriadas* and popular neighbourhoods. The informalisation process instigated at least three consecutive waves of new popular organisations representing the interests of the *informales*: the associations of the *pobladores* (slum-dwellers) in the 1970s; the association of micro-entrepreneurs and the self-employed in the 1980s and 1990s; and the rural and urban security committees of the 1990s and 2000s. This third wave in particular led to a specific security setting and a certain relationship of confidence between residents and the police. As a result, relative non-violence and a shared frame for citizenship security prevails in the city despite the overall indicators of poverty, inequality and socio-spatial differentiation.

Buenos Aires and Mexico City are examples of megacities with relatively low 'objective' indicators of violence but with a widespread sense that official public security strategies are flawed and unable to mitigate the common perception of insecurity and fear. In Buenos Aires, this echoes the recent period of social upheaval generated by the economic and political crisis of 2001–02. In Mexico, the environment of widespread drugs-related crime and violence, the endemic fragmentation and corruption of the police, and the militarised response by the Mexican state to the security crisis in other cities and regions in the country contribute to a sense of apprehension, if not siege, in the nation's capital. Examples of resilience in these two cities come close to the mitigation type, mainly in the form of social mobilisation and protest directed at the state.

In Buenos Aires, social movements against police violence and impunity have a stable and firm tradition of street protest and public denunciation. This follows the Argentinean tradition of *piqueteros*, protesters against government abuse or failure to provide essential services or public goods (Massetti 2004; Villanova 2012). The more politically oriented protest movements follow the tradition established by the mothers and grandmothers of the Plaza de Mayo, reclaiming information about their disappeared children and grandchildren during the decades of dictatorship. The Movimiento de Dolor (Movement of Pain), a social movement of victims and their family members protesting against impunity and violence, emerged in the beginning of the 1990s. After a while, the complex network of complicity between corruption and impunity among police institutions, judges, public prosecutors and politicians led to the creation of this protest movement, which had a repertoire of marches, public protests and occupation of public spaces (Denissen 2008: 106–7). This movement was slowly institutionalised in the form of a loose cluster of victim and/or family committees (ibid.: 113). Several of them published documents and proposals for improvement, whole others distributed flyers (ibid.: 131–2). Besides being involved in juridical approaches, all committees utilise street marches, participate in open-air masses (as in

COMPARISON OF FIVE MEGACITIES | 49

2004) and other commemorations, and sometimes erect monuments or sculptures (ibid.: 150–9).

In Mexico, similar forms of protest movements have been emerging more recently. In May 2011, marches for Peace with Justice and Dignity were organised in around 40 Mexican cities (Naveau and Pleyers 2012: 118–19). Afterwards, in 2011 and 2012, the Movement for Peace with Justice and Dignity played a role in dialogues with the national government and in organising new marches and manifestations. The entrepreneurial non-governmental organisation (NGO) México Unido Contra la Delincuencia was a favoured partner in government circles during the tenure of presidents Fox and Calderon (Loeza Reyes and Pérez-Levesque 2010: 145–6). Protests against *femicidio* (Wright 2005) and, quite recently, against the disappeared students in Guerrero are also clear examples of mitigation by demanding that the state, which is perceived as deficient, offers redress for violence that the state itself permitted or created.

Rio de Janeiro provides an example of recovery. Towards the end of the 2000s, opinions about the security situation in Rio started to change. The rise of the militias caused increasing concern as they were perceived as a new and potentially more complicated illegal violence actor. Massive police incursions in some *favelas* (in 2007) produced numerous casualties. In 2008, the kidnapping and torture of journalists and other abuses by militias caused public indignation and a parliamentary inquiry. The award of the two mega-events in sport in 2014 (the FIFA World Cup) and 2016 (the Olympic Games) to Rio de Janeiro and Brazil added greatly to a sense of urgency to bring about a radical shift in the way in which violence and insecurity were to be handled in the country and its megacities: a 'pacification strategy'. The objective was to recover permanent control of urban territories and communities dominated by the drug trade and militias, to promote the bringing together of *favela* residents and the police (and the state), and to introduce social policies by state institutions. The federal and municipal governments sought to recover territories and to win the hearts and minds of the inhabitants of areas that had been 'occupied for decades by traffickers and, more recently, by *milicianos*' (Willadino et al. 2011: 153). This strategy was implemented in four steps. First, urban territory was recovered, generally by special forces of the police and the army (which were considered to be less corrupt), evicting the drug gangs. Second, police presence was stabilised by setting up key police stations. Third, a high-profile Unidades de Policia Pacificadora (UPP) was established as part of the everyday routine of the community. Finally, other social services were provided.

The renewed presence of the state, and especially the UPP, considerably improved the local security situation but it has not been applauded unanimously. Cases of police abuse and corruption, and even an incidental homicide during an arrest in one of the neighbourhoods that has been part of the pacification programme, have caused the improved image of the police to deteriorate and have even created antagonism towards the presence of other state functionaries working on urban upgrading and social services projects (ibid.: 163). In the post-pacification period, land and real estate prices rocketed. Another financial consequence of the strategy is that the delivery of services such as gas, electricity, water and cable television has been formalised and regulated, because these companies now have access to territories that formerly they did not dare enter. Under the regime of the drug lords, the delivery of such services was illegal but free for decades (ibid.: 160). These side effects are the reason why there is a new trans-*favela* migration process in Rio de Janeiro. Pacification, independently of the mixed assessments the strategy inspires, explicitly seeks to achieve recovery from previously existing states of violence and insecurity. The specific design and limitations of pacification (it is selective and top-down; see Rodrigues et al. 2012) have made this at best a fragmented recovery strategy so far.

In 2013, Brazilian cities, including Rio de Janeiro and São Paulo, were the scene of civil protest movements that, among other things, demanded improved public security as part of a repertoire of claims about the state's failure to deliver public goods and services to an increasingly empowered but underserved citizenry. Despite such calls for recovery, explicitly including demands for more effective and less violent public security, law enforcement and police behaviour, most Brazilian cities continue to face the dual challenge of high violence levels and ineffective, mostly reactive, security approaches. In terms of resilience, this boils down to coping and mitigation.

São Paulo offers the clearest example of this type of resilience. The spectacular drop in homicide rates in the city over the past decade raises the question of how this can be explained. There are two rival explanations. One interpretation argues that the police's improved law enforcement capabilities account for the successful reduction of lethal violence and crime after 2000. Goertzel and Kahn (2009) argue that, at the end of the 1990s, a number of reform measures directed at policing, the prison system and the control of small arms combined to explain the 'great São Paulo homicide drop'. Policing was reorganised to improve data gathering and exchange on criminal activities; this included the introduction of geographic information systems and enhanced computer technology to target policing and to identify criminals. Interagency collaboration was improved, especially between the military police and the civil police. The tightened national legislation prohibiting unlicensed firearms and the public use of firearms was more effectively enforced in the city. Imprisonments increased between 1997 and 2001. Preventive strategies such as community policing and special police units to attend (female) victims of domestic violence were put in place (ibid.: 403–4).

A different perspective is offered by researchers who have revealed the role of the PCC in establishing order in the vast periphery of the city (Denyer-Willis 2009; Denyer-Willis and Tierney 2012; Feltran 2010; 2011). Around the turn of the century, the PCC managed to establish itself as the single faction in control of drug trafficking and extra-legal coercion in São Paulo's periphery. Feltran shows, on the basis of ethnographic evidence, that this has introduced a situation in which it is 'no longer allowed to kill' (Feltran 2010: 69). His data reveal the informal but effective procedures set up by the PCC to judge minor and major infractions of the 'law' established by the PCC itself. These procedures are based on 'debates' involving local PCC members in the case of minor infractions, and more influential criminal leaders in the case of major infractions such as the embezzlement of drug money or 'unauthorised' assassinations. The curious thing is that PCC debates can assume tribunal-like characteristics, including the right of defence given to the 'accused' and their relatives and friends.

How can these two perspectives be combined? Obviously, it is impossible to explicitly correlate either improved policing or PCC justice with the decrease in lethal violence. Therefore, all evidence is circumstantial. In certain areas of the city, such as 'Cracolândia', an area of crack trafficking and other illicit business in downtown São Paulo, the improved policing strategy does seem to have had an effect, at least by day (Denyer-Willis and Tierney 2012: 22). But in the peripheries, according to Denyer-Willis and Tierney (ibid.: 26), a situation of 'contentious collusion' has emerged between the residents of peripheral neighbourhoods, the PCC and the police. In one specific neighbourhood where Denyer-Willis and Tierney carried out field research, police stations have been established but there is no active patrolling (except to collect bribes). There seems to be a tacit understanding between the police and the PCC to avoid shootouts and to condone the operations of the local drug outlets (the so-called *bocas*). Among residents, distrust of the police remains invariably high, also in view of the persistently high levels of lethal violence applied by the São Paulo police forces (ibid.). Available evidence therefore suggests that there is a fragile stalemate, the unspoken coexistence of public and criminal law enforcement. The fragility of this arrangement is not only demonstrated by the continuation of fear and distrust that both regimes inspire among residents; it also came dramatically to the fore during the May 2006 violence spree described earlier in this chapter. This demonstrated that any disturbance of the silent pact of security between the state and organised crime can quickly spiral into widespread violence and outright panic among São Paulo's citizens. Coping and mitigation as resilience strategies thus work only as long as the key stakeholders in the power equation permit them to do so.

3 | CARACAS: FROM HEAVEN'S BRANCH TO URBAN HELL

Roberto Briceño-León*

Introduction

Caracas used to be a symbol of modernity and safety of urban life in Latin America. In the 1970s, when Venezuela had overcome the fear of the urban guerrilla and embraced the promise of prosperity and growth based on high oil revenues, the city lived in an atmosphere of hope. The huge benefits of oil income and its use in social policies predicted a future of security and prosperity. The old colonial panorama with French-style houses and mansions was transformed. Instead of the colonial urban pattern of networks of streets lined with single-story houses, skyscrapers and high office towers came to dominate the skyline, coexisting with the expanding informal shanty towns.

Until the 1990s, Caracas was still fairly safe, as was Venezuela as a whole, with a homicide rate of about eight victims per 100,000 inhabitants. Many analysts wondered how it was possible to explain the many differences between Venezuela and neighbouring Colombia with regard to violence (Deas and Gaitán Daza 1995).

The city's residents and immigrants were fortunate to find a city so safe and with such immense opportunities for prosperity amidst the economic hardship and military dictatorships in the region. There were so many benefits that a commercial advertisement launched a slogan: Caracas was an outlet of heaven. However, that situation changed very quickly. At the beginning of the present century, Caracas had become one of the most dangerous cities in the world. In the lists of homicides in the megacities of the world, Caracas appears, with 122 deaths per 100,000, as the most violent. This is even more surprising because

* The research on which this text is based was carried out with financial support from the UK government's Department for International Development (DFID) and the International Development Research Centre (IDRC), Canada. The opinions expressed in this work do not necessarily reflect those of DFID or IDRC.

the Latin American urban agglomerations that had been symbols of violence in the region, such as Bogotá, Mexico City and São Paulo, had reduced their homicide rates during the previous decade (UNODC 2014: 146).

In the Venezuelan context, one can ask to what extent, and why, Caracas is an exception. Statistically, homicide rates in Caracas Greater Metropolitan Area appear to be considerably higher than in other urban areas in the country. This does not mean, however, that violence and insecurity are not a problem in the smaller cities and towns. The national survey of victimisation and security perception conducted by the Instituto Nacional de Estadística (INE 2010: 115) reports a homicide rate of 233 per 100,000 in the Caracas Metropolitan Area, an average rate of 50 per 100,000 in all large cities, 66 in medium-sized cities, and 50 in small cities in Venezuela. Clearly, homicide rates in urban Venezuela are higher than in major Latin American urban agglomerations such as Mexico, São Paulo or even Medellín. In addition, in some smaller cities, crime cannot be contained because criminal groups or the paramilitary have taken over control. There are even a few so-called 'peace zones' where the national government has limited or prohibited the presence of the police and the military, leaving control in the hands of local groups. Nevertheless, Caracas clearly stands out.

This chapter examines the process of urban growth and expansion of Caracas and demonstrates how, despite the vast oil wealth, the metropolis could not move forwards to become a safe and inclusive city. What happened in Caracas? How can we explain how a capital city and a national society have become so fragile and aggressive, especially after successfully resisting the political violence of guerrilla campaigns and urban social disintegration that resulted from an accelerated rural–urban migration process? I will demonstrate in this chapter that the explanation for the changes that occurred with respect to violence and insecurity in Caracas is found in the fragmentation of social life and the normative institutional destruction in Venezuela after the turn of the century.[1] Two dimensions are crucial in this respect. First, the destructive measures of the national government, social and political polarisation, the actions of armed actors, the constraints faced by the police and the increase in conflict have had a significant impact on metropolitan Caracas (far more so than in other urban areas). Second, informal institutions and mechanisms of social control, which also substitute for the rule of law, are much weaker in Caracas; in other, smaller cities and towns, these informal institutions have a far greater capacity to shape daily life.

Caracas in modernising and urbanising Venezuela

Caracas is located in an elevated valley, about 3,000 feet above sea level, and is separated from the sea by high mountains that served as a defensive wall against attacks by pirate ships during colonial times. Both its fresh climate, spring-like throughout the year, and the proximity of a safe harbour transformed the city into a privileged place of residence for the political and economic elite of the colonial province, and afterwards the independent nation. Caracas was one of the port cities that, along with Maracaibo and Angostura, guaranteed the export of agricultural and mining products to Europe and the Caribbean Islands.

After independence, Caracas developed as the national centre of power. When oil production took hold of national life in the course of the twentieth century, the revenue from its export ended up in the hands of the central government, which spent most of it to expand and enhance the capital city as part of a strategy to build a modern state. Caracas was just a large town in the early twentieth century when other Latin American capitals already presented a much more complete and complex urban face. With the onset of the oil boom, Caracas became a populous city very quickly. The small historical centre was quickly overwhelmed; the new construction sites comprised both large areas of formal real estate and residences for the middle and upper classes and, in the interstices of private and public property, large areas of informal urbanisation for the low-income workers, known in Venezuela as *barrios* (popular neighbourhoods).[2]

Caracas expanded by means of three different regulatory systems. The first corresponded with formal legislation and the regulation of planned and approved development. The second ignored or violated formal legislation and resulted in a parallel informal system of norms and sanctions, based on consensus and the traditions of its inhabitants. And finally, a third regulatory system functioned as an interface between the first and the second one, facilitating the coexistence of the two normative models (Merton 1965). Informal urbanisation was neither authorised nor repressed; it was simply tolerated (Hardoy and Satterwaite 1987). This third model did not always work consistently. In some cases, the local administration permitted construction and even offered supplies; in other cases, it did not. Over time, it became even less consistent: in electoral periods the local or national authorities were more permissive than during the intervals of regular administration.

Violence and institutional crises in Caracas[3]

The situation of low levels of violence in Venezuela was stable for several decades (Ugalde 1990). It was the result of a long period of little social conflict and relatively minor crime. By the mid-1980s, the country's homicide rate was similar to that of the United States: between eight and nine murders per 100,000 inhabitants. Then the situation changed alarmingly. Two major events contributed to a significant break within the institutional framework of the country. Both were factors that produced a serious increase in violence and insecurity: the lootings of 1989 and the two coups d'état in 1992.

The Caracazo of February 1989   In Venezuela, free convertibility of the bolivar against the dollar at a fixed rate had been preserved for almost 20 years until February 1983, when a strict exchange control was imposed. The devaluation of the national currency produced an increase in the value of imports, accompanied by differential exchange rates for certain products (such as food, medicine and whiskey). In order to prevent a rise in prices, the national government established strict price regulation, which soon led to shortages and stockpiling of essential goods such as milk powder, sugar and sanitary towels.

This situation continued for several years, until the second presidential term of Carlos Andrés Pérez (1989–93), when illusions of a new oil boom and instant prosperity emerged, as had happened during his first term. However, soon after his inauguration in February 1989, an increase in the price of gasoline led to a rise in urban transport costs in Caracas and nearby suburban cities. This caused an outcry among users that quickly resulted in widespread rioting and looting. Supermarkets and food stores were plundered, but hardware shops, warehouses and appliance stores were looted as well. Within hours, Caracas was submerging in chaos and the basic rules of property and commerce were violated by hundreds, maybe thousands, of people who took what they wanted and ran away without paying.

Initially, only the large stores located in downtown areas were looted, followed by medium-sized businesses in the main streets, and finally the small shops of the shanty towns. In some cases, it produced clashes, injuries and murders in the skirmishes between owners, employees and looters. This led, from the second day onwards, to a rejection of the action by the inhabitants themselves, who were alarmed by these transgressions of boundaries. However, the intervention of the army and its use of weapons to restore order backfired and speeded up wanton violence and homicides. In a study I undertook at that time, in the Caracas morgue I counted 534 people who had been assassinated during that week. In a country that had seen a total of 1,709 murders during the previous year throughout the country, the figure of 534 violent deaths in one week and in one city was gigantic. That year ended with 2,513 murders, an increase of 804 or 47 per cent in comparison with the previous year; most of these homicides took place in Caracas (Briceño-León 1990). That is why the revolt was popularly coined the *Caracazo*.

The reasons for the revolt have been widely discussed. One theme related to what triggered the upheaval and another theme was the resulting breakdown of the model of social peace in its aftermath (López Maya 2003; Marquez 1995). Without doubt, the event marked the first institutional breakdown in Venezuelan society: the rules about property and commerce collapsed, and social constraints that served to foster respect for other people's belongings were abandoned. What was also lost was respect for life – first during the hostilities between owners and looters, and then with the repressive actions of the army against looters and many innocent bystanders.

The coups d'état of 1992   In the years after the *Caracazo*, the political crisis deepened. There were divisions in the ruling party and the changes proposed by the government failed to convince the different sectors of the population, both employers and employees, who did not want to lose what they had but rather called for the strengthening of the prevailing model for the distribution of oil revenues (Baptista 2005). In the years following the *Caracazo*, the murder rate did not decrease but nor did it increase: the situation remained stable. What could not easily been foreseen by ordinary people and the political leadership was that a group of soldiers was concocting a coup d'état to seize power and take over Caracas by force, first in February 1992 and then in November of that same year.

Twice that year the streets of Caracas were the scene of combat between military forces loyal to the government and the rebels. In the second coup attempt, in November 1992, even air strikes on strategic points of the city were carried out. The death toll in the two attempts to overthrow the government was not very high, given the extent of the fighting. The total number of victims among the military, the police and civilians was about 50 in February 1992 and more than 170 in November 1992. Nevertheless, the increase in violence affected the entire society; that year, homicides rallied nationwide by 34 per cent to 3,336 victims. In Caracas, the increase was 48 per cent, jumping from 1,041 in 1991 to 1,541 in 1992, representing close to half of the national victims.

The attempted coups d'état represented a fundamental break in the political institutional make-up of the country. The rules of the game structuring the democratic and peaceful means of access to power through elections were crushed by the military and replaced by guns and force. A significant part of the population showed sympathy for the rebel military action and even provided support to the coup. Perhaps unwittingly, violence became a legitimate means to achieve political and other objectives. Just as in 1989 it had ceased to be necessary to pay for a television set before taking it home, in 1992 it ceased to be necessary to register and win elections to achieve political power.

The political crisis that was generated was a kind of watershed, with far-reaching consequences for Venezuelan society. President Carlos Andrés Pérez was charged with fraudulent use of secret discretionary funds and, after impeachment, he was removed from office in 1993, to be replaced by an interim president. The institutional crisis contributed to the fact that violence gained momentum and began to increase (Pérez Perdomo and Navarro 1991). In 1993, for the first time in the history of Caracas, there were over two thousand homicides: 2,064 victims to be precise. The national total rose to more than four thousand: 4,292 victims.

The search for stability, 1994–99   As a result of the increase in homicides in 1994, the Pan American Health Organization included Venezuela in its list of the most violent countries in the region. With reason: the homicide rate had reached 20 per 100,000 inhabitants, twice what is considered an epidemic level. The murder rate in Caracas was 98 per 100,000, ten times higher than epidemic level.

That same year, Rafael Caldera began his second (non-consecutive) term as president (1994–99), defeating the candidates of the two major parties, one of which he had founded himself decades earlier.

The distinctiveness of his government's action was that it did nothing spectacular. In the wake of the commotion of popular revolt and coups d'états, his objective was to stabilise the political, labour and business relationships in Venezuelan society. His purpose was to restore the rule of law as a regulator of social life, and in this Caldera was successful. The economic situation was precarious because oil prices, the main source of national and government revenue, had been in steady decline. In 1998, the price of crude had reached its lowest level (less than US $10 per barrel, one-third of the nominal price of 15 years earlier). Confronted with popular discontent, government policies were initially restrictive, then were radically revised; it was as if there had been two completely different government teams operating during the same presidential period. However, the presidential policy of restoring law and order, promoting dialogue and orchestrating consensus, paid off and the violence abated. In Caracas, a significant decrease in violence was observed. The homicide rate decreased from 98 per 100,000 in 1994, to 63 per 100,000 in Caldera's last full year in office in 1998: an impressive 35 per cent fewer homicides. What happened in Caracas?

All explanations converge at the conclusion that Caldera's government succeeded in restoring normative institutionality and social cohesion after the *Caracazo* and the two failed coup attempts. It provided a possibility of peace, composure and civil security. It discouraged the use of violence and restricted the carrying of weapons. It reinforced the police in carrying out the functions of surveillance. It transferred responsibility for public security in a cluster of popular neighbourhoods in Caracas to leading politicians from the left. It condoned the ringleaders of the coup, including Hugo Chávez, and granted them amnesty so that they could join democratic electoral campaigns. It dislodged and demolished a prison building that had been a symbol of police abuse and the violation of the human rights of prisoners. It approved a change in criminal prosecution and punishment procedures, providing a new penal code that aimed at diminishing violence and maximising freedom (Ferrajoli 1990).

The population responded by supporting the campaign to reduce crime and social and political conflict. The explanation for the drop in homicides during this period can be found in the reinforcement of normative constraints whereas all other social and economic indicators pointed in the opposite direction: a clear decrease in public spending for social policies, skyrocketing inflation and an escalation of poverty and inequality. But despite all these grim indicators, the number of homicides in Caracas decreased by 34 per cent.

The Bolivarian revolution

The trend of violence reduction was strikingly reversed with the change of government in 1999 after the electoral victory of Hugo Chávez. During Chávez's first two years in office, the national number of homicides increased by 76 per cent, from 4,550 in 1998 to 8,028 in 2000. The homicides in Caracas followed a comparable pattern: from 1,436 in 1998 to 2,420 in 2000, an increment of 68 per cent. How can we explain this astonishing increase in lethal violence?

Three processes interacted to produce an upsurge in crime and violence while diminishing the effectiveness of law enforcement and favouring a certain decline in public morale. First, in July 1999, a new Code of Criminal Procedure (COPP) was introduced, declaring that detainees could only be those who were caught while flagrantly committing a crime. This legal provision caused confusion within the police forces that were not trained for its implementation and were not inclined to accept a measure that both undermined their authority and posed obstacles to police abuses. The immediate result was a policing paralysis: officers decided not to detain suspects either through fear of being reprimanded or in order to sabotage the law.

Second, the COPP stipulated that a person could not remain in detention for more than two years without being formally sentenced to a term in prison. Procedural delays were lengthy, and, in 1998, more than 63 per cent of inmates did not have an established sentence. Therefore, in order to comply with the COPP, inmates were released irrespective of their innocence or guilt. In January 1999, there was a total of 23,889 inmates incarcerated; in December 1999, only 15,529 inmates were imprisoned. In a couple of months, 8,360 prisoners had been released, 35 per cent of the entire prison population, the largest discharge in Venezuelan history (Rosales 2002). The practical consequences were severe with regard to social institutionality. It is not possible to know exactly how many of the people released from prison committed new crimes, but it is clear that the unintended message received by society was that crime would be met with impunity, not justice.

Third, the anti-normative message of the president justified the decision not to prosecute crime. For political reasons, Hugo Chávez, even at the very moment he was inaugurated, let it be known that he considered the constitution 'moribund'. Later, he justified theft by a person or a family if performed out of necessity. Subsequently, he legitimised violence, contradicting traditional Venezuelan educational advice and asserting that it was not true that violence was 'the weapon of the unwise'.

When we look at these interacting processes – the restriction and reduction of arrests, the release of detainees without pardon and the anti-normative message – we can understand why the preventive effects of the strict implementation of the law and appropriate punishment were ruptured, and why a widespread perception of impunity was generated that in turn encouraged crime and violence (Hart 2008; Altheimer 2013).

A sharp increase in violence and official censorship   The early years of the present century were characterised by great turmoil and political division in Venezuela. Several national strikes were organised by the associations of employers and employees. Then, in 2002, a segment of the armed forces attempted a coup d'état that was resolved quickly but in a very confusing way. The year 2003 began with a general strike that lasted nearly two months and led to the dismissal of more than 18,000 workers in the oil industry. Political polarisation became increasingly evident. The subject of public security was not mentioned in political disputes, and therefore it seemed not to be a problem at all. The homicide rate, however, continued to increase, and by the end of 2003 a total of 11,342 deaths and a rate of 44 per 100,000 were reached. The increase in violence was dramatic: two and a half times more homicides than in the year that Hugo Chávez had campaigned as a presidential candidate.

From then onwards, a change took place in official policy. In 2004, official statistics were no longer published. Even statistical data on the web pages of the relevant ministries were removed. The same happened with the institutional data provider, the Instituto Nacional de Estadísticas (INE or National Institute of Statistics). Even at the time of writing (May 2014), there is no official information about crime, homicides, assaults and so on. Official censorship has prevailed during an entire decade. In 2005, researchers at the national universities decided to create the Venezuelan Observatory of Violence (Observatorio Venezolano de Violencia) as an alternative source of trustworthy statistics.

Meanwhile, the Venezuelan authorities have been denying the existence of the problem. In February 2008, President Hugo Chávez accused the researchers and journalists reporting on the increase of violence during his presidential mandate of telling lies: 'a lie the size of a cathedral' (Chávez Frías 2009). In reality, the official but censored statistics for that year (2008) indicated the occurrence of 14,489 homicides, 10,000 more than in the year he came to power.

At present, the major source for the real situation of violence in Venezuelan cities is a report based on two victimisation surveys conducted by the INE (2010), the results of which were made public although in a censored form. The first survey was conducted in 2006 (based on a sample of 5,596 households) and the second in 2009 (with a sample of 16,419 households). The 2006 survey established a tentative national homicide rate of 49 per 100,000. INE's own officials assessed it as 'an average rate of incidence, not too distant from, although higher than, the rate recorded by official statistics' (ibid.: 15). Three years later, the 2009 survey indicated a homicide rate of 75 per 100,000 inhabitants. That was a remarkable increase, much higher than those in other countries: twice as high as in Colombia (34), and three times more than Brazil (22) and Mexico (22) (UNODC 2014: 126–7).

The 2009 survey (INE 2010) also established the homicide rate for the Caracas Metropolitan Area (Área Metropolitana de Caracas or AMC): 233 homicides per 100,000, one of the highest in Latin America and indeed the world. Caracas had four times higher homicide rates and twice the rate of victims of injuries than other Venezuelan cities. And, unlike the situation in other countries, such as Mexico, violence was not concentrated in the frontier regions but in the central areas of the country, where the homicide rate doubled. In terms of abductions and robberies, small towns presented a significantly lower rate of victimisation; this can be explained, despite the reduced presence of the relevant state institutions, by the presence of much more informal social control in more remote areas of the country.

Most victims of violent crimes are male, young and poor. The population segment of the poor and extremely poor are much more prone to victimisation in terms of murder (83 per cent of all homicides), injuries (74 per cent) and robberies (60 per cent). The situation with respect to abductions is different: for the segment of the extremely poor, no victims of kidnapping are mentioned, whereas 47 per cent of abductions took place in the segments of the middle classes.

In 2014, the increasing trend of violence has persisted and the official statistics continue to be censored. A more or less official reference has been published only twice. In 2012, the Minister of the Interior, Justice and Peace acknowledged in a speech to the National Assembly, without mentioning additional details, a rate of 48 homicides per 100,000 for 2011. In 2013, a new minister reported a rate of 52 homicides per 100,000 for 2012. Calculations made by the researchers of the national universities participating in the Observatorio Venezolano de Violencia provide much higher rates: 69 for 2011, 72 for 2012 and 79 for 2013 (Briceño-León et al. 2012; OVV 2013).

Caracas' fragilities: violence in times of prosperity

How can we explain this? Our thesis is that the increase in violence in Venezuela is the consequence of the obliteration of the relevant institutions caused by the government itself, despite the increase of oil revenues and the implementation of social policies.

The common explanation of the origin and evolution of the violence is centred on the existence of mass poverty and sharp inequality (Levitt 2004; Briceño-León 2005; 2008). The increase in violence in the late 1980s and early 1990s initially appeared to support this hypothesis. However, the singularity of the violence in Venezuela is that it occurs in the period of greatest wealth and of a significant decline in poverty and income inequality in the country. In 1998, just before the great increase in homicides, the price of a barrel of oil was US $10.50. By 2008 it had increased eight times to US $86.40. Despite a slight decrease during the global financial crisis, it settled again at an average of US $100 during 2013. This means that, in the decade between 1999 and 2010, US $516.3 billion flew into the country, more than three times more money than in the previous decade, from 1986 to 1998, when the country received US $149.6 billion (Maza Zavala 2009; BCV 2012).

This immense wealth and income to the central government was, according to official sources, distributed among the population to reduce poverty and inequality. According to INE sources, the proportion of poor inhabitants declined from 29 per cent of the total population in 1998 to 20 per cent in 2013. In the same period, inequality, as measured by the Gini coefficient, declined from 0.486 in 1998 to 0.398 in 2013 (INE 2014).

During these years – and despite the many social policies of the government that sought to improve the situation of poor families, providing services, credits or allowances for study or work – a socio-politic process surfaced that transformed Caracas into a lawless metropolis, an urban conglomerate where the law was replaced by force or arbitrariness. The singularity of this process is that it is largely the consequence of government actions that damaged the normative institutional structure in Caracas. Instead of being a preventive force of law and order, it triggered and instigated urban disorder, basically seeking political and electoral successes without caring too much about the negative consequences that might result from this. Below, I mention five dimensions of the process of deterioration.

First, the urban environment became the stage for social conflict and class struggle. Political leaders and government officials supported land invasions, as well as the occupation of empty buildings and construction sites. During 2007, about two thousand families invaded the Tower of David, a 45-storey office building, unfinished because of the crisis and expropriated. The government, the owner of the building, did not prevent the occupation nor did it adapt the building for residential use. The building was simply allowed to transform into a vertical *favela* that does not meet any of the existing urban regulations. The tower does not have elevators, but motor-taxi drivers bring people and their shopping up the stairs to the twenty-eighth floor. A mall of 21,000 square metres was on the brink of opening its doors in late 2008, with all legal construction permits in hand. It was the property of one of Venezuela's most successful shopping centre holding companies. Suddenly, the president announced in his weekly television programme that the mall should be expropriated and transformed into 'a clinic, a school or university' (MPPCI 2008). Without any legal procedure and without indemnification to the proprietors, the government took possession of the property. Six years later, there was no school, clinic or university established in the building. It had been used to accommodate homeless families who had lost their houses during one of the tropical rainstorms. The police do not enter these places; public security is guaranteed by concerned citizens or irregular armed groups that control the occupied spaces.

Second, motorcycles in Caracas were traditionally forbidden from driving on the highways. In 2001, the city mayor allowed motorcycle traffic on expressways; in 2003, the federal government authorised the use of motorcycles on all roads around the clock. In addition, the government allowed the import of Chinese motorcycles as 'socialist means of transport for the poor'. The purpose was political and it paid electoral dividends in gaining support for the government. However, the number of accidents and traffic incidents rose sharply. The motorbikes were converted into the main instrument for committing crimes; furthermore, bike owners also became the victims of robberies and killings. The disorder was so pervasive that, on 4 October 2011, the government issued a decree regulating basic obligations for all motorcyclists: wear a helmet, do not drive on sidewalks and wear a prescribed vest with clear identification; do not carry more than two people on the bike and never carry children. The regulations are not obeyed, but the authorities are unwilling or unable to enforce their implementation. The police do not dare to control the riders, and the citizens are too scared to protest. In the absence of law, arms and bullets resolve conflicts between bikers and the public.

Third, the relationship between landlords and tenants is regulated by an agreement that defines the mode of transfer of the property by the owner and the rent that the tenant has to pay in return. One would expect a correction for inflation; however, beginning in 2002, and during the subsequent 11 years, the rental fee has been 'frozen' by the national government. The tenant pays the same nominal amount despite an annual inflation rate of between 25 per cent and 61 per cent. In addition, the law was modified and it was established that even in cases where the tenant failed to fulfil their commitments and, for example, did not pay the rent, they could not be evicted until they found a place to move to, provided by the government or the landlord. A similar 'right' was established for those who rented a room in somebody's house or apartment. In fact, the owners, mostly smallholders who had invested their savings in these residences as their only source of income, were left to their own devices (Lovera de Sola and Lovera 2014). Some owners remained silent; others, as leverage, moved into the halls of their houses and lived there in order to demand the return of the property by their tenants; still others sought a different and sometimes violent 'solution'. That paved the way for a new kind of businessman whose expertise is 'problem solving' by means of intimidation, using their menacing presence and arms against those who do not want to hand the property back to its owners.

Fourth, the collective labour agreements between workers and employers in the construction industry currently stipulate that 75 per cent of workers required in construction projects must be chosen by the trade union. Thus, the unions became informal employment agencies with the power to designate who is entitled to be contracted. Of course, the unions compete with each other to gain control over the projects in order to assign their affiliates to the jobs. The selection of candidates is based on friendship, political affiliation or money. The worker is charged an extra fee to get the job. The financial benefits are huge and competition for project control has become violent. In 2012 and 2013, at least 136 union leaders were killed, assassinated during violent disputes over the control of employment quotas.[4] The collective labour agreements explicitly prohibit the carrying of firearms during working hours. However, criminal gangs, whose members never were affiliates, replace the corrupt union leaders and, even from prison, negotiate new collective agreements and payment for 'protection' in order to guarantee social peace and security.

Fifth, delinquent youth gangs control Caracas' popular neighbourhoods and shanty towns, regulating drug trafficking and the provision of local services and businesses. Families accept the situation, reluctantly, and live in coexistence with their local gang; they are more afraid of the gang next door (Pedrazzini and Sánchez 2001; Zubillaga 2003; Moreno Olmedo 2009). But there are also neighbourhoods in Caracas that are controlled by a particular category of gang that call themselves 'collectives'. They claim to follow the guerrilla tradition of the 1960s and 1970s, and continue to believe in armed struggle as a means to achieve power; sometimes they declare themselves to be devoted Marxists-Leninists. Sometimes they sport military uniforms and maintain social and military order in 'their' territories, implementing 'social policies' and reforms, as if they were local mini-states. Various collectives expelled the drug traffickers and cleaned up their territories; others simply took over the criminal businesses while using revolutionary phraseology. Their territories are special areas in which the state is absent; police personnel or other individuals have to have special permission to enter these zones. Their leadership has adopted an ambiguous position vis-à-vis Hugo Chávez. Some are very critical, while others accept financial support from the government that permits them to use their radio equipment and closed-circuit television; they are allowed to go fully armed when accompanying government representatives. In one neighbourhood, they erected a statue of Tirofijo (Manuel Marulanda Vélez), the founder of the

Colombian Marxist guerrilla organisation FARC. Their activities are restricted to small territorial spaces, but their socio-political influence is enormous, as it demonstrates the legitimacy of arms and brute force employed by private groupings using political symbolism. In 2013, the police arrested members of certain collectives for illegal possession of arms. In response, motorised and armed members of these collectives surrounded police stations and forced them to release the detainees. When they asked for an adequate response, the extremely frustrated police officers encountered only silence from their superiors. 'We never arrest one of those guys again', researchers were told (Ungar 2003).

Institutional destruction and the failure of citizen security responses

The failed coup attempt against the Chávez government in 2002 turned out to have far-reaching implications for the structure of order, security and control within Venezuela's 'Bolivarian' state. Old actors and agencies were transformed, and new ones were put in place or expanded in the interstices of the revolutionary project. The consequences for the military and police were several. The participation of part of these two security institutions in the coup attempt led to a purification of both forces' hierarchies and the creation of parallel bodies (such as *milicias*, paramilitary units under direct presidential control) and the emergence of the so-called *colectivos* (collectives). These collectives were urban armed actors in support of the Chavista government, modelled on the old-style urban guerrillas. These groups were initially referred to as 'Tupamaros' (mimicking the well-known Uruguayan leftist urban guerrilla of the 1960s and 1970s), after one of the most prominent of these groups (ICG 2011; Jacome 2012). The Tupamaros collectives subsequently split up; one faction transformed into a 'legal' political organisation, while others developed into armed collectives that controlled urban areas to provide security and to push out the drug traffickers (although sometimes collectives themselves took over the local drug trade). Recently, collectives such as La Piedrita and Alexis Vive have established control over territories where the police do not enter and where they openly display their weapons and use sophisticated communication technology such as radios and closed-circuit television.

After 2002, the politicisation of the military (Fuerzas Armadas Nacionales Bolivarianas or FANB) deepened to ensure direct loyalty and political support to the president. Also, the FANB was increasingly given a role in domestic public security and law enforcement. This turned out to be part of a broader militarisation and centralisation of presidential control over public administration and also over the Misiones Bolivarianas, the social and poverty alleviation programmes of the government (Kruijt and Koonings 2013). The creation of new, parallel security bodies ran counter to the growing need to reform the police in the face of the escalation of violence and crime, especially in Caracas (ICG 2011; Jacome 2012).

The police in Venezuela were traditionally highly fragmented. Until 2007, the country counted 123 different uniformed policing organisations: 24 state police forces and 99 at the municipal level. Caracas had a metropolitan police force and municipal police forces in the five municipalities of metropolitan Caracas (Briceño-León 2007: 165). In 2006–07, a national police reform was devised to address the complex legacy of police dysfunction (ibid.). The combined forces were large but inefficient, corrupt and violent, and involved in criminal activities. In addition, policing became increasingly political after the 2002 coup attempt. The police reform aimed to create a new national police force, called Policía Nacional Bolivariana (PNB). The initial implementation was slow and could not escape the tendency of militarisation and centralisation. In Caracas, the substitution of the metropolitan police by the PNB was not effective in stemming the rising tide of violence, in part because former police officers who were not incorporated into the new PNB became active in organised crime (ICG 2011: 25). In addition, the overlap of responsibilities, competition and inter-institutional rivalries between the PNB, the military, the *milicias* and even the collectives further deepened what can only be understood as institutional destruction (ibid.: 21 ff.). The failure to reform a largely ineffective judiciary and prison system added to this implosion.

In Caracas, the destruction of formal institutions has not been compensated by the functioning of informal institutions such as family, schools, religion, community leaders and, I would add, the informal operations of the police. In small- and medium-sized cities in the country, these institutions shape informal social cohesion and control: people know each other, family ties allow for a certain control over youth, schools can identify violent juveniles and teachers communicate with parents and the local police. Local leaders can more easily contain criminals or strike deals with them to prevent excessive violence. In Caracas, these mechanisms are largely absent; anonymity and a greater diversity of social actors are far more conducive to violent crime. This is reinforced by the fragmentation and internal rivalries of the different metropolitan police forces already mentioned. As I noted, Caracas consists of five municipalities and therefore has five police forces. In fact, there are seven forces if we include the PNB and the criminal investigation body (Cuerpo de Investigación Científicas, Penales y Criminalísticas or CICPC). There is no coordination between these forces. The metropolitan administration is responsible for the coordination of public security policy but, because this administration is in the hands of the national opposition, the municipal police of Libertador, which is controlled by the national government, does not participate in this effort. Furthermore, the metropolitan administration does not receive support from the national Ministry of the Interior. In sum, what is already difficult in any large city has become much more complicated in Caracas because of this institutional and political polarisation.

Defensive resilience

It would be unfair to suggest that the government of Venezuela did not propose or implement programmes to counter crime in the country and in Caracas. In the 15 years from 1999 to 2014, 22 security plans were developed, some of them especially aimed at the situation in Caracas: Plan Bratton in 2001 (when the metropolitan municipality invited experts from New York), Plan Misión Caracas (Caracas Mission Plan) in 2006, Caracas Segura (Safe Caracas) in 2008, Plan Ruta Segura (Safe Route) in 2008, Noche Segura (Safe Night) in 2009 and Autopista Segura (Safe Highway) in 2010. National programmes were devised, including DIBISE (Dispositivo Bicentanario de Seguridad or the Bicentenary Security Module) in 2010, Misión a Toda Vida Venezuela (Mission for a Full Life) in 2012 and Patria Segura (Safe Fatherland) in 2013.

What one can criticise is the fact that no evaluation of the implementation was published, nor was any explanation given as to why they were abandoned and replaced with other plans. For instance, Plan Ruta Segura was launched in response to the protests of the public transport sector about the many murders of bus drivers. The plan stipulated that an armed soldier would be present on every city bus in order to protect both passengers and drivers. A few months later the plan was suspended without explanation. Afterwards, it was rumoured in the corridors of police stations that delinquents had assaulted the soldiers, stealing their rifles. One can conclude, given the situation discussed above, that the plans presented in the last 15 years failed to reduce crime and violence. Security policies are measured by results, not by intentions, and violent crime in Venezuela did not decrease, but redoubled.

Given this situation of governmental powerlessness, residents of Caracas have only three options left: first, to restrict their daily work and other activities to specific times and places; second, to build up or get access to private security, in all its forms; and finally, to join neighbourhood actions. The citizens of Caracas are avoiding public places for fear of becoming a victim of violence; shopping malls have become the safe haven of urban leisure and activities for the middle classes. Those who live in the shanty towns come back home from work pretty early and control their outdoor visits afterwards. Schools, shops, stores and cinemas reduce their evening programmes for fear of shoplifting, burglary and kidnapping. Young people, and sometimes entire families, move to another city when threatened by gangs or criminals. Private security of varying types has been employed according to social class and income. The armoured car industry has become a thriving business despite the high cost of its products; customers need to register on a waiting list of three to six months to be able to equip their cars with protective shields. Businessmen and others who belong to the upper-middle classes hire bodyguards when they attend a party or when they come home after an overnight flight. Senior government officials and seriously rich people are protected, of course, by permanent bodyguards.

The urban landscape has been changed by the emergence of gated communities, walls around residences, gated roads and exits in the middle-class neighbourhoods, and pedestrian paths with railings in the popular *barrios* and informal settlements. Houses have adopted higher walls, electric fences or sharp barbed wire. Families in the shanty towns close their windows with cement or build up a double wall in order to prevent the entry of bullets. In general, the response by the population has been to retreat in a form of social autism. In interviews and focus groups organised by researchers, they express it in one sentence: 'Don't look, don't hear, and don't tell.' Their advice is repeated: 'Mind only your own business and your family's. Don't react, don't report, don't resist. Don't look at the heavies and the thugs.'

Nevertheless, there are people and organisations in the *barrios* of Caracas who do resist violence: mothers, schoolteachers and religious groups. In a modest way and without support from the authorities, they build barriers of containment, informal institutions that in some cases achieve ceasefire agreements between the gangs, or non-aggression pacts around schools, or a temporary cessation of hostilities during religious festivals.

Conclusion

The final result of this process of steady deterioration has been an enormous loss of life and freedom, a loss of fundamental rights, destabilising elementary principles of citizenship and even the right to the city. Formal institutional arrangements, based on law and order, were undermined by political power. The government believed that the law was contrary to its revolutionary interests, but it did not provide regulatory substitutes. The result was a loss of social order governed by recognised and sanctioned rules, the deficiency of the police, the increase of arbitrary power and, finally, widespread anomie. Personalism and authoritarianism were imposed as the new style of government. Rules and agreements were substituted by the use of force and arms. The actions had the political purpose of conquest and consolidation of power, but the consequence was an increase in common crime.

The forces of moral contention were shattered and the institutions of control and punishment, like the police and the tribunals, lost their capacity for action. This is the reason why Caracas, once considered an outlet of heaven, became an urban hell. Building up the institutional framework of law and order is what other national and metropolitan authorities did in Medellín, Bogotá and São Paulo. In the past, these urban conglomerates were much more violent than Caracas, but their governments managed to reverse the trend and reduce their violence and their homicide rate. The social order has an important material basis, but the rules that control relationships between human beings and that, formally or informally, establish mechanisms of cooperation and conflict resolution are more important (Becker 1968; Zaibert 2005; Lijphart 1999). This lesson, sadly, has not been learned in Caracas.

Studies on the historical evolution of violence highlight the importance of these institutional processes. The long civilising process that implicated the development of sensitivity, self-restraint and control of violence was a process of normative construction that accompanied changes in the power of society (Elias 1987; Eisner 2001). The loss or recovery of the legitimacy of social institutions has been used to explain variations in the number of homicides in the United States (LaFree 1998; 1999) and in Japan (Roberts and LaFree 2004). In Latin America, one explanation for the decline in homicides in São Paulo is the strict gun control implemented by the state (Goertzel and Khan 2009; Nadanovsky 2009). This explanation refers to the necessary but not the sufficient conditions. Gun control and disarmament require a normative and regulatory system capable of establishing that these actions have a moral value, but also a police force capable of enforcing them and courts to punish the offenders. This means norms and institutions. In Bogotá, the decline in murders has been explained as a result of the measures to enhance the quality of urban space, traffic regulation and restricted sale of alcoholic beverages (see Chapter 4 in this volume). But behind all this action on urban regulations or transit rules are established and enforced rules and norms. This is what former Bogotá mayor Antanas Mockus (Mockus et al. 2012) calls 'civic culture': the normative dimension of social order that reinforces the strengths and weaknesses of cities. Analysing the decrease in homicides in London, from a rate of 20 per 100,000 in the late Middle Ages to less than one homicide in the twentieth century, Gurr (1981) uses the idea of a 'huge cultural change' and refers to it as a change in the 'internal and external' system of controls.

What has happened in Caracas at the turn of the century and thereafter can perhaps be explained similarly. A major cultural change took place, but in the opposite direction: the loss of internal and external controls on aggressive and illegal behaviour. The amazing point in the comparison is how slow the processes of institution building are and how quickly they can be destroyed. But perhaps so are the social processes conducive to democracy: hard to gain and easy to lose (Dahl 1971; O'Donnell 2000; Karstedt 2006). In the mountains of the Venezuelan Andes, people have an expression that reflects this: 'It's hard to climb with a rock to the top of the mountain, but it's easy to throw it downhill.'

4 | BOGOTÁ: COUNTERING VIOLENCE WITH URBAN GOVERNMENT

Alan Gilbert*

Introduction: crime in Latin America

Latin America is a rather unsafe place. While few people have ever lost their lives in wars against foreign countries, far too many are killed by their fellow citizens. Indeed, homicide rates have risen dramatically in many Latin American cities over the last couple of decades. However, violence has not risen everywhere and Bogotá is one city where the level of violence has fallen spectacularly since a peak in the early 1990s. In this respect, Bogotá's crime history is very distinctive.

This chapter will discuss the city's recent history of violence and show that much of the received wisdom about violence provides an inadequate explanation of what has happened. Bogotá's experience shows that causation is complicated and simple explanations are rarely helpful in explaining local rises, or falls, in crime rates. The analysis covers the situation in Bogotá and Colombia until mid-2012, coinciding with the end of the presidency of Álvaro Uribe (2002–10) and the beginning of Juan Manuel Santos's first term (2010–14), and the first months of the mayorship of Gustavo Petro in Bogotá.

Crime and violence in Latin America have become major concerns of politicians and, increasingly, academics.[1] Few seem to doubt that cities are the main foci of violence and that the situation is getting worse (Koonings and Kruijt 2007; Moser 2004: 6; Davis 2006: 181; Horowitz 2005; *El Diario de Hoy* 2011). Indeed, Rotker (2002) claims that:

* I should like to thank the following for helping me to understand the crime situation in Bogotá: Hugo Acero, Ariel Avila, Rúben Dario Ramírez, Juan Carlos Flórez, María Teresa Garcés, Jerónimo Castro, Carlos Mario Perea and Eduardo Corredor.

Citizens of Latin American capitals live in constant fear, amidst some of the most dangerous conditions on earth. In that vast region, about 140 thousand people die violently each year, and one out of three citizens has been directly or indirectly victimised by violence.

There is some justification for this somewhat apocalyptic statement insofar as all but three of the top 25 most violent cities in the world are to be found in Latin America (IUDPAS 2011).[2] All of those cities have homicide rates of more than 47 per 100,000 inhabitants, compared with rates of less than three in most of Europe. However, the idea that violence in Latin America is growing everywhere is not entirely accurate. While the statistical evidence for 1980–2006 shows that homicide rates rose across the region as a whole, between 2003 and 2007, murder rates rose in the Caribbean and Central America but fell in South America (Malby 2010: 15).

While some countries have seen dramatic rises in crime, notably Guatemala, Honduras, Venezuela and most recently Mexico, others, including Colombia, have seen a fall. A similarly mixed pattern appears at the urban level. The rise in violent crime in the drug centres of Mexico, in Caracas and in many Central American cities is perfectly clear, but violent deaths are relatively rare in Buenos Aires and Montevideo. In Colombian cities, the trend in homicide rates is mostly downwards (see Chapters 1 and 2 for more detailed information).

Crime in Bogotá: changes over time

Bogotá suffers from much higher levels of violence than most cities in Europe. Some 16.6 homicides per 100,000 inhabitants occurred in the first half of 2012, compared with rates of less than three in most cities in Europe. In addition, mugging and domestic violence are common events and far too many citizens take the law into their own hands. Many explain the high levels of violence in Bogotá and other cities in Colombia in terms of their 'culture' of domestic violence, machismo and excessive drinking (Gaitán 2001). The country has had a long history of civil conflict, and the ready availability of guns means that quarrels may lead to death (Safford and Palacios 2002; Duque and Klevens 2000: 198; Malby 2010). In Bogotá, guns are used in two-thirds of killings – admittedly a rate lower than the Colombian average of 80 per cent (*El Tiempo* 2012c; *Observatorio* 2009: 142). But contrary to local belief, most *bogotanos* are no more likely to kill their fellow citizens than are Londoners (Duque and Klevens 2000: 195; Montenegro et al. 2000). If they were, then violence would be spread fairly evenly across the city. The figures show, however, that homicide has long been concentrated in the city's clubs and bars and in certain notorious black spots (Llorente et al. 2001; CEACSC 2012). Nor do most 'structural' factors explain either spatial or temporal patterns in violence in the city (Montegro et al. 2000; Acero 2003: 34; Rubio 2000). Llorente et al. (2001: 13) show that the most violent areas in Bogotá in the late 1990s were not among the poorest and there was a negative correlation between the index of misery and violence. And, since 1981, there has been absolutely no correlation between different measures of crime and unemployment, poverty and education. As Martin and Ceballos (2004: 708) point out, between 1995 and 2003, poverty and unemployment first rose and then decreased, but crime rates fell consistently. And, for a longer period, from 1970 to 1991, homicide rates quadrupled while the rate of poverty fell by half (Gaitán and Afanador 1996: 41). Since the early 1960s, education levels have generally risen while homicide first increased and then fell. What seems to have been more significant since 1960 is the national pattern, especially the fact that crime – and homicide in particular – increased rapidly throughout the country from less than 5,000 deaths per annum in the first half of the 1970s to 26,000 in the 1990s.

Bogotá's history of homicide since 1961 can be categorised into four periods. Before 1979, it was an unsafe city but one in which the death rate was fairly low. However, from 1979 until 1993, the murder rate rose first slowly and then very quickly until it reached the tragic level of 80 homicides per 100,000 in 1993. Subsequently, the homicide rate declined rapidly although it never returned to the low levels of the 1960s and 1970s. After 2008, the homicide rate began to rise again before falling once more.

1961 to 1979: an insecure and dangerous city but one that was still liveable   Crime has always been a problem in Bogotá but killings were relatively rare in the 1960s. Between 1965 and 1978, the homicide rate averaged around ten per 100,000 inhabitants, far too high but half of the national figure and low relative to that in many other Latin American cities today.[3] Much of the crime was conducted by organised gangs, some of which originated in other parts of Colombia (Ávila Martínez 2010: 10). The emerald mafia of Víctor Carranza controlled the city and perhaps kept violence in check in a way similar to the Yakuza in Japan.[4] Most injuries were the result of interpersonal conflict and domestic violence (Museo de Bogotá n.d.). The security system was weak and the police operated as part of a national organisation; the force in Bogotá was small, poorly equipped and very badly trained. If the perpetrators of homicide were sometimes caught, it was because they handed themselves in (Gaitán 2001: 86). The justice system, as now, was extraordinarily slow and unpredictable.

1979 to 1992: an increasingly violent city Homicide rates began to rise in Bogotá after 1978, dropped for a brief period, and then rose dramatically in the late 1980s. In 1994, 'Bogotá was the Latin American capital with the highest homicide rate' (Museo de Bogotá n.d.). The increase in violence in Colombia's major cities was associated with the rise of drug trafficking (Gaviria 2000; Montenegro et al. 2000). In Medellín, and later Cali, inter-gang battles for territory and official attempts to clamp down on that violence led to extraordinarily high rates of homicide: 586 per 100,000 at one point in Medellín and 149 in Cali. Although Bogotá was less involved in drug trafficking, the number of homicides escalated with Pablo Escobar's declaration of war on the state. During the late 1980s, the Medellín cartel launched a campaign of car bombs, kidnapping and selective assassination in the city. The most spectacular attacks included the Palace of Justice siege in 1985 (at least 117 deaths),[5] the killing of the editor of *El Espectador* newspaper in 1986, and a whole series of events during 1989 including the assassination of Luis Carlos Galán, who was odds on to win the presidential election, the death of the Minister of Justice, the bombing of *El Espectador* newspaper, the blowing up of a commercial flight between Bogotá and Cali (107 deaths) and the destruction of the headquarters of the intelligence services (64 dead). The drug gangs did not only attack the state. In July 1989, Gonzalo Rodríguez Gacha (*El Mexicano*), who was in charge of the military arm of the Medellín cartel and sought to control Colombia's emerald trade, attacked the Bogotá headquarters of his rival Víctor Carranza.

But it was not only the drug gangs who were killing people. The guerrilla movements also increased their activity during the 1980s and early 1990s. Rubio (2000: 172) estimates that the number of guerrillas operating nationally rose from little more than 1,000 in 1982 to over 11,000 in 1997. The FARC (Fuerzas Armadas Revolucionarias de Colombia) began to develop guerrilla units in poorer areas of Bogotá in the early 1980s (Casas Dupuy and González Cepero 2005: 253), some of which were destroyed later by members of the AUC (Autodefensas Unidas de Colombia), who also 'cleansed' the city of perceived delinquents, drug addicts and prostitutes.

Although Gaitán (1995: 386) argues that perhaps only one-fifth of all homicides in Colombia were committed directly by either drug gangs or guerrillas, he believes that they were ultimately responsible for the dramatic escalation in violence. As Gaviria (2000: 20) explains:

On the one hand, they directly generated violence through their activities, and, on the other, they indirectly generated violence through various criminal externalities: congestion in law enforcement, spillovers of knowledge, supply of weapons, and the creation of a 'culture' that favoured easy-money and violent resolution of conflicts over more traditional values.

The increase in drug and guerrilla violence was critical in occupying an already ineffective police and justice system. In 1988, only one homicide in 200 resulted in a criminal going to jail and, while the rate had improved by 1992, 98 per cent of homicides still remained unsolved (Gaitán and Afanador 1996: 47). Not surprisingly, the general public had little confidence in the security system; in 1993 only 20 per cent of crimes were reported to the police and only 1.5 per cent of those led to any kind of sanction (ibid.: 66). There was growing suspicion that many in the police force were not only ignoring criminal activity but were participating in crime themselves (Escobedo 2006: 340). The security system simply could not cope with the escalation in crime, which encouraged potential criminals to join in. And as the number of crimes increased, so did the rate of homicides.

The activities of the drug gangs also acted as a laboratory for learning. Gaviria (2000: 13) argues that ordinary criminals:

may have learned from the cartels how to buy arms in international black markets, how to launder illegal money and how to identify 'connections' inside the law enforcement agencies. Also, drug business played a prominent role in the diffusion of criminal technology and, particularly, of weapons.

And it is possible that, as the cartels' activities gained 'street cred', 'they may have played a crucial role in the erosion of morals' throughout society. This argument would explain why most kinds of crime increased in Bogotá even though the drug cartels were far less visible than in Medellín or Cali. It was the general spread of criminality throughout society, 'from the dishonest official to the burglar, the kidnapper, the taxi driver who does not respect the rules', that explained the explosion in crime and violence from 1979 to 1992 (Gaitán and Afanador 1996: 65). However, Gaitán and Afanador's (ibid.) own statistics suggest that the increase in crime and violence was very patchy. While organised criminal activity, such as bank holdups and kidnapping, did increase rapidly after 1986, less organised branches of crime, such as mugging and general robbery, did not rise at the same speed. I therefore believe that Llorente et al. (2001: 7) are correct in arguing that the extraordinary rise in national killing has to be explained primarily in terms of 'the presence and activity of irregular armed groups – drug traffickers, guerrillas and paramilitaries – as well as the deficient operation of the justice system'. Slowly, the national disease of violence spread to Bogotá, growing with the proliferation of new kinds of criminal gang.

1994 to 2007: declining violence and better governance   After 1993, Bogotá benefited from a major improvement in the quality of its administration (Bromberg 2003; Montezuma 2005; Gilbert and Dávila 2002; Gilbert 2006; Gilbert and Garcés 2008; Silva and Cleuren 2009). Through luck or judgement, the electorate voted in a series of honest and effective mayors. Over time they improved the city's finances, introduced a radical change in the transport system and for the first time generated some pride among the citizenry.

Many argue that the fall in homicides and crime was a direct result of the policies introduced by Antanas Mockus (1995–97) and developed by the next three administrations (Acero 2003; Martin and Ceballos 2004; Gilbert and Garcés 2008; Silva and Cleuren 2009; PNUD 2004; Mockus 2001). For the first time, the district administration took seriously its constitutional responsibility for tackling crime (Acero 2003: 42–3; Martin and Ceballos 2004: 710). The quality of policing was greatly improved and major efforts were made to improve social behaviour and to reduce the 'high level of divorce between the law, morals and culture' (Mockus 2001: 1). People had to learn that they could live together (*convivencia*) (Acero 2003: 16). Several important changes were made to the police service, something that was essential given that only 17 per cent of the public had any confidence in the force in 1992 (Beckett and Godoy 2010: 287). The Mockus administration dismissed large numbers of officers and closed down the whole traffic police department in 1996 to demonstrate that corruption would not be tolerated in the city. Morale within the force was improved by teaching officers about their civic duties and the problems that they would face on the streets (Acero 2003: 57). Coordination with the national authorities also improved; monthly security councils under the chairmanship of the mayor brought police commanders, the armed forces, justice agencies and human rights organisations together. The security budget increased nine-fold between 1993 and 2003 – most of the money being spent on improving the quality of staff and their equipment. New vehicles were purchased and officers on street patrol were issued with radios. Investigative capacity was improved and the better recording and mapping of crime meant that *Centros de Atención Inmediata* (CAIs) were put in strategic locations. A key objective was to bring the police closer to the people.

Between 1995 and 2003, a real effort was made to improve the way in which *bogotanos* behaved (Mockus 2001). People needed to have more respect for the law, help their neighbours and get involved in ways that would stop crime. If that occurred, fewer police officers would be needed. Several unorthodox initiatives were introduced to reduce the number of killings. A voluntary disarmament programme was launched in 1996 in response to the fact that around half of all killings involved a gun (Acero 2003: 66). The campaign led to a few guns being handed in but real progress was achieved in 1997 with a decree banning the carrying of arms (Bromberg and Gomescásseres 2009: 183–4). A second initiative was intended to curb deaths caused by drunken fights; in December 1995, nightclubs and bars were ordered to close at 1.00 a.m., the so-called 'carrot hour'.[6] Third, a public education programme tried to change the way in which *bogotanos* drove their cars, educating drivers about respecting road crossings and traffic lights and not to drink and drive. Some 150 mime artists were employed to persuade drivers not to park on white lines or zebra crossings.[7] To back this up, ten mobile units were set up in 1995 to control drink-driving and to stop people driving too fast.

Mayors Mockus and Peñalosa both believed that improved public amenities would help to create neighbourhood cohesion and pride, thereby reducing violence (Gutiérrez et al. 2009: 11). Enrique Peñalosa invested heavily in new parks, built mini-football pitches in poor neighbourhoods and established several stunning new mega-libraries. He also sought to control *bogotanos*' habit of parking wherever they wished by erecting bollards on pavements. He introduced an annual car-free day and established a network of cycle lanes. He also removed itinerant traders from many streets and squares, both to reduce crime and to improve the look of the city.[8] Beckett and Godoy (2010: 278) argue that:

> the Bogotá example shows that it is possible to take crime and disorder, and the fear they generate, seriously, and to enjoy reductions in serious crime, yet to couple policing and other security measures with broader initiatives to strengthen democratic inclusion, extend and deepen citizenship, and shore up the rule of law.

And Hugo Acero, who played a key role in introducing many of these initiatives, argues that they had a real impact.

> After eight years under three governments, the policy results have been impressive, citizen culture has changed, there is a greater commitment to development of the city and deaths from homicide and road accidents have fallen from 80 in 1993 to 28.4 in 2002 and from 25 in 1995 to 10.5 in 2002, respectively. (Acero 2003: 17)

The national context

However, not everyone is convinced that the Mockus–Peñalosa approach to crime was responsible for the dramatic fall in crime and violence in Bogotá after 1993. Three main criticisms have been put forward.[9]

National trends Homicide rates began to decline nationally in 1991, a couple of years before they began to fall in Bogotá (Acero 2011). The improvement nationally was the result of:

> a series of reforms in national security policy, in particular reform of the administration of justice and the police, strengthening of the intelligence services, the fight against criminal organisations and in general the adoption of more coherent security policies. (Martin and Ceballos 2004: 706)

Murder rates also fell in other large cities, even those that had not improved their own security systems. Particularly impressive was the decline in the murder rate in Medellín, from 586 per 100,000 in 1991 to around 46 in 2006 (Ruiz Vásquez 2009: 106). Whatever was happening in Bogotá was part of a national trend.

A return to normality Casas Dupuy and González Cepero (2005: 285) argue that 'the fall in homicide rates in Bogotá from a historical viewpoint is less exceptional than the increase that preceded it. The reduction registered from 1993 wasn't really a reduction, but a return to an earlier average.' The same argument would apply to the rise in violence in Cali and Medellín, and indeed across the country as a whole. Violence grew during the 1970s and 1980s because of the bellicosity of the drug gangs and the guerrillas. After 1992, the state managed to reduce the influence of these groups and they in turn changed tactics. The most powerful drug gang, the Cartel de Cali, eschewed Pablo Escobar's tactics of confronting the state, relying more on bribery and infiltration. While they did not abstain from violence, the level of drug-related homicides generally declined. Something similar occurred with the guerrilla movements. While the number of militants increased from little more than 1,000 in 1982 to over 11,000 in 1997, the FARC and the ELN (Ejército de Liberación Nacional) relied less on killing people and more on kidnapping and terrorism (Rubio 2000: 172). This was part of a tactical retreat, to cope with the increasingly effective security offensive launched by the national government (Martin and Ceballos 2004: 705).

Bogotá's security policies merely accentuated national trends Mockus relied heavily on educational programmes and pedagogic shock tactics to improve the quality of citizenship. However, Ruiz Vásquez (2009: 106) claims that there is no evidence 'to show the relationship between the citizen culture programmes and changes in citizen behaviour'. And, critically, homicide rates had started to decline in Bogotá in 1993, two years before Antanas Mockus became mayor and the new approach to security had even started (Ruiz Vásquez 2009: 106; Casas Dupuy and González Cepero 2005: 286). Since cultural policies usually take years to take effect, Mockus' campaign was an unlikely cause of the sudden decline in violence. In addition, Gutiérrez et al. (2009: 13) argue that, despite employing very similar security policies, 'Cali is conspicuous for having had no miracle … Homicide and crime rates remain very high.'

Llorente et al. (2001: 7) point out that a cultural approach cannot work because urban violence is not the result of public intolerance and poor citizenship. Most killings are committed by organised bands of criminals dedicated to underground activity of one kind or another. These bands vary considerably in both their organisation and their objectives (from crime to social cleansing) but share one common denominator – their use of violence. This argument is supported by the fact that most crime is committed in a limited number of places rather than being spread across the city. There is a close association between the hotspots of violence and the operation of illegal markets and outlaw activities belonging to the 'underground world' (ibid.: 16). Between 1997 and 1999, one-fifth of all homicides were concentrated in 21 of the city's 603 census districts, where only 5 per cent of the population lived (ibid.: 10).

These arguments, which are directed at Mockus' and Peñalosa's pedagogic and public space policies, do not address the point that these mayors also attacked crime in more traditional ways. Both took action in crime hotspots and, indeed, the mapping exercise conducted by the municipality's SUIVD (Sistema Unificado de Información de Violencia y Delincuencia – Unified System for Information on Violence and Crime) was instrumental in identifying those areas. They also acted against perceived concentrations of crime in, for example, *El Cartucho*, a rundown area close to the city centre known as a centre for criminal activity of all sorts. This 'community' was removed in 1998 and is now the site of the Tercer Milenio park (Beckett and Godoy 2010: 291). Their policies were much more coherent and coordinated than earlier efforts and incorporated much of received wisdom from other cities. Whatever the critics say, the cultural and space initiatives must have helped reduce crime and cut the murder rate. After all, deaths from road accidents fell from 1,341 in 1994 to 585 in 2003, the result of a major campaign to improve road safety and reduce drink-driving and the upward trend in property crime was also reversed (Ospina 2005).[10]

From 2008: a new crime surge or a mere blip?

Unfortunately, increasing discussion of insecurity under the left-wing mayorship of Lucho Garzón (2004–07) began to hit the headlines almost from the day his successor Samuel Moreno became mayor in January 2008. Between 2006 and 2010, the number of murders in the city had risen from 1,336 to 1,726 (CEASC 2012). A crime wave appeared to be hitting the city. Opinion polls revealed that 72 per cent of people felt unsafe in December 2010 compared with only 39 per cent in December 2007 (CCB 2011). The only consolation for *bogotanos* was that homicide rates were much higher in most other Colombian cities, especially in Cali and in Medellín (*Razón Pública* 2011). Several explanations were put forward to explain the deteriorating security situation.

The changing national security situation   Few doubt that the national administration of Álvaro Uribe (2002–10) was highly effective in improving security in the countryside. The 'democratic security policy' that was introduced in 2003 cut homicides, kidnappings and terrorist attacks and allowed the government to establish a permanent police or military presence in every Colombian municipality for the first time in decades. An agreement with the AUC led first to its partial disbandment and then total demobilisation by 2007. A major effort was also launched to control the FARC. But some observers suggest that the very success of the rural campaign led to former paramilitary and guerrilla groups moving to the cities (Cano 2009; Ortiz 2011); indeed, this was part of the campaign insofar as the amnesty programmes introduced in the mid-2000s brought 5,700 ex-combatants and their families to Bogotá (Ávila Martínez and Pérez 2011: 85). Some of these people engaged in criminal activity in the city, with one report suggesting that paramilitary gangs were operating in ten of Bogotá's 20 *localidades* (*Cambio* 2009).[11] Ortiz (2011: 11) claims that demobilised paramilitaries are active in the drug trade, are operating protection rackets and are involved in campaigns of social cleansing (Casas Dupuy and González Cepero 2005; Romero 2011; Escobedo 2006: 330). Their activities explain the sudden rise in violence and homicide.[12]

Of course, former paramilitaries are only part of the problem, and the Santos government is now referring to the threat posed by new kinds of criminal organisation (*bandas criminales emergentes* or BACRIMs) that are operating across the country (Ortiz 2011; *Razón Pública* 2011; *Semana* 2011b; *Semana* 2011c). These groups are seemingly better organised than gangs in the past. Former senator and then mayor Gustavo Petro claims that, 30 years ago, gangs operated independently, whereas today's organisations are interconnected and their networks have 'captured, co-opted and reconfigured the state' (*El Espectador* 2011).[13] Older established criminal bands also continue to operate in the city, where they are involved in the sale of drugs, control of prostitution, money laundering and gun running (Romero 2011). In addition, guerrilla groups continue to be active and, in September 2008, they launched a series of bomb attacks on stores that had refused to pay protection money (*El Tiempo* 2008c). Perhaps it is this very proliferation of different kinds of criminal band in the city that has led to a rise in violence. For, unlike the situation in the 1960s and 1970s, when powerful mafias controlled most forms of crime in the city, the recent proliferation of criminal groups has led to competition and violence between those groups (Ávila Martínez and Núñez Gantival 2010: 52).

Finally, there is the problem of the *pandillas* and *parches* (Zorro Sánchez 2004; Perea Restrepo 2007).[14] An official study in 2003 claimed that 691 youth gangs were operating in Bogotá with up to 12,000 members; another, in 2008, counted 1,319 youth gangs with 20,000 members (Ramos 2004; Linares 2011). Their members carry guns and knives in order to steal from people on the street, break into homes and rob businesses. For some young criminals, these are the training grounds before being recruited into organised criminal bands. What is clear is that it is predominantly young men who commit crimes. In 2006, 78 per cent of the people captured by the police in Bogotá were aged between 12 and 35 (Escobedo 2006: 270). This also explains why so many die violently: in 2011, 56 per cent of murders in Bogotá involved people aged between 20 and 34 (*El Tiempo* 2012c).

The increasing use of drugs A second explanation for the recent rise in violence is that local drug consumption is increasing. The economic recession in Europe and the USA and increasing competition from other suppliers, notably those operating in Mexico, have reduced the profits to be made from international trafficking. This has encouraged Colombian gangs to target the domestic market more aggressively (*El Espectador* 2009; Ávila Martínez and Pérez 2011).

There is scattered evidence to support the idea that drug consumption is rising in Bogotá. Linares (2011) claims that 90 per cent of *pandilla* members consume drugs, and, in 2010, the retiring police chief announced that the great majority of police arrests were related to drug use and trafficking (Caracol Radio 2010). Most worrying is the suggestion that drug use is increasing among secondary school students (*El Tiempo* 2008a; Amat 2012).

Poor policing and local administrative failures   Others claim that the recent surge in criminal activity in Bogotá is the fault of the authorities. While the national government continues its military strategy against the guerrillas in the countryside, it has failed to tackle the mafias in the cities (Angarita 2009). The local authorities have also been guilty in that they have failed to build on their earlier successes. In addition, political differences between the mayor and the national government have meant that there is little coordination. The public have long complained that Bogotá has too few police officers (*Semana* 2011a). In 2008, Bogotá had one policeman for every 514 inhabitants compared with a United Nations recommendation of one per 250 (*El Tiempo* 2008b). The number had risen to 12,000 (plus 6,000 *auxiliares*) in 2011, but many would argue that this still leaves the city under-policed (Guevara 2011); after all, New York, a city with a similar population, has 50,000 (Murrain 2010).[15] Of course, the effectiveness of the police does not depend simply on their numbers, and locals frequently complain of inefficiency and worse. Some claim that the police are bribed to turn a blind eye, they are in league with the gangs and 'one knows of some police who manage fabulous prostitution and drug businesses' (Puentes Melo 2011; *El Espectador* 2011). Public trust in the police is again in decline; while it had risen to 46 per cent in 2008, it had fallen to 27 per cent two years later. In 2011, only 27 per cent of victims bothered to report a crime and 98 per cent of reported crime remained unsolved (Bogotá Cómo Vamos 2011; *El Tiempo* 2010).

In their defence, the police argue that they have greatly improved their effectiveness and that their efforts are often undermined by the deficiencies of the justice system. In September 2010, the retiring head of Bogotá's police force complained that, during the year, the police had captured 20,485 people but only one-third of them were behind bars. Certainly, few would defend the Colombian justice system. It is far too slow and open to all kinds of abuses.

Currently, there are signs of an improvement in security in the city. Gustavo Petro, who became mayor in January 2012, has introduced several new measures to address the security situation. He has cracked down on the carrying of guns, which were linked to 65 per cent of all homicides in 2011 (*El Tiempo* 2011b), and the police have set up 43 elite groups to combat the escalating rate of mobile phone theft (*El Tiempo* 2012b). In addition, he has stepped up the *cuadrantes* initiative started in 2010. This is an attempt to provide proper protection for the population in specific areas of the city and seems to have helped reduce feelings of insecurity (*El Tiempo* 2012b). And, in August 2012, he made a controversial announcement that he hoped to decriminalise drug use and to create treatment centres for addicts (*Semana* 2012). Only time will tell whether or not these measures are working, but recent indications are that crime and violence are no longer increasing. During the first half of 2012, the homicide rate of 16.6 killings per 100,000 inhabitants was the lowest since the late 1970s (*El Tiempo* 2012b). Recent victimisation surveys also show that most forms of crime seem to be diminishing (*El Tiempo* 2012a). If this trend continues, it will be clear that the worrying rise in crime and violence after 2008 really was a blip and not a return to the bad old days of the early 1990s.

Conclusion

It seems that the actions of organised crime best explain the rise and fall in violence in Colombia. The rapid increase in deaths in the 1980s, both nationally and in Bogotá, was linked primarily to the operations of the drug cartels and the guerrillas. When the national government responded to the guerrilla and drug threats, homicide rates rose from moderate levels in the 1960s to the horrifying levels of the early 1990s. Negotiation with some armed groups, a crackdown on the guerrillas and better directed security measures led to violence falling during the 1990s. In Bogotá, homicide rates also rose in the late 1980s and fell during the 1990s. The decline was faster than in most other cities and was hastened by an impressive set of local actions that improved the physical infrastructure, the effectiveness of the police and public attitudes. However sensible those policies were, they would not have been so effective without complementary changes in national security policy. The decline in homicide in most of the country's major cities was linked to the fall of Pablo Escobar, the changing tactics of the remaining drug cartels and increasing control over the guerrilla movements.

Bogotá's experience contravenes received wisdom about crime in Latin America in several ways.

First, it shows that trends in crime and homicide fluctuate; at times they may rise but later they may fall. Bogotá's homicide rate of around ten deaths per 100,000 inhabitants in the 1960s, rising to 80 in 1992 and around 17 currently (2012), demonstrates this clearly.

Second, the evidence from Bogotá undermines the idea that there is a 'culture of violence' among the population at large. Most killings are linked to the activities of organised crime. Drug dealing increases insecurity and struggles between gangs contribute enormously to general crime rates and particularly to homicide. Effective policing and military intervention help control that violence but it is extremely difficult because of the resources that the drug gangs can mobilise against the authorities. Many stories are told of how drug gangs outgun the public security forces and how they both bribe and threaten the authorities.

Third, Bogotá's security policy after 1995 did not reduce crime and violence on its own. And, while it shows that local policy can improve public morale, cut the number of road deaths and accelerate positive national trends, it also shows that local authorities need a supportive national policy. While the Uribe government did not help Bogotá directly, it did reduce the level of drug, paramilitary and guerrilla activity nationally. It is difficult to reduce local violence if there is a wave of criminal activity nationally.

Fourth, Bogotá shows the advantages of establishing a reliable and trustworthy system of statistics; good data are needed for effective intelligence-based investigation. They help the police identify where crime is occurring and what kinds of crime need to be tackled. In Bogotá, they show that the main perpetrators and victims of violence are young men. Reliable data also help to lower the acrimony of political debate about whether or not criminality is rising or in decline. Since crime is news, violence and robbery are usually reported in a sensational way, and politicians are highly sensitive to stories about crime, a trustworthy source of statistics is essential. And while opinion polls can be helpful, too many surveys are poorly compiled and exaggerate feelings of insecurity. Publication of the fact that only 16 per cent of Latin Americans rated 'the state of citizen security' in their country as 'good' or 'very good' is likely to exacerbate fear (Latinobarómetro 2010: 90). Perhaps it is the way in which the opinion polls are compiled that explains why, in Bogotá and Quito, insecurity has become the number one issue for the cities' mayors.[16]

Fifth, so-called structural factors – such as inequality, poverty, poor levels of education and unemployment – are less than helpful in explaining what has happened in Colombia or in Bogotá over the last 50 years. Indeed, experience in Bogotá supports work in other parts of the world in playing down the importance of income (Fajnzylber et al. 1998; Cardia et al. 2003: 22), unemployment (Hojman 2002: 122; *The Economist* 2011), social inequality (Heinemann and Verner 2006: 16), urbanisation (Gizewski and Homer-Dixon 1995) and size of city (Geyer 2007; Gilbert 2000). Colombia has long been a poor and unequal country and its major cities have reflected those problems. Yet the changes in crime and violence over recent years have little direct relationship with these structural indicators.

Sixth, the fact that Bogotá suffers from less violence than other cities in the country supports research from other places that it is the individual characteristics of cities that determine their crime rate. In the United States, violence is more common in the south and in cities with large African-American populations (Geyer 2007). While high rates of homicide are usually found in cities with high rates of gun ownership, alcohol and drug use, inequality, low education levels and male unemployment, local differences still make a difference (Renner 2001; Safford and Palacios 2002).

Seventh, Bogotá shows that crime is not the preserve of the poor. If poor areas suffer more than their share of crime and violence, this is largely because they cannot afford to pay for private security. If poverty caused crime, it would be spread more widely across the city. In Bogotá, most criminal acts are committed in the central area, along the main bus routes and in places where the major crime syndicates operate.

Eighth, a firearm is used in the majority of homicides in Colombia and is the preferred weapon for organised gangs. It seems obvious that the easy availability of guns leads to more deaths than occur in countries where few people own them. As such, it is clearly vital to control access to firearms. Unfortunately, that is difficult to achieve when the arms traffic is run by sophisticated gangs.

Finally, Bogotá's crime history suggests that Colombians, and indeed Latin Americans generally, are not inherently violent. Violence is something that occurs when something upsets the status quo – political disputes, the removal of a crime kingpin, the introduction of a market for drugs and so on. It is not even good for criminals, because, as the mafia and yakuza have learned, violence is bad for business (Ávila Martínez and Pérez 2011).

Rising violence is not inevitable and recent figures on crime in Bogotá show that the police are able to take effective action against crime and that better governance helps to reduce the climate for crime. Growing violence is not associated directly with urbanisation or with structural factors such as unemployment. Nor is it a phenomenon that afflicts big cities more than smaller ones. As such, the future of violence in Latin America is not preordained. Let us trust that the doom-mongers take heed of that observation!

5 | SAN SALVADOR: VIOLENCE AND RESILIENCE IN GANGLAND – COPING WITH THE CODE OF THE STREET

Wim Savenije* and Chris van der Borgh

Introduction

Over the past decades the street gangs Mara Salvatrucha (MS) and 18th Street Gang (18st) have become extremely powerful actors in El Salvador and its capital city. These transnational gangs – which have their origins in Los Angeles and a substantial presence in the countries of the Northern Triangle of Central America (El Salvador, Honduras and Guatemala) – not only use violence to fight each other, but also to build up local power bases in neighbourhoods they consider their territory. The use of violence includes deadly force, but also threats to and intimidation of local residents, and extortion of small enterprises and bus companies. In the face of the weak law enforcement capacity of the police (and in a number of municipalities also of the military), basic civil liberties, such as freedom of movement, are not guaranteed. What's more, the possibility of using public space to socialise is severely restricted. Neighbourhood residents, especially young people, need to take into account the 'supremacy' of local chapters or cliques of the gangs. To achieve resilience – that is, to lead normal or ordinary lives when confronted by the all-pervading presence and control of the gangs – they need diverse coping strategies.

This chapter explores how neighbourhood denizens who are not members of a gang deal with the gangs' presence and control. It discusses how young people perceive gang power, how they relate to gang members, how gang presence affects their social lives and what strategies they develop to socialise with their peers. It also shows how

* This research was assisted by a grant to Wim Savenije from the Latin American Drugs, Security and Democracy Fellowship Program administered by the Social Science Research Council and the Universidad de Los Andes in cooperation with the Open Society Foundations.

a supposed cessation of hostilities or a truce between the main gangs, which promised to diminish harassment of the non-gang population, has impinged on young people. The chapter first provides some background information about the gang phenomenon in the Metropolitan Area of San Salvador (El Área Metropolitana de San Salvador or AMSS) and discusses briefly the concept of resilience of non-gang youth vis-à-vis the gangs. The next section sketches the power of gangs in popular neighbourhoods,[1] emphasising the ways in which youth perceive this control. It moves on with an examination of the coping strategies that non-gang members employ. In the face of gang presence, youth develop strategies that tend to restrict their movements and sociability, while there remain few spaces of sociability open to these young people that are not affected by the presence of gangs. The last section argues, again from the experiences of ordinary youth, that, 18 months after the gang truce, the opportunities for youth to socialise are still profoundly affected by the presence and impositions of the gangs.

The focus on everyday experiences and resilience in the face of serious gang presence and violence can help to broaden the gaze of academic inquiries and public policies to include the struggles faced by ordinary youth in attaining ideals that have become more and more difficult to realise in the context of gang-dominated popular neighbourhoods. Social research can expose the daily struggles of these young people, while public policies should support them to achieve a different future.

The evidence presented in this chapter is based on a series of interviews (individual and group) with ordinary youth living in 13 different neighbourhoods in the AMSS where different gangs are present. These interviews are part of a long-term research initiative looking into gangs and security forces in popular neighbourhoods in Central America. A number of questions in these interviews addressed the ways in which the activities of young non-gang youth are influenced by the gang presence. Thus, instead of the more usual way of looking at collective efforts to deal with gangs and gang control, the main argument of this chapter focuses on the perspective of ordinary youth: on the situations and threats they face and on the individual adaptions and strategies employed to deal with the (perceived) power of local gangs. The majority of these interviews were carried out between August 2011 and November 2013.

Gangs and a gang truce in El Salvador

The peace agreements that concluded the civil war in 1992 brought an end to the political violence but other forms of violence persisted or increased. In the 'post-war' period, the homicide rates, which were among the highest in the world, became a key concern of Salvadoran governments. Although precise data about the perpetrators of homicides are scarce, there are strong indications that over the past two decades gang-related violence has accounted for a substantial proportion of murders in El Salvador.[2] In addition to this, the growing presence of – predominantly – the MS and 18st and their capacity to use force have deeply influenced the lives of residents in popular and marginalised neighbourhoods.

These gang structures have their roots in Los Angeles, one of the principal destinations of the large flow of migrants – most of them illegal – to the United States that started in the 1970s and continues today. Although this migration preceded the civil war, the war was a key reason for leaving; other motivations included the pursuit of jobs, better opportunities and family reunification (Bibler Coutin 2007: 152). During the 1980s, scores of Salvadoran youngsters, growing up in poor migrant neighbourhoods, started to join existing gangs such as the 18st, a gang largely of Mexican origin. Eventually, young people of Salvadoran origin formed street-oriented groups that later became known as the MS (Savenije 2009; Ward 2013). Just like the 18st, the MS became a 'home' for youth originating mainly from Central America, especially from the Northern Triangle.

In the 1990s, many gangsters[3] were deported after being arrested and founded gang chapters or 'cliques' (*clikas*) in their native countries (Zilberg 2011). This deeply influenced the gang phenomenon in El Salvador, as well as in the other countries of the Northern Triangle (Savenije 2009; Cruz 2010). Deported gangsters formed cliques of the MS and 18st in the towns and cities where they appeared. In the years that followed, many existing local gangs also converted into chapters of these two large gangs (Savenije and van der Borgh 2009). Through these cliques, the MS and 18st control (parts of) neighbourhoods or even cities. In 2011, the PNC estimated a total number of gang members in El Salvador of 28,130, of whom some 10,400 were in prison.[4]

Gang proliferation has been particularly strong in the AMSS, which consists of 14 municipalities including San Salvador, the country's capital. The AMSS hosts some 1.7 million inhabitants, which is approximately 28 per cent of the entire Salvadoran population (DIGESTYC 2013). Gangs are present in a large number of neighbourhoods and are considered by the national authorities to be a serious security threat (van der Borgh and Savenije 2015). However, there is great variation with regard to gang presence and violence. The poorest municipalities experience a greater gang presence and a disproportionate number of the homicides; however, even in the most violent parts of the AMSS, there are neighbourhoods where gang presence is much less marked. It is fair to say that gang presence is generally strongest in the most disadvantaged neighbourhoods (Savenije and Beltrán 2012: 18–20), where opportunities for young people are scarce, where social control has eroded and where the authority of the government is limited. In these places, the gangs also have a growing support base, consisting of local wannabes, relatives and friends.

Government efforts to stop gang-related violence and to disrupt gang control over neighbourhoods have so far had limited effect. The gang phenomenon had already started to grow in the first half of the 1990s, but serious government policies only began to develop when gang structures were already firmly in place. The administrations of President Francisco Flores (1999–2004) and President Antonio Saca (2004–09) emphasised zero-tolerance approaches, which included deploying the military on the streets and locking up large numbers of supposed gang members (FESPAD 2004; Wolf 2011). These policies were often criticised for being ineffective, and the need for social and preventive policies was stressed (Jütersonke et al. 2009). Although the latter is what the centre-left Funes administration (2009–14) proposed, during the first years of Mauricio Funes' term in office repressive approaches continued to dominate (van der Borgh and Savenije 2014).

During the past decade, as a result of these repression-oriented security policies, a large number of gang members have been imprisoned and a major part of the gang structures moved into the prison system. The jails have become an important meeting ground for homeboys belonging to the same gang. This has led to improved consultations between gang leaders from different parts of the country, but also to new relationships between jailed leaders and those in the neighbourhoods. While information about these relationships and the power balance between gangs is scarce, one can argue that gang leaders in prisons have a considerable ability to impose their wishes on the homeboys roaming the streets (Savenije and van der Borgh 2014)

While the MS and 18st are sworn enemies, occasionally the leaders of these gangs have shown a capacity to cooperate and even to start a dialogue with the Salvadoran government (van der Borgh and Savenije 2015). In this regard, a major turnaround took place on 9 March 2012, when they announced a cessation of hostilities. Although government officials initially denied any involvement in the deal, it soon became clear that the Minister of Justice and Public Security, Munguía Payés, had facilitated the truce. He endorsed mediation by his adviser and former guerrilla commander Raúl Mijango and Monsignor Fabio Colindres, the army bishop (Sanz and Martínez 2012). They initiated talks with long-standing gang leaders who were imprisoned and isolated in a prison with relatively high security in Zacatecoluca. These leaders agreed on the need for a reduction in violence and on the idea of a cessation of hostilities between the gangs, while also formulating a list with general requests to the Salvadoran authorities.

An important step in the facilitation process was the transfer of 30 gang leaders to ordinary prisons (*El Diario de Hoy* 2012). This enabled these leaders to interact freely with the imprisoned rank and file of their gangs, and to communicate and enforce the truce on the streets. Within days, the murder rate fell from around 14 to around five homicides a day.[5] The cessation of hostilities was considered a first step in a national process of pacification (*Crónicas Guanacas* 2012a; *El Faro* 2012) and talks continued between the facilitators and the gang leaders about the next phase, known as 'Municipalities Free from Violence' (Municipios Libres de Violencia or MLV).[6] The basic idea was to bring the process of pacification to the municipal level, where gangs would not only cease hostilities but would also reduce their criminal practices, including homicides, extortion, robbery, assault and abductions, would allow free passage to citizens and would hand over their arms, among other things (*Crónicas Guanacas* 2012b).

However, the process became stuck in June 2013, after a new Minister of Justice and Public Security, Ricardo Perdomo, took office (Sanz and Dada 2013). Perdomo publicly distanced himself from this approach, seeing it mostly as a ploy by the gangs to protect their interests in the drugs trade (Martinez and Sanz 2014). Furthermore, Raúl Mijango and his team were denied further access to the prison system, hampering their work. While the initiatives to communicate with imprisoned leaders were thwarted, tensions inside and between gangs resurfaced and the homicides increased (Marroquín and Quintanilla 2014). In the period until June 2014, the truce gradually eroded. Although the pacification process led to some interesting initiatives, it never really affected the local power base of the gangs. In most neighbourhoods, control and extortion by gangs kept pace or even intensified.

Resilience facing the code of the street The hazards for young people living in neighbourhoods with a high degree of gang control largely exceed those in neighbourhoods where this control is weak or absent. On streets and in public places, gang members gather, control the movements of the passers-by and impose their rules; but they also charm other youth, invite them to hang around or ask them for favours. The threat of violence by the gangs and the incitement to join can be pervasive. In these situations, simply avoiding becoming victimised or getting tangled up in gang-related behaviour may be critical in achieving more positive goals (Zimmerman and Brenner 2010: 300), such as going to school, having regular employment or practising sports. In gang-infested neighbourhoods, young people encounter almost daily threats to their self-regard, well-being and growth. Simply achieving things that in other, less controlled neighbourhoods would be seen as relatively 'normal' can therefore be interpreted as resilience (Masten 2001: 228).

Recent literature considers resilience as positive development and successful adaptation in the face of adverse conditions (Zautra et al. 2010: 4; Zimmerman and Brenner 2010: 284). It stresses that, even if resilience can be seen as an individual outcome, it is not the result of passive personal strategies but of the combined efforts of individuals and their social context to reduce the negative consequences of the adverse conditions surrounding them (Murray 2010; Ungar 2012). The success of these efforts depends largely on the capacity of the social environment to make available and accessible opportunities for positive developments in ways that are appealing to young people and take into account their skills and abilities (Ungar 2012: 14–19).

While much attention of state institutions, non-governmental organisations and academic researchers is usually directed to the question of how to deal with gangs and how to stop or prevent violence, the fate of non-gang youth living in gang-controlled neighbourhoods has largely been neglected. However, despite the adverse conditions and limited opportunities in society for the youths of these neighbourhoods, a majority of the young people 'make the effort and seize what little opportunity may arise' (MacLeod 1995: 259). Acknowledging the difficulties, they persist because most 'lack the resources to run from the problems that surround them' (Newman 1999: 229). They strive for good outcomes despite the presence and control of the gangs by going to school, studying at university, accepting poorly paid jobs, participating in sport, community or cultural activities, meeting friends from other neighbourhoods and so on. Hence, they try to lead 'normal lives' and struggle to achieve the middle-class ideals cherished in wider society.

Social and economic support from family, neighbours and friends is essential for young people to flourish, but scarce in gang-infested neighbourhoods. In addition, youth need to deal directly with the challenges posed by gangs, while at the same time gang control negatively affects their support structures. In these cases, the resilience of young people is about taking advantage of the limited opportunities available for positive development, while taking into account the control of the gangs and resisting the temptations they may offer.

Code of the street The difficulties and threats ordinary youth encounter result from the sway that the code of the street holds over popular neighbourhoods. The norms and required skills of gangs are often opposed to those of mainstream society (Anderson 1999: 33; Short 1997: 63). Ironically, gangs can be seen as 'street elites' who 'conduct violence as agents of aristocratic privilege devoted to the oppression of the poor' who live in what they claim to be their territory (Katz 1988: 166, 121). The idea of aristocratic privilege captures well the importance the gangsters attach to respect – that is, being treated with due deference, especially by other young people but also by adult neighbourhood residents (Anderson 1999: 33; Savenije 2009: 46). This not only includes being treated correctly in interpersonal contacts, but also being looked up to as a representative of the gang as a whole.

Adherence to the code of the street permits gang members to obtain both a positive self-image and resources in the midst of situations of poverty and social exclusion (Savenije 2009). It is part of an alternative system for developing identities and building self-esteem through which the youth can achieve respectable status (Wilkinson 2003:

223; Vigil 2002: 26). At the heart of the system is gaining respect, being respected by others and defending the respect that one deems is merited. In the context of the street, all three are attained by using violence – or by being openly disposed to use it (Anderson 1999: 68). Although confronting rivals and defending their territory are important ways for members to gain respect in the gangs, controlling daily events in their neighbourhood is also imperative. At stake here is not only the need to shield themselves from the security forces and to protect their illegal economic activities, but also to preserve a credible posture as 'street elite'. However, concerns about being disrespected lead to respect for residents being easily violated (Short 1997: 65).

In the context of strong local gang presence, the strategies of young people go far beyond the pragmatic dealings with gangs (code switching) described by Anderson (1999), where they adapt to the street mores when in the neighbourhood but display the values of wider society while at home, school or work. In these situations, the reign of the code of the street has often been extended into strong control by the gang over the whole neighbourhood. It then goes beyond the individual gangster who wants to be respected; any perceived offence against one of their homeboys easily becomes an affront to the gang as a whole. The gang itself must be respected. Under a clear threat of violence, the residents must obey the directives set out by the gang and the imperative not to interfere in gang affairs. The following section focuses on the different kinds of control the gangs exercise over the lives of young people, and the next takes a look at the efforts, skills and strategies that youth develop in order to avoid disrespecting gang members, attracting their attention or openly infringing gang directives.

Gang control in popular neighbourhoods

For many young people in popular neighbourhoods, gangsters are 'the owners of the street'.[7] They are not only armed and hang around on street corners, in alleyways or in the few parks and football fields situated in the most densely populated urban areas, they also control the movements of people in their territory, especially non-residents visiting the neighbourhood and the patrolling security forces. Their presence profoundly affects the lives of ordinary youth, because the spaces they move through and where they meet with friends are under the watchful eyes of the gangs. In the long history of inter-gang conflict, both the MS and 18st have proved to be capable of using extreme violence. Ordinary residents are afraid that this violence will also be used against them if they act or are perceived to act against the interests of the gangs. This fear reinforces the capacity of the gangs to monitor what happens in the neighbourhoods and to extort with near impunity local individuals and businesses.

The presence of police or military patrols is hardly considered a guarantee of some kind of security. They face severe difficulties in doing their work and obtaining intelligence in gang-controlled neighbourhoods, mainly because of a gang prohibition on talking to the police or the military. Even a casual conversation on the street can cause a gangster to enquire why individuals are talking. If one asks residents about what kind of relationship exists between neighbourhood residents and the security forces, one of the most common answers is: 'There is no relationship.' As Gutiérrez et al. (2009: 137) observed, in gang-dominated neighbourhoods, the security forces are 'almost foreign, acting alone in unfamiliar territory'.[8] In this sense, their presence is largely irrelevant for the habitants. Ordinary youth have to find their own way to deal with the gangs.

It becomes abundantly clear who considers themselves the proprietors of the neighbourhood and plainly in control; graffiti alluding to the names of the gang and the local clique take the form of impressive murals. Some contain an explicit message to the population to keep silent: *'Ver, oir y callar'* ('Watch, listen and be silent'). Occasionally, they even acquire some threatening force, with phrases such as '… *si de la vida quieres gozar'* ('… if you want to enjoy life') or, a little more explicitly, '… *o morir'* ('… or die'). Frightening they may be, but it is not immediately clear what these messages are meant to convey. Even without explicit warnings, people in the neighbourhood already know that it is dangerous to act against the interests of the gang or talk to the security forces. They are clear messages of control directed at neighbourhood residents but possibly also at wavering members: here, we are all-powerful and nobody can touch us.

Control through monitoring In their efforts to protect their territory against external threats, gang members are suspicious of people from other neighbourhoods and especially intolerant towards young people from areas controlled by rival gangs. 'I had friends who lived in Las Arboledas. One day they [the gangsters] put a pistol to my head and said that if I came back again they would kill me.'[9] To control the boundaries, the gangs use roughly the same tactics as the security forces – they check the identity and origin of passers-by. They ask incoming young males for their names, where they come from and what they are doing in the area. To verify the answers, they frequently ask for their identity card to check their neighbourhood of residence. To make sure that a visitor does not belong to a rival gang, they sometimes demand that he takes off his shirt to demonstrate that he has no gang tattoos. The treatment of girls is less intrusive, but they can also be asked to show their identity card.

To control their sometimes extensive territories, the gangs tend to use children to keep watch and warn them of visitors. Normally these are children or teenagers – also called '*gatos*'[10] or '*postes*'[11] – who enjoy hanging out with the gang members and who inform them if, for instance, police or military patrols, strangers or trucks with supplies to local shops enter the neighbourhood. The gangs are always looking for young people who want to join them and who, in the meantime, can do them all kinds of favours, especially by taking on the more arduous jobs. Young children can easily and inconspicuously engage in surveillance activities, but they might also collect extortion money. They are paid small amounts of money and given mobile phones, clothes and other items, and the most trustworthy steadily get closer to the gang and eventually are invited to join.

> Being young one doesn't think. The gangsters give them things and they start doing errands for them. If they [the children] do them a job – that is to say, if they notice them when someone enters – they give them things, for instance mobile phones. And in this way they draw them [towards the gang].[12]

Control through extortion Extortion is one of the most important sources of income for the gangs. In the zone they consider their territory, the gangs usually demand money ('*renta*') from public transport and trucks that carry supplies to local shops. Stallholders, small stores, garages and workshops do not escape from paying the gangs either. The extensive extortion networks make it more difficult for ordinary youth to find or accept a job. Not only are there few businesses offering jobs in these zones, but it has also become more complicated for young people to start their own business or accept work that requires travel to other neighbourhoods. If they have to enter a new zone, they have to arrange safe access with their clients and negotiate their presence with the local clique. In all cases, they probably will have to pay extortion money. Not paying the *renta* is perceived as an affront to the gang and punished severely.

Restricted movement and sociability

While some youth are attracted to the gangs from a relatively early age, others learn to evade them. While the former like to hang out on the streets, to share in the power and feel protected by the gangs, the latter want to finish school, go to university or find a decent job. Gangs can make life very difficult for ordinary youth. Showing respect to gangsters, obeying their directives and not interfering with gang business are basic requirements, but implementing these requirements can seriously restrict the routines and leisure activities of non-gang youth. Not complying, however, can have even more far-reaching consequences. An admonishment or beating is a normal punishment, but people can also receive serious threats, be raped or be killed.

When young people pass through the streets of the neighbourhood or meet with friends on street corners, in the alleyways, parks or football fields, they get physically closer to the gangs. However, talking, joking or being friendly with the homeboys may generate the idea that the person is interested or can be drawn into the gang. Ignoring them, on the other hand, can be interpreted by gang members as disrespectful. Ordinary youth have to tread a fine line: 'One can neither be very close, nor very distant'[13] – or, in other words, 'neither talk too much, nor don't talk with them at all, because that is to look for problems'.[14] Getting too close can lead to unwanted attention; being too distant can be interpreted as offensive. It is vital not to generate conflicts. The whole gang usually backs up the homeboy who takes offence at what someone says or does. It is a delicate balance: not frequenting public spaces too much, but not locking yourself up at home either; being polite with the gang members but maintaining a respectful distance at the same time; being careful and controlled in the face of the possible threats they pose.

> I say hello, that's all. Sometimes I ignore them, depending on what they say to me. I've to be cautious with the jokes they make. Depending on how one responds, they get closer and then start inviting you.[15]

Restricted movements   If maintaining good relationships in the neighbourhood is a basic requirement, evading rivals is imperative. Young
people cannot enter residential zones controlled by opposing gangs.
This could be the neighbourhood on the other side of the road or the
one that separates theirs from the centre of town. By entering, they
could be considered 'spies' who will pass on information about the
neighbourhood to enemies, or, worse, they might be mistaken for
members of a rival gang. 'It is safe, provided that it is not territory of
the rival gang. There they consider us spies. They say that "They are
checking what's going on."'[16] In the best case, the individual will be
sent away, but there is also a risk that they might be beaten up – or even
killed if they are 'proved' to be part of the enemy.

When visiting family living in a conflicting neighbourhood, the
relatives have to receive them at the entrance. The gang regularly lets in
a person from another locality if they are accompanied by relatives who
testify to the good intentions of the visitor. Even though the person is a
relative, the gang usually checks their credentials to make sure they are
not linked to a rival gang or related to one of its members. If there are
any suspicions, the person will face questions or consequences.

For the same reason, it is dangerous to study at a school or college
in territory claimed by an opposing gang, or to participate in sport
or other kinds of events. The gangs may fear that the visitors pass on
information to their enemies and make them vulnerable to violent
attacks or incursions.

> Many [students] go to zones they consider secure, that is to
> say, where the same gang is located. The students from this
> neighbourhood go to Santa Lucia secondary school, where the
> same gang hangs around [the MS]. There are only a few that
> attend the INSAM, which is the secondary school of San Martin
> and controlled by the opposing gang [the 18st].[17]

In some localities, one gang controls the centre of town and prohibits
the entrance of youth coming from rival territories. This makes it
difficult or impossible, especially for male adolescents, to go to the
shops, restaurants or events located there.

Restricted sociability: gang territories becoming social divides   It is difficult to maintain friendships with peers who live in neighbourhoods

controlled by opposing gangs. If it is complicated to visit relatives, it is almost impossible to visit friends or schoolmates, or to participate in sport activities or community events in other neighbourhoods. The risk of being beaten up if they stroll into another neighbourhood has an unexpected corollary for some youth. Resenting these dangers, some come to perceive and internalise the conflicts between gangs as common rivalries between the young people of different areas. 'Because of the neighbourhood where I live, I cannot enter other neighbourhoods. I was upset by that and I felt resentful; although I did not belong to a group [gang].'[18] This makes it even more difficult to become friends with their peers from other areas and can even reinforce violent rivalries between different educational centres.

In the same way, is it dangerous to have a girl- or boyfriend who lives in a conflicting territory. The boy in particular runs the risk of being beaten up if he visits his girlfriend, and, if he keeps ignoring the warnings and threats, he can even get killed.

> A neighbour was dating a boy. He visited her regularly. [One day] the gangsters came and grabbed him from the door of the house. They got him out; they lifted his shirt and asked 'Where do you live?', 'Where are you from?' They interrogated him and they took him away.[19]

Although girls are perceived as being less of a threat, they can also be threatened and told to keep away from their boyfriend's neighbourhood or can be questioned in their own area because of their visits to rival territory. It is particularly dangerous for girls to get romantically involved with police officers stationed in or near their neighbourhoods. They will almost automatically be considered to be informers and will be treated as such. 'A girl of 17 years old started going out with a cop, as his girlfriend. Suddenly, after a few months she disappeared. They found her corpse in the ravine without her tongue.'[20]

Local youths must be careful in how they dress. Although some find it fashionable to use styles associated with big city, urban or street life, as shown frequently on MTV, in television series or movies, boys from the popular neighbourhoods must be cautious about not dressing in a similar style to the homeboys, talking in the same way or even walking as they do. Even if ordinary young people think it looks 'cool' to do so, it can be – and repeatedly will be – interpreted in another way.

Gang members can see it as a sign of interest in gang culture, and consequently approach the youth to try to draw them into the gang. On the other hand, it can also be interpreted by a rival gang as a sign of being a gangster, and therefore as being the gang's enemy. Homeboys 'walk different, talk different – therefore this is very, very complicated; not so much to dress up like them, but to find a more modest way of dressing, talking, walking'.[21] If the youngster is not very interested in getting nearer to the gang or, later on, becoming part of the gang, he will be pressured to adopt another style. If he does not comply, he usually will receive some warnings and beatings to reinforce the need to change.

Girls have to be careful not to dress too strikingly or sensually. Through their looks, they attract the attention not only of the ordinary boys, but also of the gangsters who pass much of their time quite unexcitingly on the streets. Their advances can be something the girl appreciates, drawing her closer to the gang. If she rejects their overtures, the situation can become complicated. Gang members often do not accept no for an answer and insist, pressing her to concede. If she continues rebuffing them, her dress and way of presenting herself can be interpreted as a provocation, increasing the risk of a violent response.

If a youth or some member of his family is a police officer or employed in the army, it is important to conceal the fact. If the gang becomes aware of this situation, the person's life will be in danger. Obviously, he or she cannot leave or come home in uniform, nor can they travel on public transport wearing a uniform. It is vital that nobody in the neighbourhood knows their occupation, not even close associates. Even a small conflict between friends, rivalry between classmates or jealousy between lovers can provoke someone to leak the information to the local clique. 'The gangsters think that [the military] are disgusting … If they knew that I'm a soldier, they'd kill me.'[22]

Remaining spaces of sociability   The power the gangs have acquired in a large number of popular neighbourhoods restricts the social relationships and movements of non-gang youth. Often, they understand very well the risks that accompany certain types of conduct, but, even so, frequently their parents consider the public spaces too dangerous and do not allow them to hang around. It is fair to say that, to protect their children, parents often reinforce the rules decreed by the gangs. In popular urban areas, there are few spaces left where young people can connect freely, without fear of gang interference.

Frequently, parents do not let their children play outside, or only in front of the house. Even meeting friends to play football is habitually viewed with caution. 'I have them [my sons] at home ... Only at school they have the opportunity to play with friends, because I don't let them leave and wander around the neighbourhood. I don't like that.'[23] Although the houses are usually small, lots of children and young people in gang-infested neighbourhoods spend their spare time locked up at home watching television, playing video games or simply doing nothing. Now and then their friends come to visit them to play or to do their homework together, but for many their social interactions are restricted to relatives and schoolmates.

The natural place to interact with others and make friends is school or college. Often these institutions are a relatively safe place where adults supervise the interactions and where there are regular visits from the security forces to check for the presence of gang members. But, inevitably, they are also haunted by the gangs, who consider them an integral part of their territory. Trouble typically arises if the school or college accepts students unknown to the local clique, or if it gives bad marks to gang-related children. Additional problems arise when gang-related students threaten their teachers or start to extort or recruit schoolmates. So even in this relatively supervised space, youngsters cannot assume that they will be cut off completely from the power of the gangs, and their ability to avert conflicts remains an important skill.

The shopping mall is one of the few places where it is safe for young people from different neighbourhoods to meet and interact. Friends, schoolmates and lovers can congregate in relative tranquillity. In particular, the food court, individual restaurants and the green zones outside the mall are places where people can assemble quite easily if they have money to spend. Private security agents control these privately owned spaces and guarantee safety. Suspicious-looking individuals are normally asked or forced to leave. 'I don't go to other neighbourhoods; I can find only death there ... With my friends, I meet in Unicentro or Metro, Plaza Mundo o Galerias. Always in a shopping centre.'[24] The shops inside thrive precisely because of the mall's image of security and quietness, and they do not want to see gangsters roaming around. This is why the malls offer the ordinary youth a kind of security that their neighbourhood or the security forces cannot provide.

Insecurity, gang truce and ordinary youth

Although the gang truce caused the homicide rate to fall drastically, it hardly changed the daily risks faced by neighbourhood youth. In fact, some feel that they are even more exposed. Although the truce primarily involved a cessation of hostilities between the gangs, it promised a broader process of pacification that was supposed to lead to a reduction in territorial control and the threat of violence towards ordinary people. However, the ongoing threat of violence against citizens and the extortion of local businesses have not stopped, and have been addressed only minimally. Without the truce taking into account the fate of the local population, the changes for ordinary non-gang youth can be only limited or are simply absent. As one young man said: 'As ordinary people we don't have a truce.'[25]

The neighbourhoods considered to be conflicting territories are still off limits, even for boys and girls who have nothing to do with the gangs. 'If [the truce] really functioned, we as youth could simply visit other communities, but that is not the case even with the truce in place.'[26] Therefore, the risk of being stopped and frisked by gangsters belonging to a rival gang remains disturbingly high. 'My brother still lives the same danger. The other [gang] stops and frisks him. They even lift his shirt to check if he has tattoos.'[27] Non-gang youth are still simply left to their own devices.[28]

In general, the gangs are reluctant to discuss the distress and fear of common people, because, without a plausible threat of violence, their local power base and income from the extortion business would decline. Even Minister Munguía Payés, who facilitated the truce, confirmed openly: 'The gangs don't want to talk about the topic of extortions, because from this money they make a living, with this money they maintain their families' (Chávez et al. 2013).[29] Without a renunciation of violence against the population at large, the cessation of hostilities between gangs remains largely irrelevant for the daily life of ordinary youth.

A number of young people – especially, but not only, those who have found themselves in conflict with the local clique – look to a more radical alternative: leaving their neighbourhood. Some go to live with relatives (grandparents, uncles and so on) in communities with a less pronounced gang presence; others try to leave the country. Gang control and (the threat of) violence have now also become important motivations to migrate to the United States (UNHCR 2014). From

2011 onwards, there has been a strong surge in the number of often unaccompanied children crossing the border of the United States illegally, 74 per cent of whom come from Mexico and the Northern Triangle (Gordon 2014). The US Border Patrol anticipated that, during the fiscal year 2014, 90,000 unaccompanied children could be apprehended. The principal reasons 'that send children to the United States are family reunification, poverty and fear of violence from local criminal organizations' (Villiers Negroponte 2014). In the case of El Salvador, these organisations tend to be street gangs or *maras* (Departamento 15 2014; UNHCR 2014: 32).

Conclusion: resilience in gangland

Seen through the eyes of ordinary youth, gangs exercise pervasive control over the neighbourhoods they inhabit. With the help of aspiring young children, gangs dominate neighbourhoods as their territories and control the visitors, especially young people from what they consider enemy territory. They also extort local businesses, public transport and suppliers. The absence of a credible presence of the security forces facilitates a situation in which youth who wish to live 'normal lives' have to devise ways to cope with the presence of the gangs.

To succeed in a gang-dominated neighbourhood requires a delicate balancing act between being attentive to gang members without coming too close and a skill in averting conflicts. Young people mentally map the territories of the different gangs to avoid entering neighbourhoods that could be dangerous for them. But they also must be cautious about adopting urban subcultural styles. Boys should not use a style of dressing, talking or walking that is too similar to that of the gangs; girls must not dress in too striking a fashion.

However, adapting to the gang's imposed limits can have serious consequences for young people's sociability. Streets and other public spaces in their own neighbourhood are often avoided. Attending school or college outside the neighbourhood, or even courting a girl or boy from another area, can be hazardous. Home, school and shopping malls are the few remaining places where they can meet their peers relatively safely. In different ways, protecting themselves from gang aggression often signifies for ordinary youth diminished interactions with their peers. Even the geographical boundaries between different gang territories can become internalised and reified by non-gang youth. As these start to function as social boundaries, they can become sources of resentment between young people of different neighbourhoods, making friendships more difficult and reinforcing social isolation.

The social and psychological costs of living in popular gang-infested neighbourhoods and of achieving some kind of resilience in the face of the omnipresence of gangs and the threat of violence are high. However, the pacification promised by the cessation of gang hostilities could counter the ensuing social isolation by reducing territorial control and practices of monitoring and extortion adopted by the gangs. The reality on the ground, though, seems to be unchanged. The failure to renounce the use of violence against the population renders the truce between the gangs largely irrelevant for ordinary youth.

Gang control in marginalised popular neighbourhoods makes positive development and the attainment of good outcomes difficult for young people. They not only have to take into account the presence of gangs, to cope with the code of the street, and to grant respect to the individual gang members. The consequences are much more profound. The gangs' pervasive control and the omnipresence of the threat of violence touch the whole social fabric of the neighbourhoods. Family relationships, friendships, schools and local businesses all are affected. Coping with the gangs seems to have become a way of life, a practice considered normal, with the social consequences sometimes barely noticed anymore. After almost two decades of 'post-civil war' gang life, in quite a few neighbourhoods the young people do not know or remember what life without gang control looks like. For them, the gangs are (and have always been) a daily hazard one simply has to deal with. However, with growing gang control over their neighbourhoods, the opportunities for social development and relationships with other non-gang youth become more and more restricted.

6 | SAN JOSÉ: URBAN EXPANSION, VIOLENCE AND RESILIENCE

Abelardo Morales Gamboa

Introduction

On 6 April 2014, a historic majority of Costa Ricans voted in the second round in favour of Luis Guillermo Rivera Solís, candidate of the Partido Acción Ciudadana (PAC or Citizen Action Party), for the presidency of the republic. The defeated candidate of the ruling Partido de la Liberación Nacional (PLN or National Liberation Party) was Rolando Araya Monge, previously the mayor of San José.[1] Also, the political left could call the elections a triumph; in the first round, eight weeks before, it had significantly increased its number of parliamentarians from one to nine members. The result reflected a vote of hope for change. It was also a vote of punishment against corruption, and against the deterioration of the social infrastructure, quality of life, social coexistence and the opportunities of upward mobility that characterised Costa Rica as a middle-class society within a Central American environment of exclusion.

The political background of this electoral landslide was the fact that, during the past three decades, Costa Rica – and especially San José – had experienced the growth of tertiary activities, demographic evolution and diversification, and a process of accelerated urban expansion. The losing presidential candidate, a member of one of the traditional political clans, had been a city councillor since the 1980s, and then the municipal executive and the mayor of San José until 2013. This electoral defeat, the largest one in the history of Costa Rica's democracy, reflects the relationship between the discontent of the Costa Ricans and a number of urban problems in the capital. Although the former mayor and defeated presidential candidate was not entirely responsible for these problems during his tenure, they revealed the decline in the perception of Costa Rica as a peaceful and equitable nation.

Indeed, the outcome of the presidential elections of 2014 provides an opportunity to analyse the social changes during the past 30 years in urban Costa Rica, especially the relationship between metropolitan expansion and the characteristics of integration, social coexistence and governance in the Greater Metropolitan Area of San José (Gran Área Metropolitana or GAM). In particular, I will consider the link between urban expansion and the process of territorial fragmentation and socio-spatial segmentation. I will pay special attention to the residential segmentation of migrants, as well as the deterioration of peaceful coexistence due to the relative increase of social violence and crime. Although homicide rates in Costa Rica, and in particular in the GAM of San José, have been low compared with those in other countries in Central and South America, the issue of the recent increase in homicides and other forms of crime and the expansion of criminal phenomena such as street gangs, drug trafficking and human trafficking have been causing concern about the sustainability of San José as a relatively non-violent, safe and inclusive city (OIJ 2013). I will also reflect on social responses, both at the institutional level and from the urban residents, and especially the strategies of the poor.

San José has transmuted over the last 30 years from a medium-sized city into the central nucleus of a metropolitan system whose development has resulted in changes in forms of social coexistence and urban governance. These transformations are characterised by the expansion of the country's infrastructure, its population growth and the abandonment of rural lifestyles. One can observe far-reaching changes in urban land use as a consequence not only of globalised economic activities and cross-border labour migration but also of the various expressions of insecurity and violence that are a legacy of the Central America civil wars and, subsequently, derive from the emergence of transnational organised crime. These three dynamics have blurred the image of San José as the provincial capital of Costa Rica, a peaceful and equitable city surrounded by coffee plantations.

The first urban and political centre of Costa Rica during the Spanish colonial era was the city of Cartago; a few years after independence in 1821, these functions were transferred to San José in an effort to resolve a series of disputes between the respective local elites.[2] The city consolidated its economic importance and eventually became the capital of the nascent Costa Rican state, under the impetus of the coffee boom that started in the mid-nineteenth century (Quesada

2007: 28). Since then, the processes already mentioned have generated other changes in the functions and features of the national capital and the formation of the GAM.

Urban development was characterised by the establishment of the country's four major cities in the central region (Alajuela, Cartago, Heredia and San José), each one the capital of a province of the same name with smaller suburban population centres.[3] Originally, these cities were established in valleys within a system of mountains and rivers with deep depressions; for a long time, these served as barriers to connectivity and hindered the possibilities of easy inter-urban transport (Pujol and Pérez 2012). These main towns and intermediate cities and urban corridors began to require land that previously had been used for agricultural cultivation. Eventually, this led to the creation of an integrated metropolitan area, GAM, spread out across Costa Rica's Central Valley.

Social characteristics of the Greater Metropolitan Area

The territory of the GAM comprises the 31 cantons of the four sub-metropolitan provincial capitals mentioned above and the surrounding urban centres, although in some cases it excludes certain outlying districts of some of these cantons. For a small country, the metropolitan enigma is one of the larger challenges within Costa Rica's contemporary development trajectory. Costa Rica has an area of 52,000 square kilometres and the GAM occupies 1,967 square kilometres, i.e. just 3.8 per cent of the national total. However, in this area, 52.7 per cent of the country's population is concentrated and nearly 60 per cent of external migrants, which in turn represents 10 per cent of all the inhabitants of the GAM. In 2011, the total population of the GAM was 2,268,248 inhabitants, more than half the country's total population of 4,301,712 (INEC 2012; see Box 6.1 for details).

The demographic growth of the GAM was constant from the 1950s onwards, due to the natural growth of the population and to rural–urban migration that contributed to the expansion of the peri-urban areas. Since the 1980s, this expansion has been reinforced by international migration. Nevertheless, in the period 2000–11, population growth was less than 1 per cent (INEC 2012). The urban economy is based on real estate development related to the expansion of new residential areas and tourism. This has encouraged the construction and financial intermediation activities associated with urban land markets. Gradually,

---

Box 6.1 The four urban centres of the GAM

Metropolitan Area of San José: the cantons of San José, Escazú, Desamparados (partial), Aserrí (partial), Mora (partial), Goicoechea, Santa Ana, Alajuelita, Vázquez de Coronado (partial), Tibás, Moravia, Montes de Oca y Curridabat and La Unión. The latter is formally a canton of Cartago but pertains functionally to the Metropolitan Area of San José.

Metropolitan Area of Cartago: the cantons of Cartago, Paraíso (partial), Alvarado, Oreamuno and El Guarco (partial).

Metropolitan Area of Heredia: the cantons of Heredia (with the exception of the district of Vara Blanca), Barva, Santo Domingo, Santa Bárbara, San Rafael, San Isidro, Belén, Flores and San Pablo.

Metropolitan Area of Alajuela: the cantons of Alajuela, Poás and Atenas (partial).

Source: PRUGAM (2008).

---

the rural surroundings of the ancient towns have disappeared; as a consequence of this transformation, the lifestyles of the population have changed as well.

Since the GAM is not an integrated system but a regional complex with several urban centres, the problems of integration are twofold: spatial fragmentation; and social and cultural segregation. The fragmentation of urban space is due not only to the existence of physical barriers between the old towns and areas of new urban expansion and construction, but also to the fact that urban growth has taken place without previous planning. Urban expansion originated in the older population centres and basically followed the evolution of urban land prices, residential expansion and the development of intra-urban corridors between and around the four metropolitan areas. Deficient planning reproduced the fragmentation of the territory. At the same time, the absence or weakness of social policies produced various forms of socio-spatial segregation, with poor people in the most vulnerable territories (Pérez 1998). Moreover, in some cases, the postponement of solutions to the complex problems of infrastructure and connectivity increased the risk of population segments informally settling in those spaces reserved for the future construction of infrastructure. Social tension and violence resulted from overcrowding, transport congestion and awareness of the fact that all opportunities for physical and social mobility were blocked (Sánchez Lovell 2010).

In the period under consideration, the urban environment deteriorated, transport infrastructure collapsed and residential areas went downhill. All this generated a sense that the city was full to capacity. While the fabric of rural life disintegrated, barriers emerged with respect to the old forms of coexistence and the conventional attachment to norms, social control and social integration, opening up an avenue into social conflict and paving the way for an increase in violence and crime. Some years ago, the Consejo de Seguridad Vial (CONAVI), the public entity in charge of traffic security, projected on screens the following slogan: 'Costa Rica: a country without an army but with a war on the roads.' This was prompted by the high rate of road accidents and the number of victims. Besides the problems of fragmentation and segregation, there is the fragility of a common identity among the various constituent parts that make up the GAM. Although all urban expansion emerged around ancient rural villages, nestled in agricultural plantations, at present individual areas have different rhythms of development and different economic, demographic and political conditions. Additionally, local identities refer to different, sometimes even antagonistic, territorial roots, which frequently limit territorial cohesion (Van Lidth de Jeude and Schütte 2010).

Residential segregation as an expression of urban exclusion

Exclusion is related to the growing level of residential segregation. The concept of socio-spatial segregation is defined as 'the degree according to which two or more groups live apart from the other, in different parts of the urban environment' (Massey and Denton 1988: 282). In the GAM, problems of residential segregation are also associated with fragmentation, mainly observed in relation to: (1) the existence of residential areas isolated by large river canyons; (2) rural enclaves in some liminal areas; (3) areas with steep slopes and unstable hillsides in almost the entire periphery located on the mountains and in river canyons; and (4) areas prone to flooding and the risk of displacement due to (informal) housing construction on riverbeds. A study conducted in 2004 (FUPROVI 2004) showed that the relationship between fragmentation, segregation and governance was one of the main causes of the deepening exclusion of the informal settlements. These patterns of spatial segregation and vulnerability are compounded by the familiar mechanisms of social exclusion: (1) difficulties of access to markets, particularly to labour markets and the benefits of formal employment; (2) exclusion from the benefits of public policies that would ensure integration and social citizenship; and (3) lack of social networks, whether in terms of civil society or neighbourhood or family circles. In the urban environment of the GAM, situations prevail in which different forms of exclusion are combined and reflected in the phenomenon of residential segregation. As is the case in many Latin American cities, this segregation shows a division between the formal sector of regulated land ownership and the informal sector, which has no regulation of land tenure or other forms of spatial occupation. While the former benefits from the provision of adequate services and infrastructure and attracts residents with high incomes and stable jobs, the latter has infrastructure and services of low quality and is where low-income population segments without stable jobs or with no jobs at all are concentrated.

At the same time, up until the mid-1990s, several land occupations took place by people desperate for housing. The traditional system of settlement distribution by a paternalistic state broke down, while the construction of subsidised popular housing became an attractive speculative market. The presence of immigrant workers, averaging at 15 per cent of the urban economically active population (EAP), also served as an incentive for the expansion of informal housing (FUPROVI 2004). Both informal construction in areas overrun by land occupation and the formalisation of these invasions led to the spatial concentration of low-income residents and drove the segregation of this population segment and the functional separation of spaces occupied by people with a higher income.

Lack of adequate information has been mentioned as one of the problems relating to the informal or precarious settlements. Another impediment is the lack of knowledge about the characteristics of these informal residents and their living conditions (Proyecto Estado de la Nación 2013). Based on census information and other data from the housing sector, Mora (2013) estimated that the number of such settlements is 418 and that 296,149 people are concentrated there: the equivalent of 7 per cent of the country's population. Families living in vulnerable conditions are located in specific areas of the urban territory, where noticeable physical deterioration is accompanied by deficient interventions by public institutions. The vulnerability of the residents of these popular neighbourhoods is manifested in high rates of demographic dependence (53 dependants per 100 residents), a significant proportion of female-headed households and adolescent mothers, low educational levels and serious problems of overcrowding in housing (Morales 2007; Mora 2013; Proyecto Estado de la Nación 2013).

In 2008, a study was conducted on the entire GAM using a household survey that, among other issues, calculated the index of social inclusion on the basis of employment and inhabitants' access to public and social services, infrastructure and other services. While the study allows us to differentiate five social territories, ranging from the highest level to the lowest level of inclusion, in the GAM as a whole there is a great deal of heterogeneity, as segments of the urban population with high living standards coexist 'with numerous and crowded nuclei of poverty in slums' (PRUGAM 2008). The condition of these settlements is typical of the forms of occupation based on informality. One can make a distinction between the transformation of initially single-family homes into multi-family 'sub-units', mostly in the central parts of the GAM, where crowded families whose incomes do not allow them to obtain a formal home are concentrated; the construction of residential establishments with subsidised state funds; and the informal occupation of land in precarious conditions, traditionally known in Costa Rica as slums (*tugurios*) – the latter are shanty towns with poor infrastructure. Three reasons are mentioned for the expansion of this residential system: first, a drop in income, and especially the increase of income inequality and diminishing access to services; second, the lack of state capacity and state resources to provide accommodation and services for this housing sector (due to the financial crisis of the state); and third, the lack of planning and institutional coordination, aggravated by corruption. It is estimated that approximately 45 per cent of the families living in these settlements are foreign immigrants, and 16 per cent are multi-families. Most of them have no access to subsidised housing (MIVAH 2007). This segment is at the mercy of real estate agents who obtain their main income from informal land speculation with urban lots that are unmarketable through formal channels.

Foreign immigration and residential segregation in the GAM

Immigration has become one of the most egregious problems of the GAM in Costa Rica. Immigration started at the end of the 1980s (Morales and Castro 1999; Morales 2007) and was an outcome of the aforementioned transformations of the last 30 years, both in Costa Rica and in the rest of the Central American region. Important causal factors have been the fragile Central American post-war economic and social situation, the diversification of regional labour markets and the formation of cross-border labour corridors (Morales 2007). The transformation of the GAM produced a demand for labour in the sectors of real estate construction and services (Morales and Castro 1999; 2006; Morales 2007; Robles and Voorend 2013).

The relationship of immigrants to the urban problems discussed here are connected to three themes: (1) residential segregation due to the existence of two urban land markets, one formal and the other informal; (2) problems relating to the effect of immigration on patterns of social cohesion among the inhabitants of the metropolitan area, such as problems relating to perceptions of fairness and security; and (3) institutional and social responses to the problems posed by immigration in the sphere of urban governance.

Not all migrants are squatters – i.e. invaders of private or public land – but they have stimulated the expansion of the informal housing market. This market is the terrain where transactions of lots and housing units take place, operations that cannot be registered legally due to the absence of property titles. Their residential areas are not ghettos in the strict sense of the word, because they live in registered places previously inhabited by poor Costa Ricans. Nevertheless, the percentage of migrants living in these peripheral areas surpasses national averages. While, at the national level, the average number of immigrants is 9 per cent, it is three times higher in the poor residential areas and reaches more than 40 per cent of all residents in extremely poor settlements (FUPROVI 2004; MIVAH 2007).

However, there are differences in the presence of immigrants between poor traditional communities and new residential areas. The presence of immigrants in the oldest popular neighbourhoods, usually located in the metropolitan centres, becomes part of the city landscape; it correlates with income poverty, the deterioration of dwellings and the poor state of urban infrastructure. In this scenario, immigrants assimilate and coexist with the rest of the poor residents to a certain extent. Not all immigrants are extremely poor occupants of the housing units available to them, but, in general, they live together with such occupants (Morales and Castro 2006).

While the disparity between Costa Ricans and Nicaraguan immigrants can be noted in the macro-social sphere, the dynamics of slum settlements reveal a mixed problem: Costa Ricans are also in a situation of vulnerability and risk in terms of socio-economic and housing deficiency. These may differ in degree but not in kind from the situation of the Nicaraguan immigrants. Among Costa Ricans, a segment of the urban population also faces problems of employment and income. They have failed to find a solution to the problem of housing and are therefore forced to live in popular neighbourhoods and slums. For Nicaraguans, the slum is an option given their particular condition as members of an immigrant group: they have no financial means, nor rights to state subsidies, and they do not have social networks to meet their demands. However, living in precariousness is an option that is perceived as temporary, to reduce costs and meet other needs: for instance, sending money to family members in their country of origin. For Costa Ricans who occupy these spaces, their situation is not the result of a choice between competing options; it relates to structural factors that have generated new forms of inequality linked to Costa Rica's insertion into globalisation.

Urban inequality in San José assumes qualitatively different expressions and differences of degree according to the characteristics of each social group: as immigrants, according to sex or age, and even based on their ethnic traits. But it is not a question of a completely rigid residential segregation – although access to better-quality housing in more favourable urban zones is more difficult for households headed by Nicaraguans – which would imply a more serious context of marginalisation or exclusion. There are no ethnic or national ghettos in the lower-class residential areas; most of the immigrants living in these settlements are incorporated into the social division of labour, which explains their greater functional integration (Beriain 1995). On the other hand, various expressions of moral integration are also evident – from the establishment of pair bonds with local individuals to people working together, in very varied situations, to construct a living in the popular neighbourhoods. Additionally, the formal recognition of children born in the country also becomes a way of establishing the right of residence, even in precarious conditions.

Violence, crime and insecurity

In a country that abolished the army in 1948 and that respects human rights, the relatively recent increase in social violence, conventional delinquency and organised crime ruptured peaceful Costa Rica and started to affect the erstwhile small-town quiet of San José and of the country's other cities. Social violence appeared in connection with an upsurge of property crime such as common theft, with or without the use of violence. Higher levels of violence were generated by local and international criminal gangs, by the practice of kidnappings and extortion, by other increasingly refined ways to assault businesses and banks, and, in particular, by the theft of vehicles to cater to an extensive black market (OPS 2004).

Organised crime started to increase in the 1980s with the establishment of clandestine arms-trafficking networks in the Colombia–Central America–Southern Mexico corridor. Eventually, this led to the formation of complex arrangements of drug trafficking and money laundering (OIJ 2013). Since the mid-2000s, there has been an increase in drug-related lethal violence, such as assassinations, and the emergence of the so-called *sicarios* (hitmen). In the mid-1990s, only 15 per cent of people killed in the country were victims of the *sicariato*, but in 2010 that figure was already 40 per cent (Arias and Solano 2012). A culture of fear arose among the local population. The presence of 'illegal' immigrants encouraged manifestations of xenophobia towards this group, which was blamed as the perpetrators of all wrongdoing affecting Costa Rican society.

In fact, the recent increase in crime, violence and insecurity in Costa Rica and the GAM is connected to the expansion of (international) organised crime and related phenomena such as urban gangs. Homicide rates for Costa Rica rose during the 2000s, from around 7 per 100,000 inhabitants in 2005 to approximately 12 per 100,000 in 2008–10; since then, the rate has dropped a few points to around 9 per 100,000 in 2012 (PNUD 2013: 48). These figures are, of course, significantly lower than in the neighbouring Central American countries, which, with the exception of Nicaragua, have experienced homicide rates classified as high (ibid.: 47). Two-thirds of the homicides in Costa Rica are committed using firearms (compared with close to 80 per cent in other Central American countries). Still, in a recent national survey, Costa Ricans have rated crime and insecurity as the second most important national problem, after corruption and before unemployment (OIJ

2013: 63). As far as the subnational variation in this rate is concerned, registered homicides for the province (not the city) of San José in 2011 and 2012 were 10 per 100,000, slightly above the national average and higher than in other provinces in the ambit of the GAM (6 for Alajuela, 5 to 6 for Heredia and 3 to 4 for Cartago).

The relatively low indicators of lethal urban violence do not mean that factors leading to violence are absent from Costa Rica. An already cited report issued by Organismo de Investigación Judicial (OIJ) in collaboration with the United Nations Office on Drugs and Crime (UNODC) (OIJ 2013) provides data that indicate a clear correlation between localised homicide rates and the sale of drugs, especially crack cocaine. As a result, registered homicide rates in specific urban areas within the GAM are significantly higher and belie the image of relative security that emerges from the national-level statistics. In 2012, for the canton of San José, a homicide rate of 58 per 100,000 has been recorded, with victims concentrated in parts of the city where gangs operate and local drug trafficking occurs (ibid. 2013: 71); this is the highest local urban rate in the country. The next highest rate is in the canton of Limón (46 per 100,000 in 2012), a town on the Atlantic coast and the principal entry port for marijuana imported from Jamaica. Nevertheless, OIJ and UNODC (ibid. 2013: 72) state that most of the youth gangs active in San José 'limit themselves to a range of minor crimes such as vandalism, petty theft, infraction of public order, assaults, and small scale drug peddling'. As a rule, the large-scale drug-trafficking groups are dominated by foreigners (Mexicans and Colombians) who seek to maintain a low profile as far as the use of violence is concerned. The local gangs do not tend to establish the types of territorial control known in other cities of the region (ibid. 2013: 26, 72).

Governmental and social responses

These perceptions gave rise to a series of police control campaigns that contributed, between 2008 and 2010, to discouraging the immigration of Nicaraguans, who then began to discover other destinations such as El Salvador and Spain. The crime level, however, did not decrease, because the causes of violent crime were not linked to immigration (Sandoval 2002).[4] But still, among politicians and in public opinion, the idea circulated that the country was invaded and that such an invasion, according to statements by the Minister of Public Safety, Rogelio Ramos, was 'a problem of national security'.[5]

Organised crime had developed a very close relationship with the arms and drugs trade; it revealed, from the very beginning, the fragility of the political and police institutions that organised crime tried to infiltrate. On the other hand, the Costa Rican authorities did not want to adopt a public security policy based on the zero tolerance (*mano dura*) approach that was dominant in other Central American countries. While, as a result, the security apparatus was not completely effective in confronting organised crime, at least it maintained the levels of criminality and violence below those experienced in neighbouring countries, including Mexico and Colombia.

Although there is a debate about whether the country has managed to effectively reduce the number of assaults and the homicide rate, these remain the lowest in the Central American region. The homicides rate, which in 1989 was only 4 per 100,000 inhabitants, had increased by 2008 to 11.1 per 100,000, and since then has remained in double figures. The country has not returned to the low crime and violence levels of the previous decades, but from 2010 to 2011 the data suggest that it has 'reached a point of stability with a downward trend in terms of victimization (specifically related to killings) and the perception of insecurity' (Arias and Solano 2012: 103).

Despite the weak evidence of causality between immigration and insecurity, social responses to the problems of development and coexistence in the urban space of the GAM remain incoherent and lack comprehensiveness. Although this system of GAM governance was established as a legal construction to try to regulate urban development of the city cluster in the Central Valley of Costa Rica, its heterogeneity has hindered the establishment of common parameters for managing the complex problems of infrastructure, economic development, social exclusion and cultural diversity. The relative success in stabilising delinquency and crime is attributed to police strategies focused on specialised intelligence operations, the creation of courts of flagrante delicto to prosecute offenders immediately and a reorganisation of police functions. To these measures, an increase in budgetary resources was added.[6] But the other problems remained unsolved: the stabilisation of security has been the result of a strategy of containment of crime, without any immediate possibility of reversing the trend.

Urban saturation, poor connectivity and the collapse of urban infrastructure had reached the limits of sustainability, generating a feeling of chronic setback and paralysis. The defeated presidential candidate was unable to convince the electorate that he was a resolute 'problem solver' after having been in charge of the management of the most important metropolitan area of the country for more than 20 years. The new government elected in 2014 assumed these responsibilities in the midst of an asphyxiating fiscal situation. It had to resolve the inadequacies of the road network and the public transport situation, and put an end to the complex problem of lack of housing and public spaces. It had to work towards a more integrated urban system, following a national urban development plan that was designed in the context of a regional and urban planning project for the GAM of the Central Valley of Costa Rica. This project was implemented between 2002 and 2008 with funds from the European Union. However, consecutive governments at the time decided not to implement the project's requested recommendations, although the project's main objective was to 'improve the efficiency of the urban system of the Central Valley, the principal Costa Rican economic space, reducing the current environmental, social and economic costs arising from an irrational and unsustainable territorial model' (PRUGAM 2008: 28).

Social segregation of the urban space of the GAM is linked to the problems of social exclusion; this, in turn, is connected to the fact that, during the process of economic growth and capital accumulation, the commitment to redistributive justice – on which the stability of the Costa Rican political system is based – was forgotten. Problem solving through popular housing programmes was left to the logic of the market, leading to clientelism, abuses of power, and even corruption and the appropriation of public funds destined for poor families (Pérez 2012). The integration of immigrants into the city was achieved only through their assimilation into labour markets, mostly for informal work and characterised by need-driven enforced subordination. The city did not allow foreigners to become citizens, especially those who had entered the country as 'irregulars', 'undocumented people' or simply as 'illegals', especially when, regardless of their immigration status, they were seeking entry into the informal housing system.

It is possible, however, to perceive some remedies that can reverse the pattern of exclusion and strengthen prospects for social integration. These are twofold: institutional actions and the actions of urban residents. Institutional actions are various, but the principal measures start with an integral proposal for the social integration of migrants, as a result of new legislation in 2010 on migration and foreigners.

This legislation reflects respect for human life, for cultural diversity, for gender equity and solidarity, and above all for human rights. With these ideas, public sector institutions such as the Directorate-General for Migration and Foreigners as well as the Deputy Minister of the Interior, the Ministry of Education, the judiciary and the Ministry of Labour and Culture[7] have initiated programmes to improve the integration of migrants. These programmes include several activities in the residential neighbourhoods of the GAM where immigrants live.

Several institutions have intervened to overcome the lack of integration and security in the popular neighbourhoods. Such actions have improved the involvement of the neighbourhoods' poor residents in local solutions to problems such as deficient infrastructure and insecurity.[8] One can see the positive effects reflected in interviews with community members and neighbourhood leaders, such as the leaders of the communities *La Esperanza de León XIII* and *Triángulo de la Solidaridad*. In both cases, the electricity provider, the state-owned Compañía Nacional de Fuerza y Luz (CNFL), implemented, with community participation, a project of public lighting and power infrastructure. 'If they had not been present, I believe that we would still be as in the era of the caveman, but they made the equipment available and we placed it.'[9] There have been more of such initiatives. Both civil society institutions and local grassroots organisations have been started since the mid-1990s to develop so-called community safety programmes under the auspices of the Ministry of Public Security (Zamora 2006). Many of the initiatives were begun by community organisations within the popular neighbourhoods, in part to overcome the stigma of being viewed as cradles of crime (Sandoval 2005).

The existence of communal social capital is illustrated by the expansion of social networks, reciprocity and the creation of mechanisms of mutual trust among the inhabitants. This is especially visible in local initiatives in the field of communication,[10] the strengthening of identities and the pursuit of shared social representations. Although these actions do not have a direct impact on fragmentation, residential segregation or exclusion, they will be the strategic elements that will advance the promotion of human rights and the expansion of the social citizenship of those who are excluded from the city, be they nationals or immigrants.

7 | KINGSTON: VIOLENCE AND RESILIENCE

Rivke Jaffe*

Introduction

The Jamaican capital of Kingston is known as one of the world's 'murder capitals'. The Caribbean island's highest homicide rates are found in the inner-city areas of Kingston as well as in secondary towns such as Spanish Town and Montego Bay. While, in recent years, the homicide rate has been near 60 per 100,000 inhabitants, the rate in inner-city areas is estimated to be over 150 per 100,000 citizens (Figueroa et al. 2008: 99).[1] Much of this violence is associated with the politically affiliated gangs that control these areas, but high rates of violence and an accompanying sense of insecurity are pervasive beyond these marginalised areas, throughout Kingston and more broadly in Jamaican society. Kingston can be understood as a fragile city, where high levels of urban insecurity are associated with problems relating to existing governance arrangements (see Muggah 2014).

This chapter gives an overview of Kingston's vulnerability and resilience to violence and insecurity. It explores the factors commonly identified as explaining Kingston's extreme levels of insecurity. In addition to factors found more generally throughout the region – government disinvestment under structural adjustment, poverty and social exclusion – Kingston's urban violence has political historical roots that are specific to Jamaica. Longstanding connections between party politics, electoral violence and organised crime shaped the current situation in which criminal leaders known as 'dons' rule over large sections of Downtown Kingston.

To understand how urban resilience takes shape in contexts of pervasive insecurity, the chapter discusses recent government and popular responses. Government responses have been increasingly repressive and include militarised policing tactics. Jamaican law enforcement

---

* Sections of this chapter have been published previously in the *Singapore Journal of Tropical Geography* (Jaffe 2012) as part of a longer article on security privatisation in Kingston.

tends to rely on 'tough policing'. High rates of fatal shootings by police officers have led to persistent accusations of extrajudicial killings on the part of human rights organisations. However, there is broad popular support for this use of excessive force on the part of the security forces. In addition, there have been a number of attempts to incorporate a community policing philosophy. The success of these attempts has been limited, probably because their scope was narrow and wider concerns regarding police corruption and brutality remained unaddressed. Also, beyond security policies and in conjunction with various bilateral and multilateral partners, the government has invested in broader social policy aimed at crime and violence prevention.

As well as such public policy initiatives, we can distinguish various private strategies developed by citizens to protect themselves, strategies that can be understood as forms of resilience that develop outside government. These include a reliance on private commercial security and neighbourhood watch organisations among elite and middle-class Kingstonians. In low-income inner-city areas, non-state security initiatives have involved the emergence of extra-legal 'self-help' law and order provided by dons. These various public and private responses to violence can be read as forms of resilience and attempts to overcome urban fragility. In 2010, a violent government 'incursion' led to the extradition of one of Jamaica's most prominent dons and a nationwide debate on the links between Jamaican politics and organised crime. Yet despite many political pledges to 'dismantle the garrison', this nexus is still largely intact, and the root causes of the island's violence and insecurity remain largely unaddressed.

Understanding the roots of urban violence

Kingston dominates the island politically, culturally and economically. With a population of around 650,000 people, the Kingston Metropolitan Area (KMA), which comprises the administrative districts of Kingston and St Andrew, is a sprawling agglomeration that accounts for about one-fifth of the Jamaican population. During the twentieth century, rapid rural-to-urban migration and a lack of effective urban planning led to the emergence of numerous informal settlements. Commercial and residential areas for the wealthier classes developed in the north-eastern part of the city, known as Uptown Kingston, while poverty and poor-quality housing and services became spatially concentrated in the southern and western areas of Downtown.

The border between these two halves, which is often located across the hubs of Cross Roads and Half Way Tree, is a strongly symbolic one, reflecting the city's polarisation in terms of class. The legacy of slavery is evident in the extent to which this broad socio-spatial divide is inflected by race. The connections between skin colour, class and urban space still reflect a racialized spatial order. Downtown Kingston and the inner-city communities found there remain associated with low-income, darker-skinned 'black' Jamaicans, compared with Uptown Kingston or 'upper St Andrew', which is seen as the domain of the wealthier classes and of lighter-skinned, mixed-descent 'brown' Jamaicans (Howard 2005; Clarke 2006).

Kingston's deep socio-economic inequalities have been exacerbated by over three decades of neoliberal policies. Following Jamaica's independence from Britain in 1962, the two main parties, the Jamaica Labour Party (JLP) and the People's National Party (PNP), both actively pursued developmentalist policies and programmes that dramatically increased popular access to public education, housing and healthcare. However, starting in the late 1970s, structural adjustment as mandated by the International Monetary Fund (IMF) severely curtailed many of the initiatives that these successive governments had developed. Structural adjustment involved massive budget cuts and the privatisation of many public services, resulting in restricted access to formerly public goods, a move that affected less affluent Jamaicans in particular. Informal sector employment increased as formal sector employment, and specifically public sector employment, contracted sharply, while the labour force participation rate dropped in general and in particular for women (Gordon et al. 1997).

Over the same period, crime rates began to rise dramatically, as for various reasons the state security forces became less effective in preventing and tackling crime (Harriott 2000; 2008). Beverley Mullings (2009) draws explicit connections between 'the processes of neo-liberalization taking place in the Jamaican economy, the spatial transformations in social reproduction and the rising levels of social disorder since the 1980s'. She notes two new sources of income that alleviated the crisis in social reproduction, following neoliberal withdrawal of the state in the 1980s and 1990s. The state's disinvestment in education, health, housing and food was somewhat compensated, first by remittances sent home by (female) Jamaican migrant workers, and second by 'gang welfare', which was also fed in part through (illicit) transnational economic flows. She argues, however, that both trends can be associated with the increase in disorder and violence, as the trans-nationalisation of the household meant that children grew up with limited supervision and care and gangs took on a state-like role in welfare provision.

While authors such as Mullings have associated the steady increase in violent crime in Jamaica with structural adjustment and increasing inequality, it is more often explained through reference to the particular features of the country's political system. While the connection between insecurity and neoliberalism is a more general one that resonates with the situation throughout urban Latin America, much of Kingston's contemporary violence has its roots in so-called 'garrison politics'. This is a specific type of electoral turf politics achieved through communal clientelism. Politicians use state resources to secure votes, and supply loyal communities with material benefits such as housing or employment, concentrating supporters in politically homogeneous enclaves known as 'garrisons'.

In the 1960s and 1970s, the JLP and the PNP both created party-loyal garrison communities through inner-city housing schemes where units were allocated to party supporters. Local strongmen (who later became known as dons) received money and weapons from their political patrons, and oversaw the distribution of these and other clientelist benefits. In return, they operated as neighbourhood-level enforcers, who ensured that residents would vote for the 'right' party. In the 1970s and 1980s, the enmity between PNP and JLP gangs in Kingston's garrison communities led to frequent eruptions of violence, especially during elections, resulting in hundreds of deaths.[2] The combination of political tribalism and garrison politics, as Figueroa et al. (2008: 119) note, has been:

> the incubator for the promotion of and legitimization of criminal
> perpetrators of violence as well as those who have become
> embroiled in inter and intra-community violence and its seemingly
> endless cycle of reprisal and counter-reprisal.

Much of the current insecurity can be traced back to these links between political parties, organised crime and electoral violence. Since the 1980s, however, the relationship between politicians and dons has shifted (Sives 2002). As politicians had reduced access to material resources to distribute to their constituencies, the dons found other sources of income in the international narcotics trade as well as in local extortion rackets, the construction business and the entertainment industry. While the influence dons wield varies considerably across inner-city neighbourhoods, in many Downtown areas they are important local leaders and critical mediators in state–citizen relations. The association between organised crime and politics continues, despite the increased financial independence of the dons. Dons can mobilise voting blocs around election time as well as suppress urban unrest; in exchange, their illegal activities may enjoy protection from judicial scrutiny.

Many inner-city Jamaicans perceive state services to be available only to privileged segments of the population. The more successful dons, however, can provide services such as financial support, employment and security, sometimes by linking to formal state actors and sometimes by replacing them. Dons' own financial resources and access to the means of violence allow them to provide services directly. In addition, their connections to political parties and local members of parliament (MPs) remain important. Many dons hold regular 'treats' around holidays or at the start of the school year, during which they distribute food, school supplies and various other gifts. They may also assist residents in gaining employment by pressuring either the MP or locally operating businesses to give them a job. They are also central to the informal provision of security and justice, outlined in more detail below. While many politicians have pledged to sever the ties between party politics and organised crime, the connections have remained. Dons and their organisations play a strong governance role in Downtown Kingston and other marginalised urban areas throughout Jamaica, resembling state-like entities in their assumption of public service provision. However, given their enduring entanglement with state actors such as politicians, bureaucrats and the police, they are not so much parallel polities as part of an emergent and unstable hybrid state (Jaffe 2013).

In May 2010, however, the Jamaican Prime Minister Bruce Golding agreed to extradite Christopher 'Dudus' Coke to the United States on drugs and weapons trafficking charges. Dudus was the country's most prominent don and leader of the JLP garrison of Tivoli Gardens. Soon after Golding had signed the extradition request, armed men began to barricade the entrances to Tivoli Gardens in an apparent attempt to prevent Dudus's arrest. Elsewhere in the capital, gunmen attacked police and police stations. In response, Golding declared a state of emergency for Kingston and adjacent areas, and a joint police and military operation forced its way into Tivoli Gardens. In what became known as the Tivoli incursion, the security forces killed over 73 civilians. Dudus was not captured until a month later; he was extradited immediately and is currently serving a 23-year sentence in a US federal prison.

This incursion and the state of emergency appeared to be a sea change in the relations between the Jamaican state and the dons. Given the historically tight ties between the JLP, the garrison of Tivoli Gardens and Dudus, few people would have expected a JLP government to attack the don and the neighbourhood so violently. Following Dudus's extradition, the security forces began a large-scale campaign to remove dons and to 'dismantle the garrisons' in the inner-city neighbourhoods, with some initial signs of success. However, a few years later, dons seem to be slowly regaining their initial level of power.

Responses to urban insecurity

A range of government and popular responses to violence and insecurity can be noted. On the part of the government, national and urban security policies have tended to rely on the repressive policing tactics popular throughout the region. In addition, starting with the 2010 Tivoli incursion and the state of emergency, we can recognise an interest in a form of policing that combines repressive and preventive elements. There is, however, a less dominant but still consistent interest in 'softer' policing, propagated in the form of 'community policing'. In addition, Jamaican policing has been subject to privatisation and pluralisation (Loader 2000), and so, as well as state responses and public security provision by the police and the military, various types of private security providers also play a role in policing urban space.

Mirroring developments in many other cities in the wider region, many wealthier citizens no longer rely on the state for the provision of security, turning to private security companies and retreating into gated communities and other types of fortified enclaves. In inner-city neighbourhoods, an informal, extra-legal form of privatised security has emerged. Increasingly, residents have turned to the dons for security and dispute resolution. This don-based, private form of 'self-help' law and order, which generally relies on violent retribution, is relatively popular among marginalised urban residents, who feel that the formal

justice system is biased and inaccessible and who may also benefit from
the broader social provisioning role dons fulfil.

Public policing Starting with government responses to urban insecurity, there has been a marked tendency to focus on a strong-arm,
zero-tolerance (*mano dura*) style of policing. On the whole, the Jamaica
Constabulary Force (JCF) has displayed a predilection for repressive
forms of policing. In recent years, police operations – especially those
in inner-city neighbourhoods – have become increasingly militarised,
and the tasks of the military increasingly include internal security and
law enforcement. JCF police officers are regularly joined on patrols
by Jamaica Defence Force (JDF) units, who provide armoured vehicles, communication technologies and surveillance helicopters.[3] This
regular military presence in Downtown Kingston can be understood
as what Stephen Graham (2011) calls the 'new military urbanism', a
tendency for military technologies and logic to become a seemingly
normal part of everyday life and civilian space.

This militarisation of Jamaican policing is distinct from similar
trends in Latin American countries that have recent histories of
democratisation following military rule under authoritarian regimes.
However, Jamaica's contemporary military urbanism has retained
some of the elements of colonial policing. As Anthony Harriott (2000)
points out, the JCF underwent limited reform following Jamaica's
independence from Britain in 1962. This meant that the constabulary
retained many of the characteristics of a colonial police force. The
police have continued to function in a largely punitive style and are
still broadly seen as upholding a highly unequal social and political
order; consequently, their operations tend to enjoy limited legitimacy,
especially among the residents of low-income neighbourhoods.

Rates of police brutality, including extra-judicial killings, have been
consistently high, suggesting a police culture supportive of summary
executions (see Amnesty International 2008). Despite the establishment
of an Independent Commission of Investigations (INDECOM) tasked
with investigating police abuses, very few officers have ever been
convicted. There has also been widespread public support for these
seemingly state-sanctioned killings. This was apparent in the popularity
of 'badman' police officers such as Isaiah Laing, Keith 'Trinity' Gardner
and Renato Adams. Adams, for instance, led the JCF's special Crime
Management Unit (CMU); after multiple allegations of extra-judicial

killings, the CMU was disbanded, but Adams was acquitted following a controversial trial.

There have been some attempts to introduce 'soft' policing. Starting in 2003, a major USAID-funded 'community policing' pilot project was implemented in Grants Pen, an inner-city neighbourhood located (perhaps not coincidentally) in Uptown Kingston. In a much publicised effort, the US $3.5 million Democracy and Governance project involved the construction of a new policing and service centre in the area, while selected JCF officers received training in community policing philosophy from US police trainers. While the project was intended to increase trust between police and residents, another objective was to encourage residents to share information on crime as a more efficient way of allocating scarce police resources. Despite initial successes, the project foundered following concerns over integrity within the JCF; even among the hand-picked community policing officers, there appeared to be links to organised crime (Harriott 2009). Beyond these attempts at community policing, within the broader security strategies there have also been various types of social welfare projects, often aimed at preventing inner-city youth from becoming involved in violent crime. Such community development projects, implemented by organisations such as the Jamaica Social Investment Fund (JSIF) and funded through partnerships with bilateral and multilateral agencies, emphasise social programmes, mediation and conflict resolution and social support services.

In the wake of the Tivoli incursion and Dudus's extradition, a more repressive type of preventive policing became evident. During the state of emergency, the security forces implemented 'curfews' in inner-city neighbourhoods during which they indiscriminately rounded up hundreds of male residents. While these men were never charged with any crime, they were detained and 'processed', arrested without charge and held overnight in the National Arena. These men were photographed and fingerprinted before being released. This collection of biodata and visual identifiers, permissible only through the suspension of the law that the state of emergency entailed, was apparently aimed at creating a database of potential criminals.

This practice is suggestive of what Lucia Zedner has termed 'pre-crime', a type of policing that 'shifts the temporal perspective to anticipate and forestall that which has not yet occurred and may never do so' (2007: 262). This involves a move away from post hoc crime-solving to a pre-crime society, in which crime is seen as a risk that can be understood and managed through actuarial calculations, similar to those that insurance companies make. Policing increasingly becomes pre-emptive, aimed at crime prevention and future offenders, rather than necessarily engaging with actual perpetrators or victims. Given that these statistical calculations of risk are inherently repressive, they can be seen as involving 'prepression', a combination of prevention and repression (Schinkel 2011). The databases that form the actuarial archive produce images of risky subjects and risky geographies that criminalise and legitimate intervention in certain groups and spaces.

In Kingston, the criminalised populations and areas in question are clearly dark-skinned, low-income men and inner-city neighbourhoods. The security forces clearly engage in place-based policing, reflecting and reproducing ideas of criminogenic spaces, where residence plus gender equals future crime risk. Citizens are framed as potential criminals based on their location in Downtown Kingston and 'suspicious' markers such as skin colour or styles of clothing.

Another form of repression also emerged during the 2010 state of emergency, when the police began to publicise lists of 'persons of interest' who were summoned to police stations. These persons were alleged dons or gang members, who were listed by their real names but sometimes only by their aliases. The newspapers and television news shows put out calls for people known as 'Killer', 'Glasses' or 'Titty Man', stating their general or exact address. Those who showed up at the police stations were held for a little while, processed and generally released as the police had no evidence on which to detain them beyond what the state of emergency allowed: they were not suspects, just persons of interest. Some of those who did not attend were killed in alleged 'shootouts' in the months that followed.

Private security provision   As in other cities throughout Latin America and the Caribbean, Jamaica's increase in criminal violence and insecurity has given rise to a proliferation of private security firms. Companies such as King Alarm, Guardsman, Marksman and Hawkeye are highly visible throughout Kingston, both on the billboards advertising their services and in the uniformed armed response units that race through the city on motorcycles. The gated luxury condominiums and exclusive commercial plazas that have been developed by private investors in Uptown Kingston over the last few decades rely heavily on these private security firms. Over 15,000 private security guards patrol the island (Chan 2010), compared with the 8,364 members of the JCF (JCF 2010).

In some other contexts, private security guards are relatively privileged in comparison to police officers, with higher wages and access to better equipment (patrol cars, weapons and communication systems, for example). In Jamaica, however, many private security officers are paid less than the minimum wage and work in conditions forbidden by Jamaican labour law. They work double shifts, are denied leave and are often armed with no more than a baton. Many of these guards are men from inner-city communities who have difficulty finding employment in other sectors because of area stigmatisation; however, their association with high-crime areas is seen as a benefit in security work. Their place of residence does have other repercussions, as it limits cooperation between private security companies and the police. The fear that inner-city residents have of being branded an 'informer' – someone who talks to the police – means that guards who live in don-led communities have a strong incentive to avoid cooperating with the public security forces.

Extra-legal 'self-help' security While significant work has been done regionally on formal private security, much less is known about the dynamics of informal security provision. Private security services and the fortified enclaves they protect are not accessible to the majority of the urban population. Whereas wealthier Kingstonians have the option to select a gated community to live in and a security firm to work for them, the options of the urban poor are much more limited. They cannot afford the services of private security firms, nor do they expect much from the police, who are perceived to be unresponsive and corrupt. Many residents of Kingston's inner-city neighbourhoods have little choice but to turn to the forms of security offered by dons. Jamaica's dons are both the source of much violence and the only form of protection many of the urban poor have against this same violence. They offer a form of 'self-help' law and order known as 'community justice' (or, more disparagingly, 'jungle justice'), providing both security and dispute resolution. There are many differences between the formal and informal privatisation of security, from the agency of those receiving security services, to the concrete ways in which these services are rendered.

While media representations often depict dons as ruthless autocrats, many dons can rely on a significant level of support from residents. This is related in part to their social provisioning role in terms of social security and employment, as outlined above. However, their most important function to residents appears to be the provision of physical security and an alternative form of justice. They provide protection and punish offenders in neighbourhoods where many residents perceive the police as unreliable, uncaring and corrupt. Dons scare off potential violators both within and outside their area by punishing perpetrators swiftly and often violently. The offences they punish include theft, rape, domestic abuse and physical assault within the community. Other types of behaviour that contravene the don's order are voting for the wrong party or 'informing' (talking to the police). First offenders or those whose transgressions are slight may get off with a warning. More serious infractions lead to violent punishments ranging from beatings to a gunshot in the leg to execution, as well as non-violent sanctions such as fines or expulsion from the neighbourhood (Charles and Beckford 2012).

Dons such as Dudus were lauded for maintaining order and 'splitting justice' in an impartial manner. One major difference with the formal justice system is, of course, the fact that one man determines what is fair and just, rather than an institution. There are indications, however, that community justice is undergoing codification and institutionalisation, with standardised punishments for certain crimes and a system of local courts in which groups of elders preside along with the don (Duncan-Waite and Woolcock 2008: 27–9).

The informal justice system – crime being prevented and punished by criminal leaders – can be seen as a somewhat perverse form of resilience to a pervasive atmosphere of insecurity. However, the system of community justice is not only a grassroots response to high levels of crime. There are strong indications that the JCF encourages the informal provision of security and justice, for instance by referring both victims and perpetrators to this system.

Conclusion

The persistently high levels of violence that have been plaguing Kingston for decades are concentrated in the city's poorest neighbourhoods. This spatial concentration of insecurity both stems from and exacerbates the social exclusion of those who live in these 'criminogenic' areas. The inability of the government to address these issues is related to the enduring ties between state officials, politicians and organised crime. Given this combination of insecurity, social exclusion and ineffective governance, Kingston can be considered a fragile city. However, these interconnected problems are not restricted to the urban scale: such issues are obviously embedded in the national polity and its history of garrison politics, but also in transnational flows of illegal drugs, weapons and money.

This chapter has addressed the various strategies that government agencies and citizens develop to cope with crime and urban violence. In addition to repressive and social welfare responses on the part of government agencies (often at the urging of bilateral and multilateral donors), citizens also develop their own coping strategies. Kingston's middle-class and elite residents tend to retreat into fortified enclaves and rely on private commercial security, with similar effects on the urban landscape as have been documented throughout Latin America. Less attention has been paid to 'perverse' coping strategies such as the community justice system, where criminal dons punish a broad range of transgressions – some of which are illegal under Jamaican law, some illegal only under their own system of rule. While dons are an important factor in causing violence, their local legitimacy demonstrates the extent to which Kingston's marginalised populations rely on them in coping with this same violence.

8 | SANTO DOMINGO: CRIMINOGENIC VIOLENCE AND RESILIENCE

Lilian Bobea

Introduction

Up to the early 2000s, Dominicans were very aware of the high levels of violence in Kingston, Jamaica (UNDP 2012) and San Juan, Puerto Rico (Nervares-Muniz 1996; Gumo Vargas De Negro et al. 1975), but they perceived themselves to be generally safe in the rapidly spreading metropolitan area of Santo Domingo. At the time, criminal and social violence was percolated through the mass media only as an epiphenomenal issue, largely produced and consumed by those inhabiting the 'disorganised' interstices of an otherwise liveable and vibrant city. Although this idealistic perception was true for many in the middle- and upper-class strata, it was experienced differently by those living in the marginalised *barrios* located at the border of the Ozama River, in the middle of the Duquesa dump, in the rundown neighbourhoods surrounding the *cementera* (cement plant), and in the margins of the industrial pole of Herrera. In these slums, where people relate with the state primarily through its coercive form, social, political and institutional violence occurred daily, affecting nearly 37 per cent of the population.[1]

In fact, since the late 1970s, as the Dominican Republic moved towards democracy after 50 years of authoritarian rule, those contrasting security perceptions have been reinforced by decades of relatively low national homicide rates of 13 per 100,000 inhabitants. This overall national rate, however, coexisted with a highly concentrated level of victimisation in the most populated *barrios* of Santo Domingo. The transition to democracy favoured competitive politics for the first time in decades, and also brought modernisation of the state and liberalisation of the economy.[2] Those changes, however, were accompanied by economic and political informalisation, a society more exposed to organised crime and the 'democratisation of violence' (Kruijt and

Koonings 1999), replacing the former situation in which violence was largely a state monopoly aimed at political dissidents. Moreover, with the systematic increase in corruption and the use of extra-legal force by bureaucrats, the police and the military became more systemically embedded in criminal activities. By the early 2000s, the Dominican security scenario had changed drastically; by 2004 it had reached a tipping point (Moser 2012; Moser and Horn 2011) when the homicide rate reached an unprecedented 25 per 100,000, an increment of 75 per cent over the three preceding years. By this time, the metropolitan areas of the Distrito Nacional (National District) showed the highest rate of violent death in the nation (43 per 100,000 inhabitants).[3] What were the political, economic and structural factors that led to the huge increase in violence in the Dominican Republic?

Criminogenic violence and transgressive ecosystems

The upsurge in criminogenic violence resulted from the concurrence of at least four factors: (1) rapid changes in the pattern of development and disorganised urban growth; (2) the transforming influence of organised crime; (3) the emergence of multiple unregulated illicit actors and activities; and (4) the lack of a comprehensive public strategy to enhance citizen security.

The *first factor* was the rapid demographic change – along with economic and developmental changes – that accentuated inequality and exclusion. Between 1970 and 1990, the national economy was transformed from an economy largely based on agro-industrial exports (80 per cent of its gross domestic product (GDP) was agricultural products) to one increasingly reliant on services (about 67 per cent).[4] The new economy soon became dependent on income generated by tourism, free export zones (*maquilas*), services and remittances. The logistical and administrative centres for this newly emergent service economy were concentrated mainly in the cities of Santo Domingo and Santiago. The new economic model had an impact on the Dominican social structure: the agricultural population, which had been 55 per cent of the economically active population (EAP) in 1970, had fallen by 2000 to 16 per cent. The segment of manufacturing and industrial jobs rose from 14 per cent to 24 per cent in the same period, while the segment of the EAP in the service sector grew from 31 per cent to 60 per cent. The new economy created a more exclusive pattern of labour insertion that affected mostly those with lower educational levels. Around 63 per cent of the population was in no condition at all to be part of the new economic model, and it benefited from it even less. Additionally, the neoliberal model that accompanied the post-authoritarian transition resulted in a shrinking of the state's administrative capacities and conditioned its good governance capabilities. For many Dominicans, modernity has consisted of an end to their lives as *campesinos* (farmers) with no possibility of finding a replacement job that offers dignity and consistency of employment. It has also meant that the state has surrendered its control of the economy to the private sector, without adequately providing social services to an increasingly urban, informal and transnational society.

The *second factor* was the encroachment of organised crime. At the macro-economic level, drug-trafficking activities unfolded alongside the new development model, where the source of wealth came basically from the external sector in combination with the delivery of internally generated services. The Dominican Republic does not produce drugs, but with the growth of international drug trafficking, the country emerged as part of the global distribution network and relied on work performed by a new subclass in the new division of labour and informal niches within the production–consumption chain. The rise of drug-trafficking activities benefited well-positioned public and private agents, allowing them to accumulate wealth based on their positions. At the same time, the emerging organised crime networks offered a precarious alternative source of income for thousands of Dominicans affected by unemployment and scarcity. Similarly, organised crime activities (drug trafficking and money laundering) became a source of illicit accumulation for middle- and upper-class individuals, politicians and bureaucrats.

The *third factor* was the autonomy of rogue official agents who became precursors of these trends. This tendency became evident as the Dominican Republic moved from authoritarian rule towards a more liberal, democratic state. The transition to democracy in the late 1970s, from an authoritarian civilian government to a liberal one, did little to push for a decisive rupture with the corrupt political, military and police elites that had deep roots in the old authoritarian system. Nor did the new democratic model impose sanctions on the past actions of the military or the police. With civilian rule came a new scenario in which violent, criminal actors colluded with state structures and exploited loopholes in state institutions. It fomented the rise of symbiotic relationships between private criminal actors and corrupt public officials, themselves part of the criminal network. Rogue state officials became embedded in the emerging vortex of organised violence and criminal activities. As the involvement of these corrupt officials expanded in illicit and criminal activities, organised crime itself was able to penetrate deeper into the institutions that these officials represented.

I have dubbed the orientation of these criminal actors towards the state and the political system, as well as the collusion of private and public criminal actors, *statetropism* – a neologism based on the concept of heliotropism – and I use this term to describe the illicit entrepreneurship of corrupt officials and functionaries who protect illicit businesses.[5] By statetropic, I mean that criminality is functionally attracted to the state as an instrument of articulation, protection and benefit seeking. Instead of confronting the state, this new criminality builds a network of alliances within and around it to the point where the state is put in the untenable position of being responsible for deterring crime while at the same time being exploited by an organised criminal elite. Statetropism is reinforced by illegal practices such as police vigilantism against vulnerable urban citizens and high-level corruption linked to complex criminality. As the Dominican Republic was drawn into the global network of drug trafficking, more and more political and entrepreneurial actors gradually entered into a highly competitive arena, seeking economic and political power and pushing for the privatisation of several state functions, including security. This, in turn, opened windows of opportunities that encouraged more disaggregation, dispersion and informalisation of state functions as well as the liberalisation and, eventually, the autonomy of bureaucratic sectors. These trends affected the higher ranks of the armed forces and medium- and lower-ranking police officials, as well as judicial personnel, making it easier for these public servants to establish lucrative bonds with organised criminal networks.

Successive administrations failed to respond adequately to this trajectory, which had the effect of officially – though implicitly – accepting illicit and corrupt practices within the lawless spaces of local and intra-state realms. This in turn led to the emergence of a phenomenon already described by some scholars as violent alternative authorities (Clunan and Trinkunas 2010; Koonings and Kruijt 2009; Arias 2010). These alternative governabilities were based on the opportunities offered by drug-trafficking enterprises operating at territorial levels and already embedded in the new economic and political spheres of Dominican state and society. In this regard, it is essential to recognise that, while most studies of criminal violence examine the effects that illicit dynamics exert over licit agencies and spaces (Arias 2006; 2010; Arias and Goldstein 2010), there is another side to be considered: how the licit realms impact on the illicit ones. This is a complex area that requires analysis of the ways in which new institutional and social arrangements, both formal and informal, facilitate the emergence of new illicit actors and open up new opportunities for criminal activities along with a growing accumulation of illicit capital.

The *fourth factor* was the lack of a holistic and inclusive national policy relating to citizen security. The transition to civilian rule had the effect of breaking apart many state agencies while at the same time centralising power in the executive branch. This disaggregation aggravated the lack of governmental coordination; in addition, it encouraged more privatisation of state functions, especially those related to justice and security. As shown below, the overwhelming use of private security forces to guard bank facilities, businesses and middle- and high-income residential areas competes with the role assumed by active public police officers who have formed 'companies' offering paid protection to functionaries, their families and businesses, while receiving their salaries as public employees. Likewise, in poor neighbourhoods, protection and security against robbers and criminals are usually provided to residents by drug-sellers and *capos* in exchange for access to their neighbourhoods and silence.

Despite attempts at reform in the field of citizen security, both the justice and the enforcement system continued to be based on privilege and discriminatory access, leading to formal and informal privatisation. Other indicators reveal the erosion of security, especially linked to policing issues: (1) the growth of the private security sector; (2) the arms build-up among ordinary citizens; (3) the lynching of suspects; and (4) the militarisation of public security. Closely linked to these issues is a resilient institutional culture inherited from previous regimes that has long relied on vigilantism, corruption and authoritarian practices, and the underlying distrust of official agents in the efficacy of their own system of justice.

These conditions promoted a kind of autonomy for public actors to work on their own pecuniary and political interests, a situation aggravated by past practices that conferred more power and responsibilities on the security forces. The outcome was to make these forces the sole designers, regulators and promoters of their own roles and institutional missions. The delegation of public policies to the security forces drastically diminished the ability of ordinary citizens – and even some sectors of the state, such as the congress – to monitor the actions and activities of the security forces and the judiciary. In the absence of vibrant policies promoting a professional, effective and accountable bureaucracy – particularly in the security forces – institutional inertia accentuated adversarial relations that emerged to set the state, the emergent political system and civil society at odds.

The interaction between illicit – and sometimes violent – state and non-state actors on the one hand and ordinary citizens on the other conforms to what I call *transgressive ecosystems*. I characterise a transgressive ecosystem as a socio-spatial construct that involves a series of political, economic, cultural and relational components as well as formal and informal institutions at the national, transnational and local levels. These systems are affected by: (1) a multiplicity of criminal groups, including private as well as autonomous state actors; (2) illicit dynamics such as street crimes, juvenile delinquency and violence; (3) implicit and explicit rules and regulations; (4) territoriality; and (5) a political nexus and connections to organised and disorganised crime and corruption. In these scenarios, complex criminality combines elements of organised and disorganised crime; it deploys regulatory violence by criminals as well as by private and public security agents. Despite promoting violence in a context of urban fragility, these transgressive ecosystems also distribute benefits widely.

To the degree to which these new social orders purposefully court and incorporate agents of the state, they again propel statetropism as a pattern of organised criminal behaviour that repositions the state as a Janus-faced criminal agent. A transgressive ecosystem 'ionises' some state agents, changing their valence to negative and permitting them to combine freely with criminal elements. Preconditions that foment transgressive ecosystems and statetropism include police autonomy, partisanship fragmentation and competition among criminal actors. These factors enhance a criminal structure, creating opportunities that favour the formation of niches for alternative as well as overlapping forms of governance. Ultimately, these elements contribute to new social orders that include violent entrepreneurs operating in local sites.

As Moser and Horn point out, these scenarios call for more accurate, realistic and effective violence-reduction interventions (Moser and Horn 2011: 1).

Criminality and the violence boom in the Dominican Republic and Santo Domingo City

With the consolidation of democracy between 1990 and 2000, the Dominican Republic experienced qualitative and quantitative changes in citizen security. These changes were reflected in an increase in criminal violence and a growing perception of insecurity on the part of Dominican civil society. An immediate effect of the heightened violence was seen in the citizen security landscape in the Santo Domingo metropolitan area, the National District and the secondary city of Santiago de los Caballeros.

Due to inconsistencies and precariousness in the country's crime statistics, the basic indicator used here to measure trends in criminality is the abrupt increase in the number of violent deaths, and the causes of those deaths. So, the national homicide rate for the year 2005 was 26 per 100,000 inhabitants, which was double the homicide rate registered only four years before (13 per 100,000 in 2001). Concomitantly, there was a change in criminal patterns, with an increase in armed assaults and homicides; between 2006 and 2010, these accounted for 67 per cent of the national homicide total (Bobea 2011).

The increase in criminality nationwide matched a rising trend for civilians to have arms. This trend was especially marked after 2000: the legal register grew from 30,515 registered weapons in 2000 to 159,648 in 2006 and 206,707 in 2011 (ibid.). At the same time, the perception of national insecurity also underwent a dramatic increase. In 1997, 51 per cent of the Dominican population stated that they felt less safe than five years earlier; this percentage jumped to 75 per cent in 2004, then oscillated somewhat, and in 2010 was 73 per cent (Morgan et al. 2012).

The violence profile is unquestionably urban. Official statistics show the following picture for 2011: 36 homicides per 100,000 inhabitants in Santo Domingo City; 35 per 100,000 in the province of Santo Domingo with its five municipalities; and 25 per 100,000 nationally (Ayuntamiento 2011). When looking at the levels of direct and indirect victimisation in comparison with other Latin American and Caribbean metropolitan areas, the city of Santo Domingo has a higher percentage of people who declare that they have been a direct victim of crime (23 per cent) compared with Kingston (9 per cent), Trinidad and Tobago (16 per cent), Caracas (16 per cent) and Port-au-Prince (22 per cent) (Morgan et al. 2012: 113).

Data for the National District (Ayuntamiento 2011) illustrate the predominance of the citizen insecurity factor, expressed by the fact that, by 2008, National District inhabitants ranked 'citizen safety' as the country's third most significant problem, after 'high cost of living' and 'unemployment'. However, by 2009 and 2010, citizen safety was considered the county's principal concern, as expressed by more than half of National District residents (56 per cent and 54 per cent respectively), followed by 'the drugs predicament' (40 per cent). By 2010, both of these issues scored much higher than unemployment (27 per cent) and 'poverty and lack of opportunities' (10 per cent).

This increasingly urban criminogenic pattern is spatially and temporally differentiated between neighbourhoods. Even though changes in the security situation in the National District affected diverse social strata, their impacts were felt more deeply by lower-income communities in the urban areas that had greater concentrations of relative and absolute poverty. My research in these impoverished areas between 2005 and 2011 revealed that residents identified alleys as the most insecure urban spaces. These alleys are located between houses, food and alcohol stands, grocery stores, liquor stores and gambling houses. Most of the latter stay open very late and frequently are the scene of illegal drug transactions, prostitution and armed clashes.

Widespread perceptions regarding the increase in violent crime have also become more entrenched over the years. Official data from the District City Hall (Ayuntamiento 2011) show that, by April 2009, 69 per cent of the inhabitants of the National District's more impoverished areas had noticed an increase in crime over the previous year. That opinion was also shared by 61 per cent of middle- and upper-class residents of the capital city. The general perception of the increasing incidence of crime (including felonies and misdemeanours) spiked in 2011, when 80 per cent of National District residents said that they believed crime had skyrocketed and metastasised within the metropolitan area. Residents of marginalised zones of the National District gave as the main reason for the increase in crime the fact that 'the state and the politicians have not been able to confront crime in an efficient way'. A second reason was 'the increase in drug traffic, drug use and the devaluation of life' (ibid.).

Socio-spatial factors and manifestations in the National District

In spite of the apparent homogeneity of social conditions in the most precarious neighbourhood blocks of the National District, the education levels and ability to find work are indicative of great differentiation. Some neighbourhoods have the lowest school registration rates; these affect up to 70 per cent of residents due to the poor coverage of education services. Almost all these neighbourhoods lack junior high schools or vocational schools, so only elementary-level schools are available. Therefore, residents – especially the youngest jobseekers – have very limited capacity to enter the formal job market. Similarly, several national studies (Vargas 2008) have revealed that the work that is most frequently available to these residents requires few educational qualifications and includes jobs such as waste collection and recycling, masonry and street food sales. None of these economic endeavours contributes significantly to the personal or financial development of these citizens.

This precarious insertion into the job market is also due to the meagre employment opportunities in these zones. The percentage of the EAP in these communities ranges between 70 per cent and 80 per cent, but the employment rate is only 49 per cent.[6] This is what the neighbourhood dwellers I interviewed emphasised when they pointed out that the young people 'cannot find opportunities in the *barrios*'. The only 'opportunities' lay in the informal sector of the economy (conservative estimates place employment in the informal sector at 60 per cent for marginalised neighbourhoods), within which the urban poor see themselves as being pressured to diversify their employment strategies to earn some income (Vargas 2008). This suggests that informal economic activities, especially those in impoverished neighbourhoods where there are few alternatives for work diversification, encourage a complementary structure of opportunities, mostly among the youngest, for illicit (criminal) informal activities, with more routinised and widespread informal jobs surrounding the transgressive ecosystem. Examples of illicit informal activities include the violent robbery of mobile phones, stealing and recycling public electric wire, and intermittent and small-scale drug selling. These activities then complement other activities that are beyond the divide between the lawful and the unlawful, such as prostitution and gambling. The informal labour market is characterised by the progressive uncertainty and contractual inconsistency that place individuals in niches that make them invisible as citizens and reconfigure them in the public and official eye as criminalised subjects. In the local sphere, while the marginalised subjects (many of whom already lack birth certificates or personal ID and are stigmatised by a criminal record for minor crimes) are protagonists in a process of citizen disenfranchisement, political and bureaucratic subjects experience a process of de-institutionalisation.

However, the re-dimensioning of violence in these urban scenarios cannot be explained only by the way in which the various actors are reconfigured. That is why it is convenient to distinguish between the social and political agents and the unlawful and violent agencies with which they interact, as well as the functions that their violent and lawless practices accomplish. Treating them all equally more often than not has resulted in the criminalisation of the weakest and less influential elements of the predatory enterprise, as well as in impunity and preferential treatment for those who bear greater responsibility. The systemic character of the interaction between the formal institutional and the informal para-institutional in recent years is expressed, as mention above, as statetropism. In this context, statetropic corruption is worse than 'ordinary' corruption because with every change in political administration new arrangements must be made with the emerging governing and administrative elites, guaranteeing a circularity of illicit subalternities.

In the case of statetropism, high-level corruption guarantees that agents consolidate systems that work transversally in every administration; this becomes a precondition for the survival of the political or administrative arrangements with those in power or with access to power, even if there is a change of actors. Statetropism requires long-term agreements between competitors, and any breach in these working arrangements can generate excessive violence. Consequently, every change in government administration implies a rearrangement in these illegal and unspoken agreements, raising the possibility of violence. These circumstances partly explain the escalation of criminal violence in 2004 when the government changed hands and a new political elite took office. These phenomena also explain the metamorphosis in activities considered criminal inside these social orders, which I characterised before as transgressive ecosystems.

Socio-spatial and temporal atomisation

Neighbourhoods experiencing a gradual lack of control over their inhabited space and everyday life, and being confronted with organised criminal violence, undergo a reordering of the social and temporal relationship between the violent actors, the public or private deregulated criminals, and the ordinary citizens.[7] This reordering has been made possible through practices that implicitly regulate public and private intra-community life and 'normalise' illicit and sometimes even violent activities. Neighbourhood residents experience insecurity and fear every day and feel trapped in the crossfire of violence between gangs, rival micro-traffickers and the police. Consequently, people in the *barrios* learn to 'adapt' their routines and their relationships with perpetrators, be they *pandilleros*, *capos*, common delinquents or corrupt police. Within this interplay, *pandilleros* and police officers turn themselves into virtual gatekeepers, creating no-go areas in the case of the former, while the police impose extortion fees (*peaje*) on pedestrians at the entrances and exits to the *barrio*.

Residents of Dominican *barrios* look for informal economic and social strategies to survive. The big question here is how much this process of adaptation really enforces a collective pattern of effective resilience. There is not a simple answer to this. As a 2005 survey conducted in the *barrios* indicates, between 60 per cent and 75 per cent of these populations admitted changing their routines in recent years: 'Avoid going out at certain times' (70 to 80 per cent); 'We are more alert' (50 to 60 per cent); 'Only going out at specific times and places' (40 to 70 per cent); and 'Going out armed'. All of this implies individual changes in routine. Residents avoid wandering around at certain times, especially at night. In the 13 *barrios* studied in the National District, 90 per cent of those interviewed reported feeling unsafe from 8 p.m. until 6 a.m. As recently as 2009 and 2011, people declared that they were afraid of 'Going out at night' (58 per cent and 65 per cent respectively); 'Going to work early in the morning' (45 per cent and 64 per cent); 'Going to nightclubs' (31 per cent and 50 per cent); 'Leaving their kids to walk alone to their schools' (36 per cent and 46 per cent); and 'Encountering a police or traffic agent in the street' (21 per cent and 40 per cent respectively) (Ayuntamiento 2011). All these apprehensions and restrictions effectively signal a deterioration of collective well-being through a self-imposed curfew, rigorously observed by fearful residents who are fully aware of the high risk of being outside at certain hours.

Residents have created a precise map of the danger zones. Some consider that certain zones lie outside both community and government control: 'They are not necessarily crime centres, but criminals use them to save time at night when committing their crimes', noted one resident.[8] Over time, people have learned which streets are notorious for gunfire fights and which ones the police do not patrol – either 'because they are afraid' or 'because of complicity with the violent elements'. Also, residents identify escape routes within their *barrios* in case of violence. The self-imposed curfews and the abundance of danger zones virtually impose a state of siege that restricts socio-spatial mobility inside the *barrios*. Under these conditions, the community is reconfigured. The more affluent or those residents with better opportunities to live in safer neighbourhoods move out, trying to escape what they feel they cannot change. As an interviewee confirmed:

> Here we live in continuous danger because people have
> been forced to leave their houses and move to another place
> without having any place to go because there is too much
> violence here. There are people who cannot go to work at
> 6 in the morning.[9]

On the other hand, residents also respond more collectively, although rather passively. Avoiding high-risk areas and observing the curfew at danger times reflect the daily adaptation and resilience of residents. In the local cartography, the highly insecure zones, where drug dealers operate on the corners, set borders within neighbourhoods, while police raids 'encapsulate' communities, isolating them from their surrounding areas. There are even places forbidden to the police. For residents, churches and schools are still seen as places of relative safety, unlike many small stores, public parks, amusement centres and even police stations, which are seen as places of extortion. A male resident explained:

> There is no safety any more, not even in front of your house or
> inside it. People put up fences for nothing because people have
> been killed while seated on their porches or just standing in the
> front of their houses.[10]

In poor neighbourhoods, fear grows as individuals become more aware of their own vulnerability.[11] Disorder and conflict increase among groups and magnify fear, as well as discouraging any attempts to address the causes of insecurity, all of which becomes a sign of micro-societal decline.[12] The evidence for these feelings can be found in the corrosion of intra-neighbourhood confidence and the attrition of community participation. Fear has become another currency with which to gauge the urban dweller's quality of life, as one participant in a focus group observed:

> We have a psychological fear of everyone and everything … we cannot fight off criminality since the police don't support us and then we are forced to develop friendships with those criminals. That is, we become friends because if we report them they will kill us and the police won't do anything.[13]

Witnessing a violent settling of a score, or being seen tipping off the police or reporting something to them, places a resident in the *barrio* in a high-risk situation. In many ways, feelings of extreme fear have decimated social cohesion, which in many communities is now seen as a thing of the past.[14] Gradually, resources (of age and local prestige) that used to be an important reference to inhibit excess have been diluted. In the collected testimonies of residents, we hear that, even though there were criminals within the community in the past, these criminal elements respected the key figures and leaders of those communities, including the elders who had known them as children growing up in the *barrio*. In the 'old days', these adults were acknowledged to hold 'rank', and even delinquents owed them respect.[15] Today, battles between rival lawless groups as well as lethal police persecution have brought about a trans-generational upset; concepts such as respect, power and risk have resulted in a new set of rules and have imposed new relationships that reverse traditional generational norms. Today, even community leaders fear this new brand of criminals, as they have become more and more ubiquitous and are organised in an unpredictable and different way to those of the past:

> There were drugs alright, but my mother raised eight daughters by herself and to this day we stayed out of trouble. She even left us in the care of *tigueres* [street smart people]. They took care of us and also of many of the elderly. They paid for the medicine of the sick and fed the hungry. Not now; now you cannot even neglect to look after your hard-earned belongings![16]

This recollection accounts for a longing for the pattern of social banditry, which, if not totally beneficial, at least was not as harmful to the community as today's criminality. Neighbourhood gangs rarely clashed publicly but rather were viewed as community protectors. However, the gradual expansion of micro-enterprises in drugs, especially hard drugs such as cocaine and crack, has created a new and more brutal partnership between drug use, street criminals and drug-dealing gangs, with its concomitant rise in crime rates.

Choosing the lesser evil: police and *pandilleros*

Besides the threats imposed by street gangs, police personnel also constitute a major active promoter of the massive fear and intimidation produced within the informal settlements. Policing at the local level relies on the abusive, lethal and unlawful use of force that reinforces unfulfilled popular expectations of protection and the guarantee of civil rights. Citizens frequently see the police as another deeply implicated actor of institutional violence, one that is involved in deals with micro-traffickers and uses extortion on the public. In the *barrios*, police officials responded to organised crime in two equally ineffective ways: first, by deploying the *mano dura* (iron fist), through indiscriminate round-ups of young people and the wanton use of lethal force; and second, by succumbing to the influence of the criminal gangs and aiding or protecting criminal enterprises. Behind their dual role of protectors and repressors lies a deeply rooted militarised culture that vindicates the coercive past, glorifies lethal fights against enemies, and promotes martial discipline and an *esprit de corps* that negatively conditions the police's relationship with the *pobladores*. The state thus contributes to the criminogenic ecosystems in which no single actor has a monopoly on the legitimate use of violence.

Fear, crime and violence are also manipulated politically by clientele practices to such an extent that they have had an impact on the capacity of individuals to define collectively their own interests or to revise their traditional response mechanisms. Community leaders complain about being unprotected against the risks involved in their positions; they face the dangers posed on the one hand by the drug dealers and on the other by the state's disregard for and involvement in the new criminality, including police extortion. They also encounter other threats, due to the socio-spatial rearrangement: the influence they enjoyed for decades has diminished in the face of new community interlocutors. Leaders themselves admit this:

The strikes at the *barrios* are not brought on by the organisations, but by these boys. It's the *tigueres*, however just the strikes are, which make them happen. The *barrio*'s *tigueres*, concerned by community needs, they are the ones with the guts. (Ceballo 2004: 85)

The limitations and opportunities of revisiting a political strategy for citizen security

Despite the gradual strengthening of the democratically elected governments since the 1990s and into the twenty-first century, even those forces that sought important state reforms continued to lag behind or simply did not make a real commitment to reform public security and justice. The failure of the governing elite to take comprehensive action to address growing national insecurity permitted an environment in which crime, violent conflict and complex criminality escalated. Complex criminality was increasingly linked to organised transnational crime, largely drug trafficking and money laundering. In addition, it became entwined with other criminal modalities, from extortion, kidnapping and killing for hire (*sicariato*) to the illegal arms trade, human trafficking and other illicit enterprises. This was the scenario that faced President Leonel Fernández, who served in his second non-consecutive term from 2004 to 2008. Besides demands for employment and the provision of public services, the president confronted the urgent need to improve public security. Increased security would become a standard by which the government was validated or disqualified.

Insecurity posed a challenge to the modernising project initiated by the president in the mid-1990s, which involved a proposal for state restructuring that showed important progress in the areas of administrative and public services. It was clear that the increase in real and perceived insecurity would have a direct impact on institutional confidence and the new government's credibility. In early 2005, Fernández published the politically strategic Democratic Security Plan (DSP), a proposal geared to reformulate the preventive, coercive and corrective security system. The plan was focused on citizens' concerns rather than having the traditionally state-centred orientation of previous national security policies.[17] Other reform initiatives were inherent parts of the DSP, notably changes to the criminal justice system and in the treatment of complex crime. The DSP policy makers took into account and examined as valid references the experiences of other Latin American countries. Those experiences emphasised the need to establish efficient institutional mechanisms to prevent, control and neutralise any risks or conflicts that infringed on the rights, freedoms and political guarantees of citizens. A large part of these strategies referred to the role of the police as agents of change and as the interlocutors between citizens and the state.

Among the chief goals of the DSP were reducing criminality and strengthening democracy, both reflected in this statement: 'the need to reduce violence and criminality and advance towards a society in which every Dominican citizen can run his everyday activities in an atmosphere of trust, security and respect for his human rights'.[18]

In place of reactive policies, the DSP set out in its concept paper 'actions proactive and preventive' in character. Given that the DSP demanded integration at all levels, the president argued in favour of a more consistent presence of state institutions such as the departments of education, public health and youth, along with the attorney general, to identify needs and devise solutions. The administration further advocated mainstreaming the DSP into the state structure to ensure the holistic consideration – and implementation – of the policies enacted to prevent and confront violent criminality. Finally, the institutional reforms would focus on the police along with the judicial and penal subsystems as the strategy's main axes of change.

The democratic orientation of the DSP and its concomitant criminal policy rested on two objectives: (1) to restore the social fabric, improving the relationship between the state and society at large; and (2) to integrate the citizenry and its formal and informal institutions as active players in public policy making. To achieve the first objective, the executive branch publicly rejected the use of coercion as well as torture and extrajudicial executions as ways to prevent crime; instead, it promised to adhere to constitutional principles to protect citizens. On the one hand, this approach implied the embrace of a transformation already under way from an accusatorial system to an adversarial one, where the accused cannot be sentenced before being judged. On the other hand, it required the police to undertake a role as a proactive agent in providing for citizen security. This objective raised the need for deep institutional reform, capable of restoring public trust in the police, which was largely absent. In a survey conducted in November 2005 by Newlink Political on security in National District neighbourhoods, 94 per cent of Dominicans thought that only the wealthy received police protection. The reform proposal tried to bolster a communitarian ethos, encourage effective and fair policing of everyday activities and, particularly, dignify police work.

Even with all the input and positive impacts generated in its first year, the DSP did not maintain consistent momentum, either politically or economically; its implementation therefore faced serious challenges. First of all, in order to restore mutual trust and a participative relationship between citizens and law enforcement agents, the police system needed to be organically and structurally transformed. It needed to be redefined in terms of concept and mission, endeavours that no previous administration had undertaken or shown any interest in addressing. At the same time, there was an urgent need to consolidate the governance of public security, developing civilian management capabilities, leadership and political will; none of these steps were evident. On the other side of the equation were the critical role of Dominican society and its capacity to be reconstituted to meet the demands of the DSP. Political and cultural traits of the Dominican tradition, notably clientelism and a Manichean character, had reduced interactions to either confrontation or a subsuming of collective interest to public and private corporatised interests.

A further area of concern was the mediation of the relationship between the Dominican state and society, which could basically be summed up as developing capacity at the national level for convening and resolving the interests of opposing policies regarding security and social provision. This agenda was meant to introduce popular expectations, especially among low-income sectors, through proactive and pragmatic channels. It was expressed in these terms:

> When we speak about democracy we are speaking about
> participation, then, if we are speaking about community
> participation, we are talking about everyone, both men and
> women, integration, where as a person one feels safe. Now we
> really lack it [participation]. The plan can't be intended only
> for those persons who represent the programme, but every
> stakeholder, every neighbourhood dweller should feel a part of it
> and feel responsible for this project.[19]

Even though the DSP was a political and strategic proposal formulated from above for all citizens by a group of specialists and technocrats, the potential beneficiaries of the proposal understood that its implementation would not be effective without other economic, political and social forces acting in concert to promote real participation among different social players. The government therefore needed interlocutors in the *barrios* to negotiate the social interventions and reform police style and quality of work from a community perspective. A monthly round table was convened that included representatives from the neighbourhoods being targeted by the intervention as well as from approximately 30 public institutions. In the long run, however, the government failed to meet this objective consistently, although it did reintroduce the public security debate and the DSP at the beginning of 2009, through a national dialogue that produced some 69 proposals from political parties, the business sector, the unions, non-governmental organisations, religious and community groups and state agencies (Artiles 2009).

A priority of the public policy strategy was the transformation of the national police service, which entailed a doctrinal, functional and organisational reform of the institution, considered the principal delivery agent of the system of prevention and enforcement. This institutional restructuring revolved around several axes: (1) the functional differentiation between administrative, operative and investigative police; (2) the decentralisation of spatial command to ensure a flexible and situational service; (3) the de-politicisation of the police cadre through the implementation of professional standards and promotion; (4) the modernisation of the infrastructure; and (5) the demilitarisation of the police in both real and symbolic terms. This ambitious agenda effectively depended for its success on many factors: (1) a high level of political will, consistent with and committed to the reforms; (2) an objective vision that assigned guidelines for change in a short-, medium- and long-term scheme, and thereby promoted a transformational strategic perspective over time; (3) an efficient and effective system of accountability within the framework of civil rights and respect for the rule of law; (4) both a managerial and a technical capacity to meet the new challenges and responsibilities for the system; and, finally, (5) the acceptance of these new responsibilities by the lead agency in security policy, namely the Interior and Police Ministry, in the areas of policy planning and security management along with preventive operations and the criminal investigation apparatus, and inter-institutional and community coordination.

At the level of macro-politics, the DSP was the main catalyst for the promotion of institutional change within the criminal and justice systems. In general terms, the DSP brought the debate on citizen security issues and policies into public forums. The Interior Ministry, the national police service and the attorney general defined the content of this agenda for change. Unfortunately, its main precepts were only partially shared and discussed with intermediate and lower institutional levels of both ministries and with other relevant public institutions. This situation proved to be an obstacle to change. Implementation was first trialled through *Barrio Seguro* (Safe Neighbourhood), a pilot programme whose objective was to integrate different lines of action and thematic components of the new policy. As a situational intervention, *Barrio Seguro* contributed to a reduction in the local homicide rates and consequently improved the internal mobility of residents in the more violent neighbourhoods of the capital city. It also brought to the people a sense of re-appropriation of public spaces in the *barrio*. Confidence in the police officers who were assigned to patrol these communities and their relationship improved considerably during the first two years of implementation.

Having said that, a few years after the DSP was first implemented there were at least three areas in which great deficiencies became evident: (1) in management authority relating to the political and administrative leadership; (2) in decision making, which involved strategic players; and (3) in the extent and quality of police reform. The present dramatic deterioration in security matters and the decline in citizens' perception of security can be attributed in part to the persistent disorganised situation of crime prevention and law enforcement. Among the factors that prevented the implementation of effective change were stagnation in the drive for police reform and the failure to redirect substantial budgetary and human resources to crime prevention and law enforcement, both crucial aspects of the strategic security policy.

Even more decisive was the inability to dismantle connections between criminal networks (both transnational and national) and political bodies within the state bureaucracy. The dynamism of criminal agents and agencies and their adaptability contrasted strongly with the inertia of law enforcement agencies. Thus, criminogenic trends, statetropism, impunity and corruption all tightened their hold. At the same time, the state itself lost momentum; it failed to assess procedures, learn from its mistakes and overcome obstacles. As a result, it was unable to develop a consistent citizen security policy as intended in the DSP. Another crucial obstacle to a more consistent improvement in citizen security was the limited extent of social policies aimed at the structural causes of conflict and crime. Finally, throughout the whole implementation period, political leaders were unable to shape a viable socio-political consensus and a shared commitment to change, which were necessary to achieve a measure of success with the new policies.

Conclusions on the subject of political will

During the long process of democratic consolidation, the Dominican Republic has experienced a radical change in the area of citizen security. The main characteristic of this alteration is the transformation of the social order through criminal and sometimes violent processes. That includes statetropic tendencies and transnational influence from the illegal drug trade and its synergetic relationships with other illicit activities – and even with legal ones. A key aspect of the new situation is the inability or unwillingness of the governmental and political elite to counter the widespread growth of a repertoire of criminal activities backed by high levels of impunity and corruption. This political elite faces a unique set of challenges. The first is to fully understand the social rearrangement processes that are under way and the agencies these processes have generated within the criminogenic ecosystems, and then to design effective answers to these social changes. That implies a deciphering of the way in which parallel authorities in contested fields constitute themselves, interact and win legitimacy. What are the social adaptability, organisational and assessment strategies of criminal actors? How do informal processes legitimise the status quo of those new criminogenic social orders and make viable the existing self-regulating mechanisms in the local sphere? What collaborative mechanisms do illicit actors use to establish connections with legal authorities? Understanding the symbiotic relationships in these collaborations, in specific contexts, would be a substantial contribution towards designing more effective counterbalancing mechanisms than the reforms that have already been half tried – and have been far from successful – or the traditional 'iron fist' policy, which has had no positive impact.

A second challenge is to understand that a policy that simply criminalises poverty does nothing more than strengthen the alternative power structure of illicit and criminal actors. The state needs to identify the capacities and alternative skills that can be deployed to complement approaches to social intervention and institutional re-engineering. The state must confront the dilemma that it cannot develop adequate policies without fully grasping the reach and complexity of the problems it seeks to modify, or without acknowledging that the state itself is part of the problem.

Achieving any measure of success requires a political will expressed consistently through institutional measures and effective and specialised bureaucracies handling citizen security and restorative justice in a holistic and concrete manner. Such steps would enable the state to prescribe, operationalise and assess performance that is consistent with security and lies within the framework of democratic government. The political will to do this requires a number of elements: (1) ensure the strengthening of democratic institutions by implementing and validating consensual precepts; (2) provide economic and financial support for the defined objectives; (3) strengthen local and management leadership, essential for the implementation of all key initiatives; and, above all, (4) include checks and balances – congressional and societal – as indispensable democratic attributes.

NOTES

1 Urban fragility and resilience

1 We include the (non-Spanish speaking) Caribbean in our definition and use of Latin America as a region. This follows the common practice of multilateral organisations such as the United Nations (the Economic Commission for Latin America and the Caribbean (ECLAC), the UN Office on Drugs and Crime (UNODC), the UN Development Programme (UNDP), the UN Human Settlements Programme (UN-Habitat)) and the World Bank as well as the scholarly community. In this volume we have included a chapter on the Spanish-Caribbean city of Santo Domingo (Dominican Republic) and the English-Caribbean city of Kingston (Jamaica).

2 *El Economista*, 12 July 2013.

3 For other case studies see WOLA (2011).

4 We follow here the arguments in Kruijt (2011). A very recent analysis with emphasis on Colombia, Peru, Ecuador and Guatemala is Briscoe et al. (2014).

2 Exclusion, violence and resilience

1 For fairly recent overviews, see Fay (2005) and UN-Habitat (2012).

2 Statistical inputs for the graphs in this section have been compiled from a wide variety of sources, listed below. The bibliography contains full references except for institutional sources of primary statistics (such as INGE, INEI, INDEC, SEDESOL, UNDP). It has not always been possible to check them thoroughly for reliability and compatibility. The graphs presented in

Figures 2.1, 2.2 and 2.3 should therefore be considered as illustrative for broad trends. No statistical precision is claimed. Sources used are: Atlas do Desenvolvimento Humano no Brasil, 2013 (www.atlasbrasil.org.br/2013/pt/ranking); Barradas Barata et al. 1999; CEPAL 2013; Carneiro et al. n.d.; Costa and Romero 2010; Delfini and Picchetti 2005; Garza and Schteingart 2010: 251; Eyzaguirre 1998; Hernández-Bringas and Narro-Robles 2010; IBGE; INEI/PNUD; INDEC Argentina; Jannuzzi 2001; Lima Cómo Vamos 2013; MTPE in Salgado Portugal 2007; Mucumeci 2002; ONU Habitat 2014; Reporte Económico de la Ciudad de México, April 2014 (http://reporteeconomico.sedecodf.gob.mx); Rocha 1997; SEDESOL; Sosa Escudero and Gasparini 2000; Spinelli et al. 2008; UN-Habitat 2012; UN-Habitat 2011; UNDP (through Google Public Data); UNODC 2011; Waiselfisz 2011.

3 See PNUD (2013) for geographic information system (GIS) data on Belo Horizonte that show distinctive urban spaces with substantially higher homicide rates. The Núcleo de Estudos da Violência at the University of São Paulo has done similar work for this city, generating similar results (see www.nevusp.org).

4 We draw here on Koenders and Koonings (2012).

5 The same happened in São Paulo. The unified PCC – organised crime being a parallel power institution in this megacity – publishes public statements in terms that at first appear to be pamphlets of the extreme left. For more on the origins of the PCC, see Souza (2007).

6 See Assembléia Legislativa do Estado do Rio de Janeiro, *Relatório final*

*da Commisão Parlamentar de Inquérito
destinada a investigar a ação de milícias
no âmbito do Estado do Rio de Janeiro* (Rio
de Janeiro, 2008). For the subsequent
introduction of permanent 'pacification'
policing in Batam (and a few other
favelas), see 'Polícia para mil e uma
utilidades', *O Globo*, 15 August 2009,
p. 12.

7 See Pablo Waisberg (2007) 'More
violent deaths in state hands', *Latin
America Press*, 13 June (http://lapress.org/
articles.asp?item=1&art=5189).

8 A more detailed account of causes
and consequences can be found in
Denissen (2008: 61–102).

9 We first present a summary of
Kruijt and Degregori (2007) and then
provide an update of the situation.

10 In the 1980s, the *cono norte*
accounted for 26 per cent of the
population of metropolitan Lima, the
cono este for 16 per cent and the *cono sur*
for 20 per cent (Matos Mar 2004: 132–3,
149–53).

11 This practice (called the 24 x 24
norm) was silently inaugurated in the
late 1980s and persisted during every
presidential term until the present. In
December 2013, the minister president
announced that the system will end in
2016 (Rospigliosi 2013).

3 Caracas

1 See North (1991); North et al. (2009);
Messner et al. (2012); Nivette and Eisner
(2013); and Nivette (2014).

2 See Briceño-León (1986); Briceño-
León and Acosta (1987); Bolívar et al.
(1994); Bolívar and Baldó (1995); and Rosas
Meza (2004).

3 The homicide data published in this
chapter are elaborated from CICPC data
from the Observatorio Venezolano de
Violencia at http://csis.org/files/media/
csis/events/071212_Briceno_Leon.pdf.

4 Published in the journal *El Universal*
in 2014.

4 Bogotá

1 The chapter will concentrate on
homicide because figures for most other
kinds of crime are unreliable.

2 The three exceptions are Kandahar
(Afghanistan), Kingston (Jamaica) and
New Orleans (USA). Several US and
South African cities figure among the
next 15 most violent cities. The analysis
includes only cities with over 300,000
inhabitants.

3 However, Melo (2009) presents
police figures that record much higher
figures for homicides in Bogotá,
fluctuating from 19 to 36 per 100,000
inhabitants between 1962 and 1967,
and averaging around 15 between 1968
and 1978. These numbers are surprising
given that, in recent years, the Instituto
Nacional de Medicina Legal figures are
consistently higher than those of the
police.

4 In Medellín, the extradition of
Don Berna to the United States is
blamed for the rise in violence after
2008, which was linked to the subsequent
fight for territory among gangs in
the city.

5 The Palace of Justice was actually
attacked by the M19 guerrillas but it
is often claimed that the attack was
financed by Pablo Escobar. For more
details on all these events, see http://
en.wikipedia.org/wiki/Pablo_Escobar.

6 *Zanahoria* (carrot) is a slang term
for the behaviour of sensible people.
In 2002, the 'optimistic hour' extended
nightclub opening to 3.00 a.m.

7 Signs were given out showing a
thumb that could be pointed up or
down to comment on other people's
road behaviour. Martin and Ceballos
(2004: 722) suggest that the
'thumbs-up' campaign was initially
the subject of public ridicule. Mockus'
marriage ceremony received a similar
reaction because it was held in
a circus.

8 His most notable achievement in this respect was to remove the informal and crime-ridden market that had long operated in San Victorino (Acero 2003: 93; Donovan 2002).

9 In discussing these criticisms, it should be pointed out that politics intervenes heavily in some of the opinions expressed. For example, those who wish to praise the national security programmes of President Álvaro Uribe tend to play down the significance of the actions taken in Bogotá. It must also be noted that supporters of Mockus and Peñalosa are often prominent critics of the left-wing mayors who governed after 2004.

10 Of course, the growth in private security, particularly the protection afforded to businesses and to residences in Bogotá's elite neighbourhoods, would also have contributed. In 2009, some 80,000 security guards were working in the city (Admejores Seguridad Ltda, n.d.).

11 The Corporación Nuevo Arco Iris claims that groups such as the Ejército Revolucionario Popular Anticomunista (ERPAC), las Águilas Negras, el Bloque 'Héroes de Castaño' and the men of 'Loco Barrera' are operating in different parts of the metropolitan area.

12 See Ortiz (2011). Police statistics show that almost half of the homicides in the country in 2010 (7,200 out of 15,400) were related to fighting between BACRIMS and among street gangs, some of whom are connected to the BACRIMS, for control of local drug markets. These same figures show that homicides relating to the civil conflict account for less than 4 per cent, or a little over 600 deaths.

13 However, the Secretary of Government in Bogotá denies that organised gangs are operating in Bogotá, or at least states that no gangs totally control particular areas of the city (*El Tiempo* 2011a).

14 Zorro Sánchez (2004: 17) defines *pandillas* as 'groups with ten or more members who commit crimes and who tend to generate conflict in barrios of the city'. However, Escobedo (2006: 335) warns that 'there is no consensus on the definition'. *Parches* are gangs who may or may not develop into *pandillas*.

15 However, the chief of police promised 1,300 more police officers for the capital in February 2011; this would increase the total force to 20,000 (Guevara 2011). The Secretary of Government claimed that there were 18,200 police in the city in August 2011 and an additional 3,500 to help security during the Under-21 international football tournament (*El Tiempo* 2011a).

16 Observations made in interviews by the mayors of Bogotá and Quito in March 2011.

5 San Salvador

1 'Popular neighbourhood' is a literal translation of the term as used in Latin America: *'barrio popular'*. In English, the terms 'slum' or 'urban ghetto' are also used.

2 Exact numbers are difficult to obtain. A recent report by the National Civil Police (Policía Nacional Civil or PNC) estimates that 50 per cent of the homicides over the last five years were committed by gang members (information provided to the authors by the PNC in 2011), while the United Nations Office on Drugs and Crime (UNODC) estimates the proportion as 16.8 per cent for 2012 (UNODC 2014b). However, in November 2011, the Minister of Justice and Public Security Munguía Payés, without revealing his sources, maintained that the gangs were responsible for 90 per cent of homicides in El Salvador (Castillo 2011).

3 In this chapter, the words 'gangsters', 'gang members' and 'homeboys' are used as synonyms.

4 Information provided to the authors by the PNC in 2011.

5 The national homicide rate fell from 69.9 per 100,000 inhabitants in 2011 to 41.2 in 2012 (UNODC 2014b).

6 By June 2013, some 11 municipalities had joined the initiative. Among them were five of the 14 AMSS municipalities: Ilopango, Santa Tecla, Apopa, Quetzaltepeque and Ciudad Delgado. For an overview of these MLV, see the website of Interpeace: www.interpeace-lao.org/programas-info/noticias lao/16 programa-juventud-news/111-municipios-libres-de-violencia-un-emprendimiento-local-en-favor-de-la-paz-social-en-el-salvador.html.

7 'Los dueños de las calles.' Interview, 25 May 2012, San Marcos.

8 'Casi extranjera, actuando sola, en un territorio desconocido.'

9 'Yo tenía amigos que vivían en Las Arboledas. Una vez me pusieron la pistola en la cabeza y me decían que si volvía a entrar, me iban a matar.' Interview, 10 November 2013, Soyapango.

10 'Cats', meaning novices or servants.

11 'Post', which derives from their vernacular 'postear' – standing like a post or watching.

12 'Uno de bicho no piensa. Los pandilleros les dan cosas y ellos empiezan a hacer trabajitos para ellos. Si hacen un trabajito, o sea, si les avisan que alguien llega, les regalan cosas, por ejemplo, celulares. Y así los van halando [hacia la pandilla].' Interview, 19 June 2013, San Martín.

13 'Uno no tiene que estar ni muy cerca, ni muy lejos.' Interview, 13 June 2013, Tonacatepeque.

14 'Hablarles mucho ni tampoco dejarles de hablar, porque eso es buscar problemas.' Interview, 11 June 2012, San Marcos.

15 'Yo saludo nada más. A veces los ignoro, depende de lo que me dicen. Tengo que tener cuidado con las bromas

que me hacen. Depende de cómo uno les salga ellos se siguen acercando y luego invitando.' Interview, 13 June 2013, Ilopango.

16 'Es seguro siempre y cuando no sea zona contraria. Allí los miran como espías. Ellos dicen que "se andan echando la manta de lo que pasa".' Interview, 28 June 2013, Cuscatancingo.

17 'Muchos van a zonas que consideran seguras, o sea, donde está la misma pandilla. Los de allí van al Instituto Santa Lucía, es de los mismos [la MS], y hay unos pocos que van al INSAM, que es el instituto de San Martín, que está la contraria [la 18].' Interview, 21 June 2013, San Martin.

18 'Yo por ser de la colonia que soy, no podía entrar a otras colonias. Eso me disgustaba y tenía algún rencor contra eso, aunque yo no pertenecía a ningún grupo.' Group interview, 13 November 2013, Soyapango.

19 'Una vecina estaba llevando a un muchacho. Él seguido iba. [Un día] llegan a sacarlo de la puerta de la casa. Lo sacan, le levantan la camisa, y ¿De dónde venís? ¿De dónde sos? Lo interrogan y se lo llevan.' Group interview, 13 November 2013, Soyapango.

20 'Había una chica de 17 años. Empezó a andar con un policía, de novios. De repente, a los meses, desapareció. Sólo la encontraron en la quebrada sin lengua.' Interview, 29 May 2013, Tonacatepeque.

21 'Caminan diferente, hablan diferente, entonces eso sí es bien, bien complicado; o sea no tanto vestirse como ellos, sino tener una forma más modesta de vestirse, hablar, caminar.' Interview, 28 June 2012, San Marcos.

22 'Los pandilleros piensan que [los militares] son un asco ... Si supieran que soy soldado, me matan.' Interview, 28 June 2013, Cuscatancingo.

23 '[Mis hijos,] los tengo en la casa ... Solo en la escuela tienen la oportunidad para jugar con los amigos, porque yo no

los dejo que salgan a andar de casa en casa. No me gusta.' Interview, 5 June 2012, Tonacatepeque.

24 'Yo no voy a otra colonia donde no puedo conseguir más que la muerte ... Con mis amigos me encuentro en Unicentro o Metro, Plaza Mundo o Galerías. Siempre un centro comercial.' Interview, 26 June 2013, Soyapango.

25 'Como población nosotros no tenemos tregua.' Interview, 29 May 2013, Ilopango.

26 'Si funcionara [la tregua], los jóvenes podríamos ir tranquilamente a otras comunidades, pero no es así aunque esté la tregua.' Interview, 25 June 2013, Apopa.

27 'Mi hermano sigue viviendo el mismo peligro. La [pandilla] contraria lo para, lo revisa. Incluso le suben la camisa para ver si tiene tatuajes.' Interview, 14 June 2013, Ayutuxtepeque.

28 As mentioned in the introduction, interviews for this study were conducted between August 2011 and November 2013. In this period, the nature of the gang presence and control seems to have become more tense, with more gang members on the streets, more and larger graffiti, and more warnings painted on the walls. In 2011, the interviewees were more relaxed about the gang presence, while in 2013 quite a few expressed fear about what was happening in their neighbourhood and how it affected them. For instance, this was clearly expressed by a person who was interviewed in 2011 and again in 2013.

29 'Los pandilleros no han querido tratar el tema de las extorsiones porque de eso viven, de eso mantienen a sus familias.'

6 San José

1 Solís obtained 77.8 per cent of the votes and the candidate of the ruling party only 22.2 per cent.

2 Officially, the city of San José was founded in 1737.

3 Costa Rica has seven provinces: Alajuela, Cartago, Guanacaste, Heredia, Limón, San José and Puntarenas.

4 A public report requested by the President of the Republic to the Defensoría de los Habitantes de la República, the public sector defender of human rights in Costa Rica, identifies a series of violations of human rights committed by the security forces of the country during a police operation in the La Carpio canton of the capital city, where they performed a series of 'massive and arbitrary arrests'. The final report with recommendations is available at www.iidh.ed.cr/BibliotecaWeb/Varios/ Documentos/BD_2061358847/Docs%20pr oteccion%20victimas/CR%204A%20Liber tad%20y%20debido%20proceso.pdf.

5 Statements by the Minister of Public Safety in the television news programme *Noticias Repretel*, 20 January 2004 (morning and midday editions).

6 Mario Zamora, Minister of Public Safety 2010–14, in a personal communication to the author.

7 'Fall in love with your city' is a programme run by the Ministry of Culture and Youth that aims to develop a cultural corridor in the districts and city squares to foster a greater sense of citizenship and identity among the urban residents.

8 The Constitutional Chamber issued decision 5907–05 in 2005 that nullified the paragraph of article 37 of Executive Decree 26935-G stating that Costa Rican citizenship by birth or naturalisation was required to be a board member of the board of directors of any neighbourhood development association (Asociaciones de Desarrollo Comunal).

9 Interview with a community leader in *La Esperanza de León XIII*.

10 For instance, the journal *La Voz de la Carpio*.

7 Kingston

1 The comparative average homicide rates per 100,000 are 12.5 for Africa, 16.3 for the Americas, 3.0 for Europe and Oceania, and 2.9 for Asia (UNODC 2014: 22).

2 For more on garrison politics, see Figueroa and Sives (2002), Harriott (2008) and Sives (2010).

3 See www.jdfmil.org/jdfTask/tasks.php.

8 Santo Domingo

1 According to the Oficina Nacional de Planificación, 37 per cent of the population residing in the metropolitan area belongs to low/medium, low and very low income strata. They comprise the 'poor' population that shares the space with the 34.3 per cent who belong to medium/high and high strata. While it is true that the rest of the country accounts for 65 per cent of the poor population, the concentration of the poor is markedly higher in the National District where the city of Santo Domingo is located. In addition, by 2009 the metropolitan area had a higher rate of unemployment (16.7 per cent) than nationally (14.9 per cent).

2 This is reflected in the transformation of a predominantly agricultural development model and economy to one oriented towards financial services, tourism, remittances and foreign investment in the form of free zone enterprises.

3 Data collected by the Procuraduria General de la Republica.

4 These and the subsequent data are to be found in Lizardo and Guzmán (2001: 2, 36).

5 Heliotropism refers to plants' orientation with regard to the sunlight. There are two types of tropism – positive and negative – whereby the plant moves towards the light stimulus in the first case or away from it in the second.

6 These data are included in CES (2006: 129). The extended unemployment category refers to the total of the population over the age of 10 years who are out of work (but had some degree of work activity at least four weeks before the census) and the working-age population.

7 See Shaw and McKay (1942), Bursik and Grasmick (1993), Kornhauser (1978) and Sampson and Groves (1989).

8 Resident interview at Barrio Luperon, January 2006.

9 Focus group with residents, Capotillo, 2006.

10 Focus group, Gualey, Santo Domingo, 2005.

11 Studies have addressed this aspect of information dissemination as a catalyst of fear in developed countries as well (see Skogan 1986: 215; Skogan and Maxfields 1981; Lavrakas 1981).

12 See Taylor et al. (1961), Koonings and Kruijt (2007b) and Zaluar (2004b).

13 Focus group, Guachupita, Santo Domingo, 2005.

14 In a survey conducted in the *barrios*, only 21 per cent of those interviewed declared that they were not afraid to circulate in any part of the neighborhood. People mentioned public places that were considered too dangerous to visit, among them parks and markets, and particular streets. They also mentioned that everybody stays indoors after dusk and during the night because those are the hours when shootings between gangs, robberies and violence are most frequent (Newlink Political, 'Survey on security neighborhoods: National District', November 2005 [unpublished]).

15 Group interview, *barrios* 24 de Abril and Gualey, October 2006.

16 Group interview with females from Gualey, 2005.

17 Presidential decree no. 263 of 2005.

18 Concept paper, 'Democratic Security Plan for the Dominican Republic', prepared by the advisory team of Newlink Political and Research, Miami and Dominican Republic, February 2005, p. 1 (unpublished).

19 Group interview with community leaders (Newlink Research 2008).

BIBLIOGRAPHY

Acero, H. (2003) *Violencia y delincuencia en contextos urbanos: La experiencia de Bogotá en la reducción de la criminalidad 1994–2002*. Bogotá: Alcaldía de Bogotá.

— (2011) 'Dos décadas de seguridad ciudadana: muchos menos homicidios, faltan gobiernos locales'. *Razón Pública*, 3 July.

— (n.d.) 'Gestión local de la convivencia y la seguridad ciudadana'. PowerPoint presentation. Available at: http://siteresources.worldbank.org/EXTLACREGTOPURBDEV/Resources/841042-1219076931513/ConferenciaBancoMundial.ppt.

Admejores Seguridad Ltda. (n.d.) 'Seguridad privada, es mejor prevenir ...'. Available at: http://admejoresseguridad.com/archives/808.

Aguayo Quezada, S. and R. Benítez Manaut (2013) 'Introducción: las violencias. Balance, efectos y prospectiva' in S. Aguayo Quezada and R. Benítez Manaut (eds) *Atlas de la Seguridad y de la Defensa de México 2012*. México: Colectivo de Análisis de la Seguridad con Democracia (CASEDE), pp. 11–14. Available at: www.casede.org/index.php/nuestro-trabajo/publicaciones/atlas-de-la-seguridad-y-la-defensa-de-mexico-2012.

Aguirre, M. (2009) 'Crisis of the state, violence in the city' in K. Koonings and D. Kruijt (eds) *Megacities: The politics of urban exclusion and violence in the global South*. London: Zed Books, pp. 141–52.

Alba Vega, C. and D. Kruijt (2007) 'Viejos y nuevos actores violentos en América Latina: temas y problemas'. *Foro Internacional* 189, XLVII(3), pp. 485–516.

Alcalde, M. C. (2006) 'Migration and class as constraints in battered women's attempts to escape violence in Lima, Peru'. *Latin American Perspectives* 33(6), pp. 147–63.

Altheimer, I. (2013) 'Cultural processes and homicide across nations'. *International Journal of Offender Therapy and Comparative Criminology* 57 (July), pp. 842–63.

Amat, Y. (2012) 'Petro propone despenalizar las drogas en ciertos sectores'. *El Tiempo*, 4 August.

Amnesty International (2008) *Jamaica: 'Let them kill each other': Public security in Jamaica's inner cities*. London: Amnesty International. Available at: www.amnesty.org/en/library/info/AMR38/001/2008/en.

Amorim, C. (2007) *CV-PCC: A Irmandade do Crime*. Rio de Janeiro: Record.

Anderson, E. (1999) *Code of the Street: Decency, violence, and the moral life of the inner city*. New York NY: W. W. Norton & Company.

Angarita, P. E. (2009) 'Éxitos en el campo se han traducido en inseguridad urbana'. *Revista Cambio*, 3 December.

Arias, E. D. (2006) *Drugs and Democracy in Rio de Janeiro: Trafficking, social networks and public security*. Chapel Hill NC: University of North Carolina Press.

— (2010) 'Understanding criminal networks, political orders and politics in Latin America' in A. L. Clunan and H. A. Trinkunas (eds) *Ungoverned Spaces: Alternatives to state authority in an era of softened sovereignty*.

Stanford CA: Stanford University Press, pp. 115–35.

— and C. Davis Rodriguez (2006) 'The myth of personal security: a discursive model of local level legitimation in Rio's favelas'. *Latin American Politics and Society* 48(4), pp. 53–81.

— and D. M. Goldstein (eds) (2010a) *Violent Democracies in Latin America*. Durham NC: Duke University Press.

— and D. M. Goldstein (2010b) 'Violent pluralism: understanding new democracies of Latin America' in E. D. Arias and D. M. Goldstein (eds) *Violent Democracies of Latin America*. Durham NC: Duke University Press, pp. 1–34.

Arias, R. and P. Solano (2012) *Informe nacional sobre violencia armada e inseguridad en Costa Rica*. San José: Fundación para el Servicio Exterior para la Paz y la Democracia.

Arjona, A. (2008) 'One national war, multiple local orders: an inquiry into the unit of analysis of war and post-war interventions' in M. Bergsmo and P. Kalmanovitz (eds) *Law in Peace Negotiations*. FICJC Publications No. 2. Oslo: Peace Research Institute, pp. 1–27.

Artiles, L. (2009) 'Seguridad Ciudadana en la Republica Dominicana'. Paper presented at the Work Table on Citizen Security, National Unity Summit to Face the World Crisis, Santo Domingo, Dominican Republic, 19 February. Published in *Secretara de Estado de Economia, Planificacion y Desarrollo*. Available at: www.academia.edu/7280920/SEGURIDAD_CIUDADANA_EN_LA_REPUBLICA_DOMINICANA_DESAFIOS_Y_PROPUESTAS_DE_POLITICA.

Auyero, J. (2006) 'The political makings of the 2001 lootings in Argentina'. *Journal of Latin American Studies* 38, pp. 241–61.

Ávila Martínez, A. F. (2010) 'Grupos armados ilegales, violencia urbana y mafias coercitivas: gobernabilidad y crisis democráticas' in FLACSO Secretaría General (ed.) *Gobernabilidad y Convivencia Democrática*. Quito: Facultad Latinoamericana de Ciencias Sociales (FLACSO), pp. 3–31.

— and M. P. Núñez Gantiva1 (2010) 'Bogotá cercada'. *Arcanos* 15.

— and B. Pérez (2011) *Mercados de criminalidad en Bogotá*. Bogotá: Corporación Nuevo Arco Iris.

Avritzer, L. (2002) *Democracy and the Public Space in Latin America*. Princeton NJ: Princeton University Press.

Ayuntamiento (2011) *Encuesta de Seguridad del Observatorio Ciudadano*. Santo Domingo: Ayuntamiento del Distrito Nacional. Available at: www.adn.gob.do.

Bailey, J. and L. Dammert (eds) (2006) *Public Security and Police Reform in the Americas*. Pittsburgh PA: University of Pittsburgh Press.

Baptista, A. (2005) *El Estado y el capitalismo rentístico*. Caracas: Academia Nacional de la Historia.

Barcellos, C. and A. Zaluar (2014) 'Homicídios e disputas territoriais nas favelas do Rio de Janeiro'. *Revista de Saúde Pública* 48(1), pp. 94–102.

Barrachina, C. and J. Ignacio Hernández (2012) 'Reforma del sistema nacional de seguridad pública en México (2006–2011)'. *Urvío: Revista Latinoamericana de Seguridad Ciudadana* 11 (March), pp. 79–92.

Barradas Barata, R., M. C. Sampaio de Almeida Ribeiro and J. Cássio de Moraes (1999) 'Tendência temporal da mortalidade por homicídios na cidade de São Paulo, Brasil, 1979–1994'. *Cadernos de Saúde Pública* 15(4), pp. 711–18.

BCV (2012) *Informe Económico 2012*. Caracas: Banco Central de Venezuela (BCV).

Beall, J. (2007) *Cities, Terrorism and Urban Wars of the 21st Century*. Crisis State Research Center Working Paper 9. London: London School of Economics and Political Science.

— (2009) 'Urban governance and the paradox of conflict' in K. Koonings and D. Kruijt (eds) *Megacities: The politics of urban exclusion and violence in the global South*. London: Zed Books, pp. 107–19.

—, T. Goodfellow and D. Rodgers (2011) *Cities, Conflict And State Fragility*. Crisis State Research Center Working Paper 85. London: London School of Economics and Political Science.

Becker, G. S. (1968) 'Crime and punishment: an economic approach'. *Journal of Political Economy* 76(2), pp. 168–217.

Beckett, K. and A. Godoy (2010) 'A tale of two cities: a comparative analysis of quality of life initiatives in New York and Bogotá'. *Urban Studies* 47, pp. 277–301.

Beltrane, F. (2012) 'Seguridad ciudadana y nuevas estrategias de control del delito en Argentina'. *Urvío: Revista Latinoamericana de Seguridad Ciudadana* 9 (June), pp. 102–12.

Benítez Manaut, R. (2010) 'México: seguridad nacional, defensa y nuevos desafíos en el siglo XXI' in R. Benítez Manaut (ed.) *Seguridad y defensa en América del Norte: Nuevos dilemas geopolíticos*. Washington DC and San Salvador: Woodrow Wilson International Center for Scholars and Fundación D. Guillermo Manuel Ungo (FUNDAUNGO), pp. 153–203.

—, A. Rodríguez Sumano and A. Rodríguez Luna (eds) (2009) *Atlas de la Seguridad y la Defensa de México 2009*. México DF: Colectivo de Análisis de La Seguridad con Democracia (CASEDE).

Benwell, M. C., J. Haselip and J. A. Borello (2013) 'Housing, security, and employment in post-neoliberal Buenos Aires'. *Latin American Perspectives* 40(2), pp. 146–67.

Beriain, J. (1995) *La integración en las sociedades modernas*. Barcelona: Antropos.

Bibler Coutin, S. (2007) *Nations of Emigrants: Shifting boundaries of citizenship in El Salvador and the United States*. Ithaca NY: Cornell University Press.

Bobea, L. (2003) 'Economía política de la inseguridad y desafíos a las políticas de seguridad ciudadana en la República Dominicana: Cero Tolerancia bajo la mirilla' in L. Bobea (ed.) *Entre el crimen y el castigo: Seguridad ciudadana y control civil democrático en América Latina y el Caribe*. Caracas: Nueva Sociedad.

— (2010) 'Organized violence, disorganized states' in E. D. Arias and D. Goldstein (eds) *Violent Democracies*. Durham NC: Duke University Press, pp. 161–200.

— (2011) *Violencia y seguridad democrática en República Dominicana*. Santo Domingo: Facultad Latinoamericana de Ciencias Sociales (FLACSO).

Bogotá Cómo Vamos (2011) *Encuesta de Percepción Ciudadana: Informe de resultados*. Bogotá: Ipsos-Napoleón Franco. Available at: www.bogotacomovamos.org/documentos/encuesta-de-percepcion-bogota-como-vamos.

Bolívar, T. and J. Baldo (1995) *La cuestión de los barrios*. Caracas: Monteávila Editores.

Bolívar, T., Y. M. Guerrero, I. Rosas, T. Ontiveros and J. de Freitas (1994) *Densificación y vivienda en los barrios caraqueños: Contribución a la determinación de problemas y soluciones*. Caracas: MINDUR-CONAVI.

Briceño-León, R. (1986) *El Futuro de las Ciudades Venezolanas*. Serie Siglo XXI. Caracas: Cuadernos Lagoven.

— (1990) *Contabilidad de la muerte en cuando la muerte tomó la calle*. Caracas: Editorial Ateneo.

— (2005) 'Urban violence and public health in Latin America: a sociological explanatory model'. *Cadernos de Saúde Pública* 21(6), pp. 1629–64.

— (2007) 'La policía y su reforma en Venezuela'. *Urvío: Revista Latinoamericana de Seguridad Ciudadana* 2, pp. 164–72.

— (2008) *Sociología de la Violencia en América Latina*. Quito: Facultad Latinoamericana de Ciencias Sociales (FLACSO).

— and M. Acosta (1987) *Ciudad y Capitalismo*. Caracas: Ediciones de la Biblioteca de la Universidad Central de Venezuela.

— and V. Zubillaga (2002) 'Violence and globalization in Latin America'. *Current Sociology* 50(1), pp. 19–37.

—, O. Avila and A. Camardiel (2012) *Violencia e Institucionalidad*. Caracas: Editorial Alfa.

—, A. Villaveces and A. Concha-Eastman (2008) 'Understanding the uneven distribution of the incidence of homicide in Latin America'. *International Journal of Epidemiology* 37, pp. 751–7.

Briscoe, I. and M. Rodríguez Pellecer (2010) *A State under Siege: Elites, criminal networks and institional reform in Guatemala*. The Hague: Clingendael Institute.

Briscoe, I., C. Perdomo and C. Uribe Burcher (2014) *Redes ilícitas y política en América Latina*. Stockholm and The Hague: Instituto Internacional para la Democracia y la Asistencia Electoral (IDEA), Netherlands Institute for Multiparty Democracy

(NIMD) and Netherlands Institute for International Relations Clingendael.

Bromberg, P. (2003) 'Los diez años de Bogotá: editorial'. *Revista Virtual de Red Bogotá* 12 (20 May). Available at: www.univerciudad.net/Editorial.

— and T. Gomescásseres (2009) '¿Qué fue y qué será la cultura ciudadana?' in *Cultura Ciudadana en Bogotá: Nuevas perspectivas*. Bogotá: Secretaría de Cultura, Recreación y Deporte, pp. 176–93.

Bursik, R. J. and H. G. Grasmick (1993) *Neighborhoods and Crime*. New York NY: Lexington Books.

Caballero, M. (2010) *Historia de los venezolanos en el siglo XX*. Caracas: Editorial Alfa.

Caldeira, T. (2000) *Cities of Walls: Crime, segregation and citizenship in São Paulo*. Berkeley CA: University of California Press.

Cambio (2009) 'En 10 de las 20 localidades de Bogotá hay presencia paramilitar'. *Revista Cambio*, 2 July.

Cano, A. M. (2009) 'Ciudades en desmadre'. *El Espectador*, 3 December.

Cano, I. and C. Iooty (2008) *Seis por Meia Dúzia: um Estudo Exploratório do Fenômeno das Chamadas Milícias no Rio de Janeiro*. Rio de Janeiro: Fundação Heinrich Boll.

Caracol Radio (2010) 'Colombia: se disparan cifras de homicidio en las principales ciudades del país', 5 September. Available at: www. caracol.com.co/nota.aspx?id=1353657.

Cardia, N., S. Adorno and F. Z. Poleto (2003) 'Homicide rates and human rights violations in São Paulo, Brazil: 1990 to 2002'. *Health and Human Rights* 6, pp. 14–33.

Carey Jr., D. and M. G. Torres (2010) 'Precursors to femicide: Guatemalan women in a vortex of violence'. *Latin American Research Review* 45(3), pp. 142–64.

Carneiro, D. M., I. P. Bagolin and S. Hong Tiing Tai (n.d.) 'Determinantes da pobreza nas regiões metropolitanas do brasil no período de 1995 a 2009'. Unpublished paper. Available at: www.anpec.org.br/sul/2013/submissao/files_I/i2-4b8441f907b56d71f36c5daaa3f76bfb.docx.

Casas Dupuy, P. and P. González Cepero (2005) 'Políticas de seguridad y reducción del homicidio en Bogotá: mito y realidad'. Available at: http://pdba.georgetown.edu/Security/citizensecurity/Colombia/evaluaciones/politicasBogota.pdf.

Castillo, B. (2011) 'Munguía Payés declara la "guerra al crimen"'. *Diario CoLatino*, 29 November, p. 4.

CCB (2011) *Resultados Encuesta de Percepción y Victimización de Seguridad en Bogotá*. Bogotá: Cámara de Comercio de Bogotá (CCB). Available at: www.ccb.org.co/Investigaciones-Bogota-y-Region/Seguridad-Ciudadana/Observatorio-de-Seguridad/Encuesta-de-percepcion-y-victimizacion.

CEACSC (2012) *Caracterización homicidio primer semestre 2011 y 2012*. Bogotá: Alcaldía Mayor de Bogotá, Centro de Estudio y Análisis en Convivencia y Seguridad Ciudadana (CEACSC).

Ceballo, R. (2004) *Violencia y Comunidad en un Mundo Globalizado*. Santo Domingo: Editorial Amigo del Hogar.

CEPAL (2013) *Panorama Social de América Latina*. Santiago de Chile: Comisión Económica para América Latina y el Caribe (CEPAL).

CES (2006) *Diagnostico Socioeconómico, Circunscripción Tres del Distrito Nacional: 'Una historia de exclusión'*. Santo Domingo: Centro de Estudios Sociales (CES) Padre Juan Montalvo.

Cesar, P. B. and F. Cavallieri (2002) *Como andam as taxas de homicídios no Rio e em outros lugares*. Coleção Estudos Cariocas No. 20020602. Rio de Janeiro: Prefeitura da Cidade de Rio de Janeiro.

Chan, B. (2010) 'Code red: private firms filling the security gap'. *Jamaica Gleaner*, 19 October.

Charles, C. A. and O. Beckford (2012) 'The informal justice system in garrison constituencies'. *Social and Economic Studies* 61(2), pp. 51–72.

Chávez, S., J. Santos and R. Flores (2013) 'Reducción de homicidios se mantiene. 49% menos con tregua'. *La Prensa Gráfica*, 8 March, p. 4.

Chávez Frías, H. (2009) *Revolución Bolivariana, 9 años de logros*. Caracas: Ministerio del Poder Popular para la Comunicación y la Información.

Clarke, C. G. (2006) *Decolonizing the Colonial City: Urbanization and stratification in Kingston, Jamaica*. Oxford: Oxford University Press.

Clunan, A. L. and H. A. Trinkunas (2010) 'Conceptualizing ungoverned spaces: territorial statehood, contested authority, and softened sovereignty' in A. L. Clunan and H. A. Trinkunas (eds) *Ungoverned Spaces: Alternatives to state authority in an era of softened sovereignty*. Stanford CA: Stanford University Press, pp. 17–33.

Coleman, J. (1990) *Foundations of Social Theory*. Cambridge MA: Harvard University Press.

Costa, G. and C. Basombrío (2005) *Liderazgo civil en el Ministerio del Interior. Testimonio de una experiencia de reforma policial y gestión democrática de la seguridad en el Perú*. Lima: Instituto de Estudios Peruanos.

Costa, G. and C. Romero (2010) *Inseguridad ciudadana en Lima. ¿Qué hacer?* Lima: Ciudad Nuestra.

Crabtree, J. (2005) *Patterns of Protest: Politics and social movements in Bolivia*. London: Latin America Bureau.

— and A. Chaplin (2013) *Bolivia: Patterns of change*. London: Zed Books.

Crónicas Guanacas (2012a) 'Segundo comunicado de la MS-13 y el Barrio 18'. *Crónicas Guanacas*, 12 May. Available at: http://cronicasguanacas.blogspot.com/2012/05/el-2-de-mayo-de-2012-tuve-la-suerte-de.html.

— (2012b) 'Pronunciamiento a la nación de Raúl Mijango y Fabio Colindres'. *Crónicas Guanacas*, 23 November. Available at: http://cronicasguanacas.blogspot.com/2012/11/pronunciamiento-la-nacion-de-raul.html.

Cruz, J. M. (2007) *Street Gangs in Central America*. San Salvador: UCA Editores.

— (2010) 'Central American maras: from youth street gangs to transnational protection rackets'. *Global Crime* 11(4), pp. 379–98.

Dahl, R. (1971) *Polyarchy*. New Haven CT: Yale University Press.

Dammert, L. (2007) *Perspectivas y dilemas de la seguridad Ciudadana en América Latina*. Quito: Facultad Latinoamericana de Ciencias Sociales (FLACSO).

Davis, D. E. (2006) 'The age of insecurity: violence and social disorder in the new Latin America'. *Latin American Research Review* 41, pp. 178–97.

— (2012) 'Urban violence, quality of life, and the future of Latin American cities: the dismal record so far and the search for new analytical frameworks to sustain the bias towards hope' in D. Rodgers, J. Beall and R. Kanbur (eds) *Latin American Urban Development into the Twenty First Century: Towards a renewed perspective on the city*. New York NY: Palgrave Macmillan, pp. 37–59.

Davis, M. (2006) *Planet of Slums*. London: Verso.

Deas, M. and F. Gaitán Daza (1995) *Dos ensayos especulativos sobre la violencia en Colombia*. Bogotá: FONADE, Departamento Nacional de Planeación (DNP) and Tercer Mundo.

Delfini, M. F. and V. Picchetti (2005) 'Desigualdad y pobreza en Argentina en los noventa'. *Política y Cultura* 24, pp. 187–206.

Denissen, M. (2008) *'Winning Small Battles, Losing the War': Police violence, the* Movimiento del Dolor, *and democracy in post-authoritarian Argentina*. Latin America Research Series. Amsterdam: Rozenberg Publishers.

Denyer-Willis, G. (2009) 'Deadly symbiosis? The PCC, the state, and the institutionalization of violence in São Paulo, Brazil' in G. A. Jones and D. Rodgers (eds) *Youth Violence in Latin America: Gangs and juvenile justice in perspective*. New York NY: Palgrave Macmillan, pp. 167–82.

— and J. Tierney (2012) *Urban Resilience in Situations of Chronic Violence: Case study of São Paulo, Brazil*. Report prepared for the Urban Resilience in Chronic Violence Project. Cambridge MA: Department of Urban Studies and Planning, Massachusetts Institute of Technology.

Departamento 15 (2014) 'Daniel emigró a EUA para huir de las pandillas'. *La Prensa Gráfica*, 15 June, p. 5.

DIGESTYC (2013) *Encuesta de Hogares de Propósitos Múltiples 2012*. Ciudad Delgado, El Salvador: Dirección Nacional de Estadisticas y Censos (DIGESTYC).

Donovan, M. G. (2002) 'Space wars in Bogotá: the recovery of public space and impact on street vendors'. MA dissertation, Massachusetts Institute of Technology.

Dreyfus, P. (2009) 'Vino viejo en odres todavía más viejos: tendencias regionales del crimen organizado en Latinoamérica en la primera década del siglo XXI y más allá' in H. Mathieu and P. Rodríguez Arredondo (eds)

Anuario 2009 de la Seguridad Regional en América Latina y el Caribe. Bogotá: Friedrich Ebert Stiftung, Programa de Cooperación en Seguridad Regional, pp. 175–89.

Duncan-Waite, I. and M. Woolcock (2008) *Arrested Development: The political origins and socio-economic foundations of common violence in Jamaica.* Working Paper 46. Manchester: Brooks World Poverty Institute.

Duque, L. F. and J. Klevens (2000) 'Creencias, actitudes y prácticas asociadas con la violencia en Bogotá'. *Coyuntura Social* 22, pp. 187–202.

Eaton, K. (2008) 'Paradoxes of police reform: federalism, parties, and civil society in Argentina's public security crisis'. *Latin American Research Review* 43(3), pp. 5–32.

ECLAC (2013a) *Social Panorama of Latin America 2012.* Santiago de Chile: Economic and Social Commission of Latin America and the Caribbean (ECLAC).

— (2013b) *Social Panorama of Latin America 2013: Briefing paper.* Santiago de Chile: Economic and Social Commission of Latin America and the Caribbean (ECLAC). Available at: www.cepal.org/en/publications/social-panorama-latin-america-2013.

Eisner, M. (2001) 'Modernization, self-control and lethal violence: the long-term dynamics of European homicide rates in theoretical perspective'. *British Journal of Criminology* 41(4), pp. 618–38.

El Diario de Hoy (2011) 'Inseguridad y delincuencia se extienden en América Latina'. *El Diario de Hoy*, 10 January.

— (2012) 'Trasladan de Zacatraz a la cúpula de la MS y 18'. *El Diario de Hoy*, 14 March. Available at: www.elsalvador.com/mwedh/nota/nota_completa.asp?idCat=47859&idArt=6729759.

El Espectador (2009) '¿Qué pasa con la seguridad urbana?' *El Espectador*, 8 April.

— (2011) '¿Qué hacer con la inseguridad en Bogotá? Propuestas de los candidatos'. *El Espectador*, 24 June.

El Faro (2012) 'Los voceros nacionales de la Mara Salvatrucha y Pandilla 18'. Declaration dated 19 March. Available at: www.elfaro.net/attachment/395/comaras.pdf?g_download=1.

El Tiempo (2008a) 'Así se mueve consumo de drogas en los colegios'. *El Tiempo*, 26 June.

— (2008b) 'Cai móviles: ¿para qué han servido?' *El Tiempo*, 30 July.

— (2008c) 'Petardos en el centro fueron una retaliación de la guerrilla a comerciantes que no pagaron extorsión'. *El Tiempo*, 19 September.

— (2010) '97,5% de los crímenes denunciados en Bogotá continúan en la impunidad'. *El Tiempo*, 19 October.

— (2011a) '"En Bogotá no hay bandas criminales": secretaria de Gobierno'. *El Tiempo*, 20 August.

— (2011b) 'Bogotá está inundada de armas de fuego ilegales'. *El Tiempo*, 22 November.

— (2012a) 'Percepción de inseguridad bajó 27 puntos en Bogotá, revela encuesta'. *El Tiempo*, 17 February.

— (2012b) 'La baja histórica en los homicidios en Bogotá se mantiene'. *El Tiempo*, 5 July.

— (2012c) 'Venganzas y riñas, lo que mata a los bogotanos'. *El Tiempo*, 10 August.

Elias, N. (1987) *El proceso de civilización: Investigaciones sociogenéticas y psicogenéticas.* México: Fondo de Cultura Económica.

Escalante Gonzalbo, F. (2009) *El homicidio en México entre 1990 y 2007: Aproximación estadística.* México: El Colegio de México and Secretaría de Seguridad Pública Federal.

Escobedo, R. (2006) *Los jóvenes: víctimas y victimarios*. Bogotá: Alcaldía Mayor de Bogotá, Centro de Estudio y Análisis en Convivencia y Seguridad Ciudadana (CEACSC).

Eyzaguirre, H. (1998) *La violencia intencional en Lima Metropolitana: magnitud, impacto económico y evaluación de políticas de control 1985–1995*. Lima: Instituto Apoyo.

Fajnzylber, P. and J. H. López (2007) *Close to Home: The impact of remittances in Latin America*. Washington DC: World Bank.

Fajnzylber, P., D. Lederman and N. Loayza (1998) *Determinants of Crime Rates in Latin America and the World*. Washington DC: World Bank, Latin American and Caribbean Studies.

Fay, M. (ed.) (2005) *The Urban Poor in Latin America*. Washington DC: World Bank.

Felbab-Brown, V. (2010) 'Rules and regulations in ungoverned spaces: illlicit economies, criminals, and belligerents' in A. L. Clunan and H. A. Trinkunas (eds) *Ungoverned Spaces: Alternatives to state authority in an era of softened sovereignty*. Stanford CA: Stanford University Press, pp. 175–92.

— (2013) *Peña Nieto's Piñata: The promise and pitfalls of Mexico's new security policy against organized crime*. Washington DC: Brookings Institution. Available at: www.brookings.edu/research/papers/2013/02/mexico-new-security-policy-felbabbrown.

Feltran, G. S. (2010) 'Crime e castigo na cidade: os repertórios da justiça e a questão do homicídio nas periferias de São Paulo'. *Caderno CRH* 23(58), pp. 59–73.

— (2011) *Fronteira de Tensão. Política e Violência nas Periferias de São Paulo*. São Paulo: Editora UNESP.

Ferrajoli, L. (1990) *Diritto e Ragione: Teoria del garantismo penale*. Bari: Laterza.

FESPAD (2004) *Informe Anual Sobre Justicia Penal Juvenil. El Salvador 2004*. San Salvador: Fundación de Estudios para la Aplicación del Derecho (FESPAD).

Figueroa, M. and A. Sives (2002) 'Homogenous voting, electoral manipulation and the "garrison" process in post-independence Jamaica'. *Commonwealth and Comparative Politics* 40(1), pp. 81–108.

Figueroa, M., A. Harriott and N. Satchell (2008) 'The political economy of Jamaica's inner-city violence: a special case?' in R. Jaffe (ed.) *The Caribbean City*. Kingston and Miami FL: Ian Randle Publishers, pp. 94–122.

Fiszbein, A. and N. Schady, with F. H. G. Ferreira, M. Grosh, N. Kelleher, P. Olinto and E. Skoufias (2009) *Conditional Cash Transfers: Reducing present and future poverty*. Washington DC: World Bank.

Flores Pérez, C. A. (2009) *El estado en crisis: crimen organizado y política. desafíos para la consolidación democrática*. México: Centro de Investigaciones y Estudios Superiores en Antropología Social (CIESAS) and Publicaciones de la Casa Chata.

FUPROVI (2004) *Diagnóstico para la inmigración nicaragüense en seis asentamientos del Área Metropolitana de San José*. San José: Fundación Promotora de Vivienda (FUPROVI).

Gabaldón, L. G. (2002) 'Discurso legal y discurso social: reflexiones sobre el espacio del control social formal'. *Espacio Abierto* 11(004), pp. 605–17.

Gaitán, F. (1995) 'Una indagación sobre las causas de la violencia en Colombia' in M. Deas and F. Gaitán Daza (1995) *Dos ensayos especulativos sobre la violencia en Colombia*. Bogotá: FONADE, Departamento Nacional de Planeación (DNP) and Tercer Mundo.

— (2001) 'Multicausalidad, impunidad y violencia: una visión alternativa'. *Revista de Economía Institucional* 5 (Second Semester), pp. 78–105.

— and M. Afanador (1996) *Estudio prospectivo de seguridad*. Bogotá: Misión Siglo XXI and Cámara de Comercio de Bogotá.

Garza, G. and M. Schteingart (eds) (2010) *Desarrollo urbano y regional*. Los grandes problemas de México II. México: El Colégio de México.

Gavilia, A. (2000) 'Increasing returns and the evolution of violent crime: the case of Colombia'. *Journal of Development Economics* 61, pp. 1–25.

Gay, R. (2005) *Lucia: Testimonies of a Brazilian drug dealer's woman*. Philadelphia PA: Temple University Press.

— (2009) 'From popular movements to drug gangs to militias: an anatomy of violence in Rio de Janeiro' in K. Koonings and D. Kruijt (eds) *Megacities: The politics of urban exclusion and violence in the global South*. London: Zed Books, pp. 29–51.

Geyer, H. S. (ed.) (2007) *International Handbook of Urban Policy. Volume 1: Contentious global issues*. Cheltenham: Edward Elgar.

Gilbert, A. G. (2000) 'Urbanization and security' in C. Rosan, B. Ruble and J. Tulchin (eds) *Urbanization, Population, Environment and Security: A report of the Comparative Urban Studies Project*. Washington DC: Woodrow Wilson International Center for Scholars, pp. 73–93.

— (2006) 'Good urban governance: evidence from a model city?' *Bulletin for Latin American Research* 25, pp. 392–419.

— and J. Dávila (2002) 'Bogotá: progress within a hostile environment' in D. J. Myers and H. A. Dietz (eds) *Capital City Politics in Latin America: Democratisation and empowerment*. Boulder CO: Lynne Reiner, pp. 29–63.

— and M. T. Garcés (2008) *Bogotá: progreso, gobernabilidad y pobreza*. Bogotá: Universidad del Rosario.

Gizewski, P. and T. Homer-Dixon (1995) *Urban Growth and Violence: Will the future resemble the past?* Washington DC: American Association for the Advancement of Science (AAAS) and University of Toronto, Project on Environment, Population and Security.

Glebbeek, M. (2003) *In the Crossfire of Democracy: Police reform and police practices in post-civil war Guatemala*. Amsterdam: Rozenberg Publishers.

— and K. Koonings (2016) 'Between *morro* and *asfalto*: violence, insecurity and socio-spatial segregation in Latin American cities'. *Habitat International* (forthcoming).

Goertzel, T. and T. Kahn (2009) 'The great Sao Paulo homicide drop'. *Homicide Studies* 13(4), pp. 398–410.

Goldstein, D. (2003) *Laughter Out of Place: Race, class, violence, and sexuality in a Rio shantytown*. Berkeley CA: University of California Press.

Gordon, D., P. Anderson and D. Robotham (1997) 'Jamaica: urbanization during the years of crisis' in A. Portes, C. Dore-Cabral and P. Landolt (eds) *The Urban Caribbean: Transition to the new global economy*. Baltimore MD: Johns Hopkins University Press, pp. 190–233.

Gordon, I. (2014) '70,000 kids will show up alone at our border this year: what happens to them?' Mother Jones, 3 June. Available at: www.motherjones.com/politics/2014/06/child-migrants-surge-unaccompanied-central-america.

Graham, S. (2011) *Cities under Siege: The new military urbanism*. London: Verso Books.

Guevara, C. (2011) 'General Naranjo

promete 1.300 policías para Bogotá'. *El Tiempo*, 5 February.

Guidice, M. (2005) 'Normativity and norm-subjects'. *Australian Journal of Legal Philosophy* 30, pp. 102–21.

Gumo Vargas De Negro, M. et al. (eds) (1975) *Etiologia de la Violencia en Puerto Rico*. San Juan: Technical Servies of Puerto Rico.

Gurr, T. R. (1981) 'Historical trends in violent crime: a critical review of the evidence'. *Crime and Justice* 3, pp. 295–353.

Gutiérrez, F., M. T. Pinto, J. C. Arenas, T. Guzmán and M. T. Gutiérrez (2009) *Politics and Security in Three Colombian Cities*. Cities and Fragile States Working Paper 44. London: London School of Economics, Crisis State Research Centre.

Gutiérrez Rivera, L. (2012) 'Geographies of violence and exclusion: imprisoned gangs ("maras") in Honduras'. *Latin American Research Review* 47(2), pp. 167–79.

— (2013) *Territories of Violence: State, marginal youth, and public security in Honduras*. New York NY: Palgrave Macmillan.

Hardoy, J. and D. Satterwaite (1987) *La ciudad legal y la ciudad ilegal*. Buenos Aires: Grupo Editor Latinoamericano.

Harriott, A. (2000) *Police and Crime Control in Jamaica: Problems of reforming ex-colonial constabularies*. Kingston: University of West Indies Press.

— (2008) *Organized Crime and Politics in Jamaica: Breaking the nexus*. Kingston: Canoe Press.

— (2009) 'Police transformation and international cooperation: the Jamaican experience' in N. Uildriks (ed.) *Policing Insecurity: Police reform, security, and human rights in Latin America*. Lanham MD: Lexington Books, pp. 123–51.

Hart, H. L. A. (2008) 'Prolegomenon to the principles of punishment' in H. L. A. Hart. *Punishment and Responsibility*. Oxford: Oxford University Press, pp. 1–28.

Heinemann, A. and D. Verner (2006) *Crime and Violence in Development: A literature review of Latin America and the Caribbean*. World Bank Policy Research Working Paper 4041. Washington DC: World Bank.

Helmke, G. and S. Levitsky (eds) (2006) *Informal Institutions and Democracy: Lessons from Latin America*. Baltimore MD: Johns Hopkins University Press.

Hernández-Bringas, H. and J. Narro-Robles (2010) 'El homicidio en México, 2000–2008'. *Papeles de Población* 16(63), pp. 243–71.

Hinton, M. S. (2005) 'A distant reality: democratic policing in Argentina and Brazil'. *Criminal Justice* 5(1), pp. 75–100.

Hojman, D. E. (2002) 'Explaining crime in Buenos Aires: the roles of inequality, unemployment, and structural change'. *Bulletin of Latin American Research* 21, pp. 121–8.

Holston, J. (2008) *Insurgent Citizenship: Disjunctions of democracy and modernity in Brazil*. Princeton NJ: Princeton University Press.

Horowitz, H. (2005) 'Corruption, crime and punishment: recent scholarship in Latin America'. *Latin American Research Review* 40, pp. 268–77.

Howard, D. (2005) *Kingston: A cultural and literary history*. Kingston: Ian Randle Publishers.

Huggins, M. K. (2000) 'Urban violence and police privatization in Brazil: blended invisibility'. *Social Justice* 27(2), pp. 113–34.

ICESI (2010) *Victimización, incidencia y cifra negra en México*. Análisis de la ENSI 6. Mexico City: Instituto Ciudadano de Estudios sobre la Inseguridad (ICESI). Available at:

www.oas.org/dsp/documents/ victimization_surveys/mexico/ mexico_analisis_ensi6.pdf.

— (2012) *¿Corrupción o seguridad? Un estudio sobre la actual desconfianza en la policía mexicana*. Mexico City: Instituto Ciudadano de Estudios sobre la Inseguridad (ICESI). Available at: www.fundemospaz.org.sv/a/ Biblioteca/Corrupcion%200%20Seg uridad.pdf.

ICG (2011) *Violencia y Política en Venezuela*. Informe 38. Brussels: International Crisis Group.

IDL (2012) *Más allá de los miedos: informe 2012 sobre la seguridad ciudadana*. Lima: Instituto de Defensa Legal (IDL). Available at: www.idl.org. pe/sites/default/files/publicaciones/ pdfs/Informe%20SC%202012_Final% 20corregido%20para%20web_0.pdf.

INE (2010) *Encuesta Nacional de Victimización y Percepción de la Seguridad Ciudadana 2009*. Caracas: Vice-Presidencia de la República and Instituto Nacional de Estadística (INE).

— (2014) *Síntesis Estadística de Pobreza e Indicadores de Desigualdad: Reporte a Mesa Informativa*. Caracas: Instituto Nacional de Estadística (INE).

INEC (2012) *Censo Nacional de Población y Vivienda 2011*. San José, Costa Rica: Instituto Nacional de Estadística y Censos (INEC). Available at: www.inec.go.cr/Web/Home/ GeneradorPagina.aspx.

INEGI (2013) *Boletin de prensa 288/13*. Mexico City: Instituto Nacional de Geografía y Estadísticas (INEGI). Available at: www.inegi.org. mx/sistemas/descarga/?proy=prensa.

IUDPAS (2011) *Estudio comparativo de la incidencia de homicidio doloso en ciudades y jurisdicciones sub-nacionales de los países del mundo (2010)*. Tegucigalpa: Universidad Nacional Autónoma de Honduras, Instituto Universitario en Paz,

Democracia y Seguridad. Available at: http://editor.pbsiar.com/upload/ PDF/50_ciud_mas_violentas.pdf.

Jacome, F. (2012) 'Continuidad en Venezuela tras trece años del proyecto chavista' in H. Mathieu and C. Niño Guarnizo (eds) *Anuario 2012 de la seguridad regional en América Latina y el Caribe*. Bogotá: Friedrich Ebert Stiftung, pp. 201–16.

Jaffe, R. (2012) 'Criminal dons and extralegal security privatization in downtown Kingston, Jamaica'. *Singapore Journal of Tropical Geography* 33(2): 184–97.

— (2013) 'The hybrid state: crime and citizenship in urban Jamaica'. *American Ethnologist* 40(4), pp. 734–48.

Jannuzzi, P. M. (2001) *Indicadores Sociais no Brasil: Conceitos, fonte de dados e aplicações*. Campinas: Alínea.

JCF (2010) *Jamaica Constabulary Force Annual Report 2009/2010*. Kingston: Jamaica Constabulary Force (JCF).

Jones, G. A. and D. Rodgers (eds) (2009) *Youth Violence in Latin America: Gangs and juvenile justice in perspective*. New York NY: Palgrave Macmillan.

Jütersonke, O., R. Muggah and D. Rodgers (2009) 'Gangs, urban violence, and security interventions in Central America'. *Security Dialogue* 40(4–5), pp. 373–97.

Karstedt, S. (2006) 'Democracy, values, and violence: paradoxes, tensions, and comparative advantages of liberal inclusion'. *Annals of the American Academy of Political and Social Science* 605, pp. 50–81.

Katz, J. (1988) *Seductions of Crime*. New York NY: Basic Books.

Klaufus, C. (2009) *Construir la ciudad andina: Planificación y autoconstrucción en Riobamba y Cuenca*. Quito: Abya Yala and Facultad Latinoamericana de Ciencias Sociales (FLACSO).

— (2012) *Urban Residence: Housing and social transformations in globalizing Ecuador*. CLAS Series No. 100. Oxford: Berghahn Books.

Koenders, S. and K. Koonings (2012) 'Winning the urban war in Rio de Janeiro? Citizen security and the favela pacification strategy'. Paper presented at the XXX LASA International Congress, San Francisco, 23–26 May.

Koonings, K. (2001) 'Armed actors, violence and democracy in Latin America in the 1990s: introductory notes'. *Bulletin of Latin American Research* 20(4), pp. 401–8.

— (2004) 'Strengthening citizenship in Brazil's democracy: local participatory governance in Porto Alegre'. *Bulletin of Latin American Research* 23(1), pp. 79–99.

— (2012) 'New violence, insecurity, and the state: comparative reflections on Latin America and Mexico' in W. Pansters (ed.) *Violence, Coercion, and State-Making in Twentieth-Century Mexico: The other half of the centaur*. Stanford CA: Stanford University Press, pp. 255–78.

— (2014) 'Violence, crime and insecurity since 2000: local dynamics and the limitations of federal response' in F. de Castro, K. Koonings and M. Wiesebron (eds) *Brazil under the Workers' Party: Continuity and change from Lula to Dilma*. London: Palgrave Macmillan, pp. 150–75.

— and D. Kruijt (eds) (1999) *Societies of Fear: The legacy of civil war, violence, and terror in Latin America*. London: Zed Books.

— and D. Kruijt (eds) (2002) *Political Armies: The military and nation building in the age of democracy*. London: Zed Books.

— and D. Kruijt (eds) (2004) *Armed Actors: Organised violence and state failure in Latin America*. London: Zed Books.

— and D. Kruijt (2007a) 'Fractured cities, second-class citizenship and urban violence' in K. Koonings and D. Kruijt (eds) *Fractured Cities: Social exclusion, urban violence and contested spaces in Latin America*. London: Zed Books, pp. 7–12.

— and D. Kruijt (eds) (2007b) *Fractured Cities: Social exclusion, urban violence and contested spaces in Latin America*. London: Zed Books.

— and D. Kruijt (eds) (2009) *Megacities: The politics of urban exclusion and violence in the global South*. London: Zed Books.

—, D. Kruijt and P. Valenzuela (2013) *Evaluación de la política de los países bajos en apoyo a la paz y los derechos humanos en Colombia*. Amsterdam and The Hague: CEDLA and Ministry of Foreign Affairs/IOB.

Kornhauser, R. R. (1978) *Social Sources of Delinquency*. Chicago IL: University of Chicago Press.

Kruijt, D. (2008) 'Violencia y pobreza en América Latina: los actores armados'. *Pensamiento Iberoamericano* (2), pp. 56–70.

— (2011) *Drugs, Democracy and Security: The impact of organized crime on the political system of Latin America*. The Hague: Netherlands Institute for Multiparty Democracy (NIMD).

— and C. I. Degregori (2007) 'Lima Metropolitana' in K. Koonings and D. Kruijt (eds) *Fractured Cities: Social exclusion, urban violence and c ontested spaces in Latin America*. London: Zed Books, pp. 101–16.

— and K. Koonings (1999) 'Violence and fear in Latin America' in K. Koonings and D. Kruijt (eds) *Societies of Fear: The legacy of civil war, violence, and terror in Latin America*. London: Zed Books, pp. 1–30.

.— and K. Koonings (2013) 'From political

armies to the "war against crime": the transformation of militarism in Latin America' in A. Stavrianakis and J. Selby (eds) *Militarism and International Relations: Political economy, security, theory*. Cass Military Studies. Abingdon: Routledge, pp. 91–103.

—, C. Sojo and R. Grynspan (2002) *Informal Citizens: Poverty, informality and social exclusion in Latin America*. Thela Latin America Series. Amsterdam: Rozenberg Publishers.

LaFree, G. (1998) *Losing Legitimacy: Street crime and the decline of social institutions in America*. Boulder CO: Westview Press.

— (1999) 'Declining violent crime rates in the 1990s: predicting crime booms and busts'. *Annual Review of Sociology* 25, pp. 145–68.

Latinobarómetro (2010) *Informe Latinobarómetro 2010*. Providencia, Chile: Corporación Latinobarómetro. Available at: www.latinobarometro.org/lat.jsp.

— (2013) *Informe 2013*. Providencia, Chile: Corporación Latinobarómetro. Available at: www.latinobarometro.org/documentos/LATBD_INFORME_LB_2013.pdf.

Lavrakas, P. J. (1981) 'On households' in D. A. Lewis (ed.) *Reactions to Crime*. Beverly Hills CA: Sage, pp. 67–85.

Leeds, E. (1996) 'Cocaine and parallel politics in the Brazilian urban periphery: constraints on local-level democratizaton'. *Latin American Research Review* 31(3), pp. 47–84.

— (2007) 'Rio de Janeiro' in K. Koonings and D. Kruijt (eds) *Fractured Cities: Social exclusion, urban violence and contested spaces in Latin America*. London: Zed Books, pp. 23–35.

Levenson, D. (2013a) 'What happened to the revolution? Guatemala City's maras from life to death' in C.

McAlister and D. M. Nelson (eds) *War by Other Means: Aftermath in post-genocide Guatemala*. Durham NC: Duke University Press, pp. 195–217.

— (2013b) *Adiós Niño: The gangs of Guatemala and the politics of death*. Durham NC: Duke University Press.

Levitt, S. (2004) 'Understanding why crime fell in the 1990s: four factors that explain the decline and six that do not'. *Journal of Economic Perspectives* 18(1), pp. 163–90.

LICIP (2015) *IVI – Índice de Victimización*. Buenos Aires: Laboratorio de Investigaciones sobre Crimen, Instituciones y Políticas (LICIP).

Lijphart, A. (1999) *Patterns of Democracy: Government forms and performance in thirty-six countries*. New Haven CT: Yale University Press.

Lima Cómo Vamos (2013) *Encuesta Lima Cómo Vamos 2012*. Available at: www.limacomovamos.org/noticias/descarga-la-encuesta-lima-como-vamos-2012.

Linares, A. (2011) 'Pandillas ascienden a más de 1.300 en Bogotá'. *El Tiempo*, 15 January.

Lis Ríos, A. (2011) 'Policía y autonomía: gobierno local y seguridad en Buenos Aires'. *Urvío: Revista Latinoamericana de Seguridad Ciudadana* 9, pp. 55–69.

Lizardo, M. and R. M. Guzmán (2001) 'Patrones de integración a la economía global ¿Que comercializa America Latina?¿Que hacen sus trabajadores? El caso de la Republica Dominicana'. *Santo Domingo* 23. Available at: http://odh.pnud.org.do/sites/odh.onu.org.do/files/Patrones20de20integracion.pdf.

Llorente, M. V., R. Escobedo, C. Echandia and M. Rubio (2001) 'Violencia homicida en Bogotá: más que intolerancia'. Bogotá: Centro de Estudios sobre Desarrollo Economico (CEDE), Universidad de Los Andes.

Available at: www.insumisos.com/
lecturasinsumisas/Violencia%20homi
cida%20en%20Bogota.pdf.

Loader, I. (2000) 'Plural policing and
democratic governance'. *Social and
Legal Studies* 9(3), pp. 323–45.

Loeza Reyes, L. and M. Pérez-Levesque
(2010) 'La sociedad civil frente a la
militarización de la seguridad pública
en México'. *Nueva Sociedad* 227,
pp. 136–52.

López Hernández, C. (ed.) (2010) *Y
refundaron la patria ... De cómo
mafiosos y políticos reconfiguraron
el Estado colombiano.* Bogotá:
Corporación Nuevo Arco Iris and
Random House Mondadori.

López Maya, M. (2003) 'The Venezuelan
Caracazo of 1989: popular protest
and institutional weakness'. *Journal
of Latin American Studies* 35(1),
pp. 117–37.

—, L. Lander and D. Parker (2005)
'Popular protest in Venezuela:
novelties and continuities'. *Latin
American Perspectives* 32(2),
pp. 92–108.

Lovera de Sola, I. and A. Lovera (2014)
*¿Los últimos Inquilinos?Claves para
entender la nueva ley de alquileres en
Venezuela.* Caracas: Editorial Alfa de
Caracas.

Machado da Silva, L. A. (ed.) (2008) *Vida
sob cerco: violência e rotina nas favelas
do Rio de Janeiro.* Rio de Janeiro: Nova
Fronteira.

MacKinnon, D. and K. Driscoll
Derickson (2013) 'From resilience
to resourcefulness: a critique of
resilience policy and activism'.
Progress in Human Geography 37(2),
pp. 253–70.

MacLeod, J. (1995) *Ain't No Making It:
Aspirations & attainment in a low-
income neighborhood.* Boulder CO:
Westview Press.

Mahon, R. and L. Macdonald (2010)
'Anti-poverty politics in Toronto and

Mexico City'. *Geoforum* 41,
pp. 209–17.

Malby, S. (2010) 'Homicide' in S.
Harrendorf, M. Heiskanen and S.
Malby (eds) *International Statistics on
Crime and Justice.* Helsinki: European
Institute for Crime Prevention and
Control affiliated with the United
Nations (HEUNI), pp. 7–20.

Marquez, G. (1995) 'Venezuela: poverty
and social policies in the 1980s' in
N. Lustig (ed.) *Coping with Austerity:
Poverty and inequality in Latin
America.* Washington DC: Brookings
Institution, pp. 400–52.

Márquez, P. (2003) 'Vacas flacas y odios
gordos: la polarización en Venezuela'
in P. Márquez and R. Piñango (eds) *En
esta Venezuela: Realidades y nuevos
caminos.* Caracas: Ediciones IESA,
pp. 29–46.

Marroquín, D. and L. Quintanilla (2014)
'Policía registra 827 asesinatos más
que los cometidos en 2013'. *Diario de
Hoy,* 18 July, p. 32.

Martin, G. (2012) *Medellín: Tragedia y
resurrección. Mafia, ciudad y Estado
1975–2012.* Bogotá: Planeta.

— and M. Ceballos (2004) *Bogotá:
Anatomía de una transformación:
Políticas de seguridad ciudadana
1995–2003.* Bogotá: Editorial
Pontificia Universidad Javeriana.

Martinez, C. and J. L. Sanz (2014)
'Gobierno desmantela la tregua
y los homicidios alcanzan 30
en un día'. Sala Negra, 24 May.
Available at: www.salanegra.elfaro.
net/es/201405/cronicas/15432.

Massetti, A. (2004) *Piqueteros: Protesta
social e identidad colectiva.* Buenos
Aires: Editorial de las Ciencias and
Facultad Latinoamericana de Ciencias
Sociales (FLACSO).

Massey, D. and N. Denton (1988)
'The dimensions of residential
segregation'. *Social Forces* 67(2),
pp. 281–315.

176 | BIBLIOGRAPHY

Masten, A. S. (2001) 'Ordinary magic: resilience proceses in development'. *American Psychologist* 56, pp. 227–38.

Mathieu, H. and C. Niño Guarnizo (eds) (2010) *Seguridad Regional en América Latina y el Caribe. Anuario 2010.* Bogotá: Friedrich Ebert Stiftung, Programa de Cooperación en Seguridad Regional.

— and P. Rodríguez Arredondo (eds) (2009) *Anuario 2009 de la Seguridad Regional en América Latina y el Caribe.* Bogotá. Friedrich Ebert Stiftung, Programa de Cooperación en Seguridad Regional.

Matos Mar, J. (2004) *Desborde popular y crisis del estado: Veinte años después.* Lima: Fondo Editorial del Congreso del Perú.

Maza Zavala, D. F. (2009) *La década crítica de la economía venezolana 1998–2007.* Caracas: Libros El Nacional.

McIlwaine, C. and C. Moser (2007) 'Living in fear: how the urban poor perceive violence, fear and insecurity' in K. Koonings and D. Kruijt (eds) *Fractured Cities: Social exclusion, urban violence and contested spaces in Latin America.* London: Zed Books, pp. 117–37.

Mejía Navarette, J. (2005) 'Medios de comunicación y violencia: los jóvenes pandilleros de Lima'. *Espacio Abierto* 14(3), pp. 389–404.

Melo, J. O. (2009) 'Cultura ciudadana y homicidio en Bogotá' in *Cultura Ciudadana en Bogotá: Nuevas perspectivas.* Bogotá: Secretaría de Cultura, Recreación y Deporte, pp. 88–109. Available at: www.institutodeestudiosurbanos.com/dmdocuments/cendocieu/1_Docencia/Profesores/Bromberg_Paul/Publicados/Que_Fue_Cultura_Ciudadana-Bromberg_Paul-2009.pdf.

Merton, R. K. (1965) *Teoría y estructura social.* México: Fondo de Cultura Económica.

Messner, S. F., R. Rosenfeld and S.

Karstedt (2012) 'Social institutions and crime' in F. T. Cullen and P. Wilcox (eds) *The Oxford Handbook of Criminological Theory.* New York NY: Oxford University Press, pp. 405–24.

MIVAH (2007) *Diagnóstico de los asentamientos en precario en la Gran Área Metropolitana (GAM).* San José: Ministerio de Vivienda y Asentamientos Humanos (MIVAH).

Mockus, A. (2001) *Cultura ciudadana, programa contra la violencia en Santa Fe de Bogotá, Colombia, 1995–1997.* Bogotá: Inter-American Development Bank. Available at: www.scribd.com/doc/63048/Colombia-Cultura-Ciudadana-Experiencia-Bogota.

—, H. Murraín and M. Villa (2012) *Antípodas de la Violencia: Desafíos de cultura ciudadana para la crisis de (in)seguridad en América Latina.* Bogotá: Banco Interamericano de Desarrollo and Corpovisionarios.

Moncada, E. (2013) 'The politics of urban violence: challenges for development in the global South'. *Studies in International Comparative Development* 48, pp. 308–30.

Monkkonen, P. (2012) 'La segregación residencial en el México urbano: niveles y patrones'. *EURE* 38(114), pp. 125–46.

Montenegro, A., C. E. Posada and G. Piraquive (2000) 'Violencia, criminalidad y justicia: otra Mirada desde la economía'. *Coyuntura Social* 30(2), pp. 85–131.

Montero Torres, A. (2012) 'Seguridad democrática y militarización en Colombia'. *Urvío: Revista Latinoamericana de Seguridad Ciudadana* 12, pp. 41–56.

Montezuma, R. (2005) 'The transformation of Bogotá, Colombia, 1995–2000: investing in citizenship and urban mobility'. *Global Urban Development* 1(1),

pp. 1–10. Available at: www.
globalurban.org/Issue1PIMag05/
Montezuma%20article.htm.

Mora, S. (2013) 'Hogares en asentamientos
informales: ¿Quiénes son y cómo
viven?' Special contribution for
the Nineteenth Report *Estado de la
Nación*, based on a presentation at
the symposium 'Costa Rica a la luz del
Censo 2011' ('Costa Rica in View of
the 2011 Census'). San José: Instituto
Nacional de Estadística y Censos
(INEC) and Programa Estado de la
Nación.

Morales, A. (2007) *La diáspora de la
posguerra: Regionalismo de los
migrantes y dinámicas territoriales en
América Central*. San José: Facultad
Latinoamericana de Ciencias Sociales
(FLACSO), Costa Rican Office.

— (2008) *Inmigración en Costa Rica:
Características sociales y laborales,
integración y políticas públicas*. Serie
Población y Desarrollo 85. Santiago
de Chile: Comisión Económica y
Social para América Latina y el Caribe
(CEPAL).

— and C. Castro (1999) *Inmigración laboral
nicaragüense en Costa Rica*. San José:
FLACSO Costa Rica, Fundación Ebert,
Instituto Interamericano de Derechos
Humanos (IIDH) and Defensoría de
los Habitantes.

— and C. Castro (2006) *Migración,
empleo y pobreza*. San José: Facultad
Latinoamericana de Ciencias Sociales
(FLACSO), Costa Rican Office.

Moreno Olmedo, A. (2009) 'El malandro
y su comunidad: violencia en el
barrio' in R. Briceño-León, O. Ávila
and A. Camardiel (eds) *Inseguridad y
violencia en Venezuela*. Caracas: Alfa,
pp. 274–91.

Morgan, J., R. Espinal and M. A.
Seligson (2012) *Cultura Politica
de la Democracia Dominicana y
en las Americas, Hacia la Igualdad
de Oportunidades*. Nashville TN:

Vanderbilt University, Latin American
Public Opinion Project (LAPOP).

Moser, C. O. M. (2004) 'Urban violence
and insecurity: an introductory
roadmap'. *Environment and
Urbanisation* 16, pp. 3–16.

— (2009) *Ordinary Families, Extraordinary
Lives: Getting out of poverty in
Guayaquil, Ecuador 1978–2000*.
Washington DC: Brookings Press.

— (2012) *Understanding the Tipping Points
of Urban Conflict: Participatory
methodology for gender-based and
political violence*. Manchester:
University of Manchester, Global
Urban Research Centre.

— and P. Horn (2011) *Understanding
the Tipping Point of Urban Conflict:
Conceptual framework*. Manchester:
University of Manchester, Global
Urban Research Centre.

— and C. McIlwaine (2004) *Encounters
with Violence in Latin America: Urban
poor conceptions from Colombia and
Guatemala*. London: Routledge.

MPPCI (2008) *Aló Presidente*. Programme
323, 21 December. Caracas:
Ministerio del Poder Popular para
la Comunicación e Información
(MPPCI).

MSP (2013) *Migraciones y Desarrollo
Humano en Costa Rica 2014*. San José:
Ministerio de Gobernación, Policía y
Seguridad Pública.

Mucumeci, L. (2002) 'Homicídios no
Rio de Janeiro: tragédia em busca
de políticas'. *Boletim Segurança e
Cidadania* 1(2), pp. 1–16.

Muggah, R. (2012) *Researching the Urban
Dilemma: Urbanization, poverty
and violence*. Ottawa: International
Development Research Centre.

— (2014) 'Deconstructing the fragile
city: exploring insecurity, violence
and resilience'. *Environment and
Urbanization* 26(2), pp. 1–14.

— and O. Jutersönke (2012) 'Rethinking
stabilization and humanitarian

action in fragile cities' in B. Perrin (ed.) *Modern Warfare: Armed groups, private militaries, humanitarian organizations, and the law*. Vancouver: University of British Colombia Press, pp. 313–27.

Müller, M.-M. (2012) 'The rise of the penal state in Latin America'. *Contemporary Justice Review* 15(1), pp. 57–76.

— (2013) *Public Security in the Negotiated State: Policing in Latin America and beyond*. New York NY: Palgrave Macmillan.

Mullings, B. (2009) 'Neoliberalization, social reproduction and the limits to labour in Jamaica'. *Singapore Journal of Tropical Geography* 30, pp. 174–88.

Munar, L., M. Verhoeven and M. Bernales (2004) *Somos pandilla, somos chamba: escúchennos: la experiencia social de los jóvenes en Lima*. Lima: Fondo Editorial de la Pontificia Universidad Católica del Perú.

Murrain, H. (2010) *Cultura ciudadana: Elementos para una Política*. Bogotá: Corpovisionarios. Available at: www.seduma.yucatan.gob.mx/eventos-memorias/documentos-ciudades-futuro/Dia2-Presentaciones/Dia2_sesion2_1_Henry_Munrrain.pdf.

Murray, C. (2010) 'Conceptualizing young people's strategies of resistance to offending as "active resilience"'. *British Journal of Social Work* 40, pp. 115–32.

Museo de Bogotá (n.d.) *Una ciudad más segura*. Bogotá: Museo de Bogotá.

Nadanovsky, P. (2009) 'O aumento no encarceramento e a redução nos homicídios em São Paulo, Brasil, entre 1996 e 2005'. *Saúde Pública* 25, pp. 1859–64.

Naveau, P. and G. Pleyers (2012) 'Frente a la violencia: movilizaciones ciudadanas en México'. *Urvío: Revista Latinoamericana de Seguridad Ciudadana* 12, pp. 113–24.

Neri, M. (2012) *A nova classe media:O lado brilhante da base da pirâmide*. Rio de Janeiro: Fundação Getúlio Vargas (FGV).

Nervares-Muniz, D. (1996) *El Crimen en Puerto Rico, tapando el Cielo con la Mano*. Puerto Rico: Instituto para el Desarrollo del Derecho.

Newlink Research (2008) 'Resultados de la evaluacion externa del *Plan de Seguridad Democratica*, ejecutado por el Gobierno de la Republica Dominicana, bajo la coordincion de la Secretaria de Estado de interior y Policia, la Procuraduria General de la Republica y la Policia Nacional'. Unpublished report. Santo Domingo: Newlink Research.

Newman, K. S. (1999) *No Shame in My Game: The working poor in the inner city*. New York NY: Alfred E. Knopf and Russell Sage Foundation.

Nivette, A. E. (2014) 'Legitimacy and crime: theorizing the role of the state in cross-national criminological theory'. *Theoretical Criminology* 18, pp. 93–111.

— and M. Eisner (2013) 'Do legitimate polities have fewer homicides? A cross-national analysis'. *Homicide Studies* 17, pp. 3–26.

North, D. (1991) 'Institutions'. *Journal of Economic Perspectives* 5(1), pp. 97–112.

—, J. J. Wallis and B. R. Weingast (2009) *Violence and Social Order: A conceptual framework for interpreting recorded human history*. Cambridge: Cambridge University Press.

O'Donnell, G. (1993) 'On the state, democratization and some conceptual problems: a Latin American view with glances at some postcommunist countries'. *World Development* 21(8), pp. 1355–69.

— (2000) 'Teoría democrática y política comparada'. *Desarrollo Económico* 39(156), pp. 519–70.

Observatorio (2009) *Caracterización del homicidio en Colombia, 1995–2006*.

Bogotá: Observatorio del Programa Presidencial de Derechos Humanos. Available at: http://historico.derechoshumanos.gov.co/Observatorio/Publicaciones/documents/2010/estu_tematicos/CaracterizacionHomicidio95-06.pdf.

Ohlson, T. (2008) 'Understanding causes of war and peace'. *European Journal of International Relations* 14(1), pp. 133–60.

OIJ (2013) *Tráfico de drogas y amenazas del crimen organizado en Costa Rica. Reporte de Situación. Costa Rica 2013*. San José: Organismo de Investigación Judicial and United Nations Office on Drugs and Crime (UNDOC). Available at: www.unodc.org/documents/ropan/Sitation_Report/Reporte_de_Situacion_de_Costa_Rica_de_2013.pdf.

ONU Habitat (2014) *Construcción de ciudades más equitativas: Políticas públicas para la inclusión en América Latina*. Nairobi: UN-Habitat.

OPS (2004) *La violencia social en Costa Rica*. San José: Organización Panamericana de la Salud (OPS) and Ministerio de Salud.

Ortiz, A. (2011) 'Police: BACRIMs main threat to Colombian security'. Insight Crime, 26 January. Available at: http://insightcrime.org/insight-latest-news/item/476-police-bacrim-main-threat-for-colombian-security.

Ospina, J. M. (2005) 'Políticas públicas integrales para la convivencia y seguridad ciudadana en Bogotá DC'. PowerPoint presentation at the Foro Internacional Interamericano sobre Seguridad y Convivencia (International Interamerican Forum on Security and Conviviality), Medellín, 12 September. Available at: www.iadb.org/document.cfm?id=917315.

OVV (2013) *Informe del Observatorio Venezolano de Violencia 2013*.

Caracas: Observatorio Venezolano de Violencia (OVV).

Pandolfi, D. C. and M. Grynszpan (eds) (2003) *A favela fala: Depoimentos ao CPDOC*. Rio de Janeiro: Fundação Getúlio Vargas (FGV).

Pansters, W. and H. Castillo Berthier (2007) 'Mexico City' in K. Koonings and D. Kruijt (eds) *Fractured Cities: Social exclusion, urban violence and contested spaces in Latin America*. London: Zed Books, pp. 36–56.

Parsons, T. (1990) 'Prolegomena to a theory of social institutions'. *American Sociological Review* 55(3), pp. 319–33.

Pedrazzini, Y. and M. Sanchez (2001) *Malandros: Bandas y Niños de la calle. Cultura de urgencia en la metrópoli Latinoamericana*. Venezuela: Vadell Hermanos Editores.

Perea Restrepo, C. M. (2007) *Con el diablo adentro: Pandillas, tiempo paralelo y poder*. Bogotá: Siglo XXI Editores.

Pereira, A. and D. Davis (2000) 'New patterns of militarized violence and coercion in the Americas'. *Latin American Perspectives* 111 (27), pp. 3–17.

Pérez, M. (1998) 'La gobernabilidad urbana y la estrategia centroamericana de desarrollo sostenible. El caso del Área Metropolitana de San José' in M. Lungo (ed.) *Gobernabilidad Urbana en Centroamérica*. San José: Facultad Latinoamericana de Ciencias Sociales (FLACSO), Costa Rican Office and Global Urban Research Initiative (GURI), pp. 95–150.

— (2012) *Avatares del ordenamiento territorial en Costa Rica*. San José: Facultad Latinoamericana de Ciencias Sociales (FLACSO), Costa Rican Office.

Pérez Perdomo, R. and J. C. Navarro (1991) *Seguridad personal: Un asalto al tema*. Caracas: Ediciones del

Instituto de Estudios Superiores de Adminstración (IESA).

Perlman, J. E. (2005) 'The myth of marginality revisited: the case of favelas in Rio de Janeiro, 1969–2003' in L. M. Hanley, B. A. Rubble and J. S. Tulchin (eds) *Becoming Global and the New Poverty of Cities*. Washington DC: Woodrow Wilson International Center for Scholars, Comparative Urban Studies Project and USAID, pp. 9–53.

— (2010) *Favela: Four decades of living on the edge in Rio de Janeiro*. New York NY: Oxford University Press.

Pinheiro, P. S. (1997) 'Democracies without citizenship'. *NACLA Report on the Americas* 30(2), pp. 17–23.

PNUD (2004) *Bogotá: Una experiencia innovadora de gobernabilidad local*. Volume 2. Bogotá: Programa de las Naciones Unidas para el Desarrollo (PNUD).

— (2013) *Seguridad Ciudadana: Diagnostico y propuestas para América Latina. Informe Regional de Desarrollo Humano 2013–2014*. New York NY: Programa de las Naciones Unidas para el Desarrollo (PNUD).

Polanska, M. (2010) 'Homicides and organized violence'. *Voices of Mexico* 87, pp. 95–100.

Proyecto Estado de la Nación (2013) *Informe del Estado de la Nación 2013*. San José: Proyecto Estado de la Nación and Consejo Nacional de Rectores (CONARE), Chapter 2: 'Equidad e integración social'.

PRUGAM (2008) *Plan Regional Urbano de la Gran Área Metropolitana de Costa Rica 2008–2030. Fase IIIA*. San José: Ministerio de Vivienda y Asentamientos Humanos (MIVAH).

Puentes Melo, R. (2011) 'La seguridad en Bogotá, un problema nacional'. *Periodismos sin Fronteras*, 5 February. Available at: www.periodismosinfronteras.com/la-seguridad-en-bogota-un-problema-nacional.html.

Pujol, R. and E. Pérez (2012) *Crecimiento urbano en la región metropolitana de San José, Costa Rica. Una exploración espacial y temporal de los determinantes del cambio de uso del suelo, 1986–2010*. San José: Lincoln Institute of Land Policy.

Putnam, R. (ed.) (2002) *Democracies in Flux: The evolution of social capital in contemporary society*. Oxford: Oxford University Press.

Quesada, A. F. (2007) *La modernidad entre cafetales: San José, Costa Rica, 1880–1930*. Helsinki: Renvall Institute for Area and Cultural Studies.

Ramírez, R. D. (2010) *Guía del buen gobierno para la seguridad ciudadana*. Bogotá: Alcaldía Mayor de Bogotá, Centro de Estudios y Análisis en Convivencia y Seguridad (CEACS).

Ramos, L. (2004) *Características, dinámicas y condiciones de emergencia de las pandillas en Bogotá*. Bogotá: Instituto para la Protección de la Niñez y la Juventud (IDIPRON) and Instituto Distrital de Cultura y Turismo (IDCT).

Razón Pública (2011) 'El aumento de la criminalidad: entre el Polo y el Gobierno Nacional'. *Razón Pública*, 28 March.

Renner, M. (2001) 'Environmental and social stress factors, governance, and small arms availability: the potential for conflict in urban areas' in C. Rosan, B. Ruble and J. Tulchin (eds) *Urbanization, Population, Environment and Security: A report of the Comparative Urban Studies Project*. Washington DC: Woodrow Wilson International Center for Scholars, pp. 51–72.

Roberts, A. and G. LaFree (2004) 'Explaining Japan's postwar violent crime trends'. *Criminology* 42, pp. 179–209.

Roberts, B. (2005) 'Globalization and Latin American cities'. *International Journal of Urban and Regional Research* 29(10), pp. 110–23.

Robles, F. and K. Voorend (2013) *Migrando en la crisis: La fuerza de trabajo inmigrante en la economía costarricense: construcción, agricultura y transporte público*. San José: Organización Internacional para las Migraciones (OIM) and Ministerio de Trabajo y Seguridad Social (MTSS).

Rocha, S. (1997) *Tendência evolutiva e características da pobreza no Rio de Janeiro*. Discussion Paper 536. Rio de Janeiro: Instituto de Pesquisa Econômica Aplicada (IPEA).

Roche, C. L. and J. Richter (2007) *Justicia penal y defensa pública*. Caracas: Universidad Central de Venezuela, Faculty of Law and Political Science.

Rodgers, D., J. Beall and R. Kanbur (eds) (2012) *Latin American Urban Development into the Twenty-first Century: Towards a renewed perspective on the city*. New York NY: Palgrave Macmillan.

Rodrigues, A., R. Siqueira and M. Lissovski (eds) (2012) *Unidades de Polícia Pacificadora: debate e reflexões*. Comunicações do ISER 31(67). Rio de Janeiro: Instituto de Estudos da Religião (ISER).

Romero, F. (2011) 'Nuevo paramilitarismo busca tomarse Bogotá'. *El Tuburon*, 30 January. Available at: http://latribunacolombia.blogspot.nl/2011/02/nuevo-paramilitarismo-busca-tomarse.html.

Rosales, E. (2002) 'Sistema penal y relegitimación procesal' in R. Briceño-León (ed.) *Violencia, Sociedad y Justicia*. Buenos Aires: Consejo Latinoamericano de Ciencias Sociales (CLACSO), pp. 289–311.

Rosas Meza, I. (2004) 'La cultura constructiva de la vivienda en los barrios del área metropolitana de Caracas'. PhD dissertation in architecture, Universidad Central de Venezuela, Caracas.

Rospigliosi, F. (2013) 'Seguridad ciudadana: deterioro sin pausa'. *Revista Argumentos* VII(5) (December). Available at: http://revistaargumentos.iep.org.pe/articulos/seguridad-ciudadana-deterioro-sin-pausa.

Rotker, S. (2002) 'Cities written by violence: an introduction' in S. Rotker with K. Goldman and J. Balán (eds) *Citizens of Fear: Urban violence in Latin America*. New Brunswick NJ and London: Rutgers University Press, pp. 7–24.

— with K. Goldman and J. Balán (eds) (2002) *Citizens of Fear: Urban violence in Latin America*. New Brunswick NJ and London: Rutgers University Press.

Rubio, M. (2000) 'Violencia y conflicto en los noventa'. *Coyuntura Social* 22, pp. 151–86.

Ruiz Vásquez, J. C. (2009) 'Dos décadas de prevención en Bogotá: una lectura crítica'. *Urvío: Revista Latinoamericana de Seguridad Ciudadana* 7, pp. 101–9.

Safford, F. and M. Palacios (2002) *Colombia: Fragmented land, divided society*. Oxford: Oxford University Press.

Saín, M. F. (2004) 'A failed state facing new criminal problems: the case of Argentina' in K. Koonings and D. Kruijt (eds) *Armed Actors: Organised violence and state failure in Latin America*. London: Zed Books, pp. 127–38.

— (2009) 'El fracaso del control de drogas ilegales en Argentina'. *Nueva Sociedad* 222, pp. 132–46.

Salgado Portugal, V. M. (2007) *¿Cómo ha cambiado la distribución de ingresos en Lima Metropolitana? Un análisis a partir de indicadores de desigualdad* *y polarización del ingreso 1990–2005.* Lima: Consorcio de Investigación Económica y Social.

Salles Kobilanski, F. (2012) '¿Militarización sin militares? Los gendarmes en las calles argentinas durante los gobierno kirchneristas (2013–2012)'. *Urvío: Revista Latinoamericana de Seguridad Ciudadana* 12 (December), pp. 13–24.

Sampson R. J. and W. B. Groves (1989) 'Community structure and crime: testing social-disorganization theory' *American Journal of Sociology* 94, pp. 774–802.

Sánchez Lovell, A. (2010) *Dimensiones socioculturales del malestar vial en Costa Rica.* San José: Universidad de Costa Rica, Instituto de Investigaciones Sociales (IIS). Available at: revistas.ucr.ac.cr/index.php/RDMCP/article/download/12648/11903.

Sandoval, C. (2002) *Otros amenazantes: Los nicaragüenses y la formación de identidades nacionales en Costa Rica.* San José: Editorial de la Universidad de Costa Rica.

— (2005) *La Carpio: La experiencia de segregación urbana y estigmatización social.* San José: Universidad de Costa Rica, Instituto de Investigaciones Sociales (IIS) and Escuela de Comunicación Colectiva. Available at: http://ccp.ucr.ac.cr/noticias/migraif/pdf/sandoval.pdf.

Sanford, V. (2008) 'From genocide to feminicide: impunity and human rights in twenty-first century Guatemala'. *Journal of Human Rights* 7, pp. 104–22.

Sanz, J. L. and C. Dada (2013) 'Lo que debilitó la tregua es la falta de respuesta económica y social del gobierno'. *El Faro*, 30 July. Available at: www.salanegra.elfaro.net/es/201307/entrevistas/12820/.

Sanz, J. L. and C. Martínez (2012) 'El trabajo de monseñor Colindres y Raúl Mijango era una pieza de mi estrategia'. *El Faro*, 14 May. Available at: www.salanegra.elfaro.net/es/201205/entrevistas/8541.

Savenije, W. (2009) *Maras y barras: Pandillas y violencia en los barrios marginales de Centroamérica.* San Salvador: Facultad Latinoamericano de Ciencias Sociales (FLACSO).

— and M. A. Beltrán (2012) *Conceptualización del Modelo de Prevención Social de la Violencia con Participación Juvenil.* San Salvador: Instituto Nacional de la Juventud (INJUVE).

— and C. van der Borgh (2009) 'Gang violence: comparing anti-gang approaches and policies'. *The Broker*, pp. 20–3.

— and C. van der Borgh (2014) 'Anti-gang policies and gang responses in the Northern Triangle'. *The Broker*, 3 July. Available at: http://thebrokeronline.eu/Articles/Anti-gang-policies-and-gang-responses-in-the-Northern-Triangle.

Schinkel, W. (2011) 'Prepression: the actuarial archive and new technologies of security'. *Theoretical Criminology* 15(4), pp. 365–80.

Semana (2011a) 'Bogotá necesita más policías, pero permanentes: Secretaria de Gobierno.' *Semana*, 8 January.

— (2011b) 'Las BACRIM, amenaza también para Bogotá'. *Semana*, 1 April.

— (2011c) 'La seguridad, en entredicho'. *Semana*, 23 April.

— (2012) 'La propuesta "trabada" de Petro'. *Semana*, 11 August.

Shaw, C. R. and H. D. McKay (1942) *Juvenile Delinquency and Urban Areas.* Chicago IL: University of Chicago Press.

Short, J. F. (1997) *Poverty, Ethnicity and Violent Crime.* Boulder CO: Westview Press.

Silva, P. and H. Cleuren (eds) (2009) *Widening Democracy: Citizens and participatory schemes in Brazil and Chile*. Leiden: Brill.

Simone, A. M. (2013) 'Urban security and the "tricks" of endurance'. *Open Democracy*, 14 February. Available at: www.opendemocracy. net/opensecurity/abdou-maliq-simone/urban-security-and-tricks-of-endurance.

Sives, A. (2002) 'Changing patrons, from politician to drug dons: clientelism in Downtown Kingston, Jamaica'. *Latin American Perspectives* 29(5), pp. 66–89.

— (2010) *Elections, Violence and the Democratic Process in Jamaica: 1944–2007*. Kingston: Ian Randle Publishers.

Skogan, W. G. (1986) 'Fear of crime and neighborhood change' in A. J. Reiss Jr. and M. Tonry (eds) *Communities and Crime*. Chicago IL: University of Chicago Press, pp. 203–29.

— (1988) 'Crime and community decline' in T. Hope and M. Shaw (eds) *Communities and Crime Reduction*. London: HMSO, pp. 48–61.

— and M. G. Maxfields (1981) *Coping with Crime: Individual and neighborhood reactions*. Newbury Park CA: Sage.

Slater, T. (2014) 'The resilience of neoliberal urbanism'. *Open Democracy*, 28 January. Available at: www.opendemocracy.net/ opensecurity/tom-slater/resilience-of-neoliberal-urbanism.

Snodgrass Godoy, A. (2006) *Popular Injustice: Violence, community, and law in Latin America*. Stanford CA: Stanford University Press.

Sosa Escudero, W. and L. Gasparini (2000) 'A note on the statistical significance of changes in inequality'. *Económica* 46(1), pp. 111–22.

Souza, F. (2007) *PCC: A facção*. Rio de Janeiro: Editora Record.

Spedding Pallet, A., G. Flores Quispe and N. Aguilar López (2012) *Chulumani flor de clavel: Transformaciones urbanas y rurales, 1998–2012*. La Paz: Programa de Investigación Estratégica en Bolivia (PIEB).

Spinelli, H., G. Macías and V. Darraidou (2008) 'Procesos macroeconómicos y homicidios. Un estudio ecológico en los partidos del Gran Buenos Aires (Argentina) entre los años 1989 y 2006'. *Salud Colectiva* 4(3), pp. 283–99.

Tassi, N., C. Medeiros, A. Rodríguez-Carmona and G. Ferrufino (2011) *'Hacer Plata sin plata'. El desborde de los comerciantes populares en Bolivia*. La Paz: Programa de Investigación Estratégica en Bolivia (PIEB).

Taylor, C. (2002) 'Modern social imaginaries'. *Public Culture* 14(1), pp. 91–124.

Taylor, R., S. D. Gottfredson and S. Brower (1961) 'Territorial cognitions and social climate in urban neighborhoods'. *Basic and Applied Social Psychology* 2(4), pp. 289–303.

The Economist (2011) 'Good news is no news'. *The Economist*, 2 June.

Thoumi, F. E. et al. (2010) *The Impact or Organised Crime on Democratic Governance in Latin America*. Berlin: Friedrich Ebert Stiftung, Department for Latin America and the Caribbean.

Thuilier, G. (2005) 'Gated communities in the metropolitan area of Buenos Aires, Argentina: a challenge for town planning'. *Housing Studies* 20(2), pp. 255–77.

Tulchin, J. S. (2010) 'Prólogo: seguridad en el Caribe, América Central and Norteamérica' in R. Benitez Manaut (ed.) *Seguridad y defensa en América del Norte: Nuevos dilemas geopolíticos*. Washington DC and San Salvador: Woodrow Wilson International Center for Scholars and Fundación

D. Guillermo Ungo (FUNDAUNGO), pp. 3–8.

Ugalde, L. (1990) *La violencia en Venezuela.* Caracas: Monteavila Universidad Católica Andres Bello.

Uildriks, N. (ed.) (2009) *Policing Insecurity: Police reform, security, and human rights in Latin America.* Lanham MD: Lexington Books.

UN-Habitat (2011) *State of the World's Cities 2010–2011.* Nairobi: UN-Habitat.

— (2012) *State of the Latin American and Caribbean Cities 2012: Toward a new urban transition.* Nairobi: UN-Habitat.

UNDP (2012) *Caribbean Human Development Report: Human development and the shift to better citizen security.* Panama: United Nations Development Programme (UNDP).

— (2013) *Regional Human Development Report 2013–2014: Citizen security with a human face: evidence and proposals for Latin America. Executive summary.* New York NY: United Nations Development Programme (UNDP). Available at: www.undp.org/content/dam/rblac/docs/Researc h%20and%20Publications/IDH/IDH-AL-ExecutiveSummary.pdf.

Ungar, M. (2003) 'La policía venezolana: el camino peligroso de la politización'. *Revista Venezolana de Economía y Ciencias Sociales* 9(3), pp. 205–29.

— (2012) 'Social ecologies and their contribution to resilience' in M. Ungar (ed.) *The Social Ecology of Resilience: A handbook of theory and practice.* New York NY: Springer, pp. 13–31.

UNHCR (2014) *Children on the Run: Unaccompanied children leaving Central America and Mexico and the need for international protection.* Washington DC: United Nations High Commissioner for Refugees (UNHCR).

UNODC (2011) *Global Study on Homicide: Trends, context, data.* Vienna: United Nations Office on Drugs and Crime (UNODC).

— (2013a) *World Drug Report 2013.* Vienna: United Nations Office on Drugs and Crime (UNODC).

— (2013b) *Global Study on Homicide 2013: Trends, contexts, data.* Vienna: United Nations Office on Drugs and Crime (UNODC).

— (2014) *Global Study on Homicide: UNODC Homicide Statistics 2013.* Vienna: United Nations Office on Drugs and Crime (UNODC). Available at: www.unodc.org/gsh/en/data.html.

Valenzuela Aguilera, A. (2013) 'Urban surges: power, territory, and the social control of space in Latin America'. *Latin American Perspectives* 189(2), pp. 21–34.

van der Borgh, C. and W. Savenije (2015) 'De-securitising and re-securitising gang policies: the Funes government and gangs in El Salvador'. *Journal of Latin American Studies* 47(1), pp. 149–76.

Van Lidth de Jeude, M. and O. Schütte (2010) *GAM(ISMO): Cultura y desarrollo urbano en la Gran Área Metropolitana de Costa Rica.* Cuadernos de Ciencias Sociales 155. San José: Facultad Latinoamericana de Ciencias Sociales (FLACSO).

Van Reenen, P. (2004) 'Policing extensions in Latin America' in K. Koonings and D. Kruijt (eds) *Armed Actors: Organized violence and state failure in Latin America.* London: Zed Books, pp. 33–51.

Vargas, T. (2008) *Jóvenes, delincuencia y drogas: Estudio cualitativo acerca de la delincuencia juvenil en Guaricano.* Santo Domingo: Casa Abierta.

Vigil, J. D. (2002) *A Rainbow of Gangs:*

Street cultures in the mega-city. Austin TX: University of Texas Press.

Villanova, N. (2012) 'Cartoneros y piqueteros. La lucha de los recuperadores urbanos, el Tren Blanco y el Argentinazo. Ciudad Autónoma de Buenos Aires, 1999–2011'. *Razón y Revolución. Teoría – Historia – Política* 23, pp. 97–111.

Villaveces, A., P. Cumming, V. Espitia, T. D. Koepsell, B. McKnight and A. Kellermannn (2000) 'Effect of ban on carrying firearms on homicide rates in 2 Colombian cities'. *Journal of the American Medical Association* 283(9), pp. 1205–9.

Villegas Alarcón, F. (2005) 'Las pandillas juveniles de Lima'. *Espacio Abierto* 14(1), pp. 73–95.

Villiers Negroponte, D. (2014) 'The surge in unaccompanied children from Central America: a humanitarian crisis at our border'. Up Front (Brookings Institution blog), 2 July. Available at: www.brookings.edu/blogs/up-front/posts/2014/07/02-unaccompanied-children-central-america-negroponte.

Waiselfisz, J. J. (2011) *Mapa da Violência 2012: Os Novos Padrões da Violência Homicida no Brasil.* São Paulo: Instituto Sangari.

— (2013) *Mapa da Violência 2013: Homicídios e Juventude no Brasil.* Brasília: Secretaria-Geral da Presidência da República and Secretaria Nacional de Juventude.

Wampler, B. (2009) *Participatory Budgeting in Brazil: Contestation, cooperation, and accountability.* University Park PA: Penn State University Press.

Ward, T. W. (2013) *Gangsters Without Borders: An ethnography of a Salvadoran street gang.* New York NY: Oxford University Press.

Wickham-Crowley, T. (1992) *Guerrillas and Revolution in Latin America: A comparative study of insurgents and regimes since 1956.* Princeton NJ: Princeton University Press.

Wilkinson, D. L. (2003) *Guns, Violence, and Identity among African American and Latino Youth.* New York NY: LFB Scholary Publishing.

Willadino, R., J. T. Sento-Sé, C. Gonçalves Dias and F. Gomes (2011) *Prevenção à Violência e Redução de Homicídios de Adolescentes e Jovens no Brasil.* Rio de Janeiro: Observatório das Favelas.

Williams, P. and V. Felbab-Brown (2012) *Drug Trafficking, Violence and Instability.* Pennsylvania PA: University of Pittsburgh, Matthew B. Ridgway Center for International Security Studies.

WOLA (2011) *Tackling Urban Violence in Latin America: Reversing exclusion through smart policing and social investment.* Washington DC: Washington Office on Latin America.

Wolf, S. (2011) 'Street gangs of El Salvador' in T. Bruneau and L. Dammert (eds) *Maras: Gang violence and security in Central America.* Austin TX: University of Texas Press, pp. 43–69.

World Bank (2002) *Caribbean Youth Development: Issues and policy directions.* Washington DC: World Bank, Human Development in Latin America and the Caribbean Region.

— (2013) *Shifting Gears to Accelerate Shared Prosperity in Latin America and the Caribbean.* Document 78507. Washington DC: World Bank.

Wright, M. W. (2005) 'Paradoxes, protests and the *Mujeres de Negro* of northern Mexico'. *Gender, Place and Culture* 12(3), pp. 277–92.

Ypeij, A. (2013) 'Cholos, incas y fusionistas: El Nuevo Perú y la globalización del andino'. *European Review of Latin American and Caribbean Studies* 94, pp. 67–82.

Zaibert, L. (2005) 'Prolegomenon to a

theory of punishment'. *Law, Culture and the Humanities* 1, pp. 221–46.

Zaluar, A. (2000) 'Perverse integration: drug trafficking and youth in the favelas of Rio de Janeiro'. *Journal of International Affairs* 53(2), pp. 654–71.

— (2004a) 'Urban violence and drug warfare in Brazil' in K. Koonings and D. Kruijt (eds) *Armed Actors: Organised violence and state failure in Latin America*. London: Zed Books, pp. 139–54.

— (2004b) *Integração Perversa: Pobreza e trafico de drogas*. Rio de Janeiro: Editora Fundacão Getúlio Vargas (FVG).

— and M. Alvito (eds) (2006) *Um século de favela*. Rio de Janeiro: Editora Fundação Getúlio Vargas (FGV).

Zamora, M. (2006) 'El programa de seguridad comunitaria en el contexto de la policía costarricense: apuntes y comentarios frente a su décimo aniversario'. *Seguridad Sostenible: Boletín del Institut Internacional de Governabilitat de Catalunya* 27 (7 February).

Zautra, A. J., J. S. Hall and K. E. Murray (2010) 'Resilience: a new definition of health for people and communities' in J. W. Reich, A. J. Zautra and J. S. Hall (eds) *Handbook of Adult Resilience*. New York NY: The Guilford Press, pp. 3–29.

Zedner, L. (2007) 'Pre-crime and post-criminology?' *Theoretical Criminology* 11(2), pp. 261–81.

Zilberg, E. (2011) *Space of Detention: The making of a transnational gang crisis between Los Angeles and San Salvador*. Durham NC: Duke University Press.

Zimmerman, M. A. and A. D. Brenner (2010) 'Resilience in adolescence: overcoming neighbourhood disadvantage' in J. W. Reich, A. J. Zautra and J. S. Hall (eds) *Handbook of Adult Resilience*. New York NY: The Guilford Press, pp. 283–308.

Zorro Sánchez, C. (2004) *Pandillas en Bogotá: por qué los jóvenes deciden integrarse a ellas*. Bogotá: Alcaldía Mayor de Bogotá.

Zubillaga, V. (2003) *Entre hombres y culebras: Devenir un homme et se faire respecter dans un barrio d' une ville latinoamericaine*. Louvain-la-Nueve: Université Catholique de Louvain, Unité d'Anthropologie et de Sociologie.

INDEX

www.ingramcontent.com/pod-product-compliance
Lightning Source LLC
Chambersburg PA
CBHW030331270326
41926CB00010B/1581